Advance Praise for *The Empathy Diaries*

"This is a scintillating memoir. Turkle acts at once as storyteller, ethnographer, and psychologist of her own life—one stretching from a straitened Brooklyn Jewish girlhood shadowed by an unspeakable secret to a womanhood of academic accomplishment amidst the excitements of Radcliffe, Harvard, Chicago, and Paris in the years after the upheaval of '68 and MIT just as our computer world is born. Along the way she gives us a vivid account of ideas crucial to the last half-century of intellectual life, tracing their inner history with bracing clarity."

—Lisa Appignanesi, author of *Everyday Madness: On Grief, Anger, Loss and Love* and *Mad, Bad, and Sad: Women and the Mind Doctors*

"By respecting her own emotional, social, and intellectual history with careful—even loving—attention, Sherry Turkle shows what rescue from the crisis of technological disconnect looks like. Intimate, compassionate, and critical, her book instructs, edifies, and heals. A paradigmatic personal narrative, yet *The Empathy Diaries* is a tour de force of social science, saluting and protecting the precious intangibility that no machine can match—the quality that makes us human."

—James Carroll, author of *The Truth at the Heart of the Lie*

"Like a Harvard educated Nancy Drew, Sherry Turkle searches her past for clues to her true self and hits the mother lode in this fascinating, fearless memoir. Her struggle with the legacy of long-held family secrets as she forges her own unique path to authenticity and forgiveness is a story countless women will identify with. Reading *The Empathy Diaries*, I felt my mind— and my heart—expanding. Sherry Turkle is not only a great writer and teacher—she's great company."

—Winnie Holzman, cowriter of the hit musical *Wicked*; creator of the television series *My So-Called Life*

"'Use concrete events to think about large ideas. Use large ideas to think about concrete events.' Sherry Turkle follows the advice of her professor, Samuel Beer, and *The Empathy Diaries* is the compelling result. The stages of Turkle's narrative unfold so gracefully, in prose of such candor and clarity, that it's easy to overlook how many tasks this memoir performs. *The Empathy Diaries* is about a childhood and a coming-of-age. It's about a courtship and marriage. It's also about the progress of Turkle's engagement in the dynamic and overlapping fields in which this professor of social sciences, science, and technology is a crucial, authoritative, and, yes, empathetic voice. In every way, this is a book about an education. Fans of Turkle's earlier work will certainly want to read *The Empathy Diaries*; but so too should everyone struggling in the cyber maze in which we find ourselves. A remarkable book."

—Rachel Hadas, PhD, Board of Governors Professor of English, Rutgers University–Newark

"I read it with delight. An honest, insightful, compelling, and sometimes painful account of the intellectual and emotional forces that shaped Turkle into a pioneer in the study of digital culture and how computers change the way we think about ourselves. Turkle's is not only a personal story, but also a story of our digital age."

—Alan Lightman, Professor of the Practice of the Humanities, MIT; author of *Searching for Stars on an Island in Maine*

"Sherry Turkle has been daring and original for a long time—bearing witness to the emergence of artificial intelligence but also writing forcefully, while surrounded by true believers at MIT, about its limitations. In *The Empathy Diaries*, she dares even further by investigating a tightly held family secret, affirming in the process the wisdom of the human heart. *The Empathy Diaries* tells a fascinating story—one that manages to be profound and entertaining at the same time."

—Susan Quinn, author of *Eleanor and Hick: The Love Affair That Shaped a First Lady*

"Over the decades, Sherry Turkle has provided the most penetrating analyses of the relations between the human and the computational worlds. In a remarkably revealing memoir, Turkle explores the personal as well as scholarly sources of her understandings and, in the process, provides a brilliant panorama of our time."

—Howard Gardner, author of *A Synthesizing Mind*

The

Empathy

Diaries

A MEMOIR

Sherry Turkle

PENGUIN PRESS
New York
2021

PENGUIN PRESS
An imprint of Penguin Random House LLC
penguinrandomhouse.com

Photo credits
p. 156, courtesy of Catherine Weill; p. 204, courtesy of Erica Ewing;
p. 333, by Jeanne Strongin from *Ms. Magazine*;
p. 336, courtesy of Steven Klein; p. 338, courtesy of Duncan Davidson/TED

Library of Congress cataloging-in-publication data
Names: Turkle, Sherry, author.
Title: The empathy diaries: a memoir / Sherry Turkle.
Description: New York: Penguin Press, 2021. |
Includes bibliographical references.
Identifiers: LCCN 2020025410 (print) | LCCN 2020025411 (ebook) |
ISBN 9780525560098 (hardcover) | ISBN 9780525560104 (ebook)
Subjects: LCSH: Turkle, Sherry. | Psychologists—United States—Biography. |
Empathy. | Technology—Social aspects.
Classification: LCC BF109.T86 A3 2021 (print) | LCC BF109.T86 (ebook) |
DDC 150.92 [B]—dc23
LC record available at https://lccn.loc.gov/2020025410
LC ebook record available at https://lccn.loc.gov/2020025411

Printed in the United States of America
1 3 5 7 9 10 8 6 4 2

Designed by Meighan Cavanaugh

My general policy in this book is to use real names, usually first names, until
graduate school friendships when I begin to use full names. When discussing
a public connection, for example, my teachers, I use full names. When I
thought I was discussing sensitive material, I asked individuals how
they wished to be identified and followed their preferences.
If they were not available, I chose a pseudonym.

To Rebecca and Ben:

the future

Contents

Introduction: *Le Nom du Père*   xi

Part One
1948–1968

1. Summer Palace/Winter Palace   *3*
2. The Memory Closet   *31*
3. An Unsentimental Education   *57*
4. *Dépaysement*   *79*
5. *Twelfth Night*   *103*
6. Taxis   *119*
7. Mourning   *137*

Part Two
1968–1975

8. Newspapers and Vinegar   *151*

9. Things for Thinking   *175*

10. Great Books   *185*

11. The Lacanian Village   *195*

12. *Chère-cheur*   *207*

13. The Perfect Shortcake   *221*

14. Knots   *233*

Part Three
1976–1985

15. The Xerox Room   *245*

16. Building 20   *263*

17. The Marriage of True Minds   *283*

18. Coming Apart   *301*

19. The Last Experiment   *319*

20. The Assault on Empathy   *331*

Epilogue: People Are Not Objects   *339*

Acknowledgments   *349*

Notes   *353*

Le Nom du Père

During the long hours of my grandmother's dying, I begin to read the Brooklyn telephone book. I look up the Charles Zimmermans. There are pages of them. I study the entries carefully. It's August 1975; I'm twenty-seven. For as long as I can remember, I've been both searching and not searching for Charles Zimmerman, my father, whom I haven't seen since childhood.

Now I'm searching. In the back of one of my graduate school notebooks, I begin to copy down Charles Zimmerman addresses and telephone numbers, long lists of them. My mother is dead and my grandparents, with whom I stay when I'm in New York, have only the Brooklyn telephone book, no Manhattan directory. I know that in Cambridge, Massachusetts, one of my Harvard professors has the Manhattan directory in his office. He once commented that everyone needs to have that directory at hand. At the time, this idea suggested a life of access and sophistication that thrilled me. Now, though, I feel a more practical need. When I get back to school, I ask his secretary if

I may borrow his Manhattan book. She says no, but she lets me sit with it in his office, where I carefully copy out new Zimmerman candidates.

My grandmother dies in December. At LaGuardia Airport, flying back to Boston after her funeral, my plane is delayed. Standing next to a pay phone, I study the Queens directory and copy down the information for all its Charles Zimmermans. It never occurs to me that my father might live in the Bronx or have moved out of New York City altogether.

Nearly three years later, at a picnic table in Ipswich, Massachusetts, I tell my aunt Mildred, my mother's sister, that I want to find Charlie, as he was known on the rare occasions when my family spoke of him. Can she help me?

Both during my mother's life and long afterword, Mildred, my grandparents, and I had respected my mother's wish to keep secret what she considered the great shame of her early divorce. We never spoke of my biological father. More than this, from the time I was five and my mother remarried—this was to Milton Turkle—my family lived under a regime of pretend. The rules were that although my legal name was Sherry Zimmerman, I had to say that my name was Sherry Turkle.

Mildred's struggle over what to say is visible, painful to watch. She promised my mother, before she died, to keep me away from my father. Finally, Mildred comes to a decision. "If you are going to do it, if you are decided, I should help you," she says. "Charlie once worked as a teacher. Many years after your mother's divorce, I met someone who said that he worked as a teacher." With that, Mildred stares down at her feet. I feel my aunt's love. She has given me what she can.

I met with a private investigator, a former police detective. I no longer remember his name, just his thin black hair and shiny gray suit. In the spring of 1979, I visited his small, bare office on the West Side, furnished with only a well-used lamp, a coat tree, and a steel desk. Sitting across from me, he traced out, on a clean sheet of paper, the meager details I knew about my father: his name; that he and my mother were divorced in Florida in the early 1950s; that he might be named in my adoption proceedings beginning in the late 1950s; and the precious detail added by my aunt: he had worked as a teacher in the New York City public school system.

After Thanksgiving, the detective called. He'd found a Charles Zimmerman who once taught school in Queens, he said. This former teacher is my father's age. There's also a record of a Zimmerman divorce in Branford, Florida, in 1951. The man's birth date matches that of the teacher in Queens. I remember that as we spoke, I could only take shallow breaths. I was crossing a line. My mother had not wanted me to do this. Perhaps she'd had her reasons.

I wrote a letter. My husband, Seymour Papert, helped me. We rewrote it many times. The final version left Charlie a lot of room to turn me down.

Dear Mr. Zimmerman,

I am Sherry Turkle, the daughter of Harriet Bonowitz and Charles Zimmerman, born on June 18, 1948. I was adopted by Milton Turkle, my mother's second husband, and thus carry his name.

I have reason to believe that you are my father. I have not been in contact with my father for many years. If you are my father, I would like to meet with you and renew our acquaintance. Please be in touch in whatever way you find most comfortable.

Thank you.

Sincerely,
Sherry Turkle
44 Tappan Street,
Brookline, Massachusetts
617-267-xxxx

Some days later the phone rang. Seymour answered. He reached for me, slung his arm around my shoulder. He kissed me on the forehead as he passed me the phone. "Hello, is this Sherry Turkle?" The same voice asked if I had recently written to a Charles Zimmerman in Queens.

"Yes," I say.

"This is your father."

I haven't spoken to Charlie in almost nineteen years. I saw him intermittently as a child, and then after Milton Turkle adopted me, I never heard from him again. Now he wants to see me. I grab a calendar. He gives me an address. We set a date for the following December weekend, just before Christmas.

Charlie answered the door. He looked like me. That's what I noticed first. The eyes. The mouth. I have his ears. His first words to me, right there at the door: "Did you find me through the *New York Times*?"

When I said, "No, I hired a detective," he seemed disappointed. For a moment I imagined, almost giddy, that he'd been advertising for a lost daughter.

My father turned out to be a rogue scientist. Now a retired high school teacher, for decades he had worked out of his home and had written a book in which he claimed to disprove Einstein's theory of relativity. Relentlessly, he then wrote to famous scientists, trying to get them to take his work seriously. He also advertised his self-published Einstein book in the back pages of the *New York Times Book Review*: "E=mc² is not correct. Queens high school teacher disproves Einstein. For more information write Charles Zimmerman." He provided a post office box number. This is the advertisement my father thought had led me to him. His Einstein disproof is displayed on a table in the living room. It is small and dark and blue.

After such a long time of knowing nothing about him, it was good to find out that Charlie was alive, healthy, and not homeless. The apartment where we met reminded me pleasantly of my grandparents' Brooklyn home. Here as there, an upholstered sofa and chairs were covered in plastic. There was a dining room set in a wood that looked so shiny that it could not possibly be real. It was some kind of space-age cherry.

Charlie explained that this was the home of his "woman friend," Lila. She'd been standing shyly behind him ever since he greeted me at the door, and now he introduced me. Lila is petite and pretty. I think of my mother. Tall and imposing, feminine and sociable. Charlie likes the company of women. Women like Charlie's company. Lila encouraged us to sit down at the table, where food was already spread out. She said how happy she is that this day has come, that she has encouraged it often.

For lunch, Charlie told me that I will have the traditional: bagels, lox, cream cheese. Babka. He will have a kale shake. I knew he was a vegetarian because it was the first thing he mentioned after showing me his *New York Times* advertisement. A childhood memory came back to me—drinking a cantaloupe malted with him in Prospect Park.

As a child, among the few things I had heard about Charlie was that he was a chemist and that he had given up his right to be in contact with me in exchange for being released from any obligation to pay child support. I think my mother let slip the chemist detail because it was something she could be proud of. I imagined her dreaming that a chemist husband would bring new status. She would visit the world of her parents and sister from a place of nicer things, she would be generous with them, her home could be their gathering place.

At our meeting, Charlie said that he had done graduate work in chemistry and also confirmed the story I'd been told about child support. My mother had wanted to erase her life with him, he said. He didn't suit her, and her lawyer thought that the easiest way to get rid of him was to ask for what he couldn't provide: money. You shouldn't demand money from a father in exchange for letting him see his daughter, he said.

For a moment, I saw Charlie's point of view. From there, I could imagine that he had actually been interested in me.

Then, over lunch, I began to take the fuller measure of my father. He couldn't connect over a feeling or even a food. I told him I had missed knowing him. I had longed for news from him—on my birthdays I had waited at the mailbox. He didn't say he had missed me. It was "how your mother wanted it," he said. At the table, he drank green juice but did not offer it to anyone else. Then he took small portions from several plates of pale cooked vegetables, none of these offered to the table either. I recognized only one: daikon. I'd seen it in Japanese restaurants.

As we ate—Lila and I, bagels and smoked salmon, Charlie, his eclectic array—I began to ask some questions and was relieved that he was willing to answer them. All these years, I wondered, had he received any news of me? Yes, a little. He had a friend who had worked with my mother when she was a substitute teacher at Lincoln High School in Brooklyn. Through this connection, Charlie knew I had done very well in school. He walked over to a manila folder and produced a June 1965 clipping from a Brooklyn newspaper. It reported that I'd won a scholarship to Radcliffe, and it was accompanied by a photograph. There I am in my official senior year portrait, wearing a black Grecian-style drape and staring into the middle distance somewhat dreamily.

I asked Charlie: "Did you think of writing me?"

"No," he said. "I thought your mother wouldn't have liked that."

At this, I struggled to hold back tears. I told myself that saving the clipping was how he was able to communicate his feelings of connection. But I had hoped for so much more. Then he told me that he knew that my mother died while I was in college. I don't remember him offering condolences or saying anything about her being gone. His face, I recall, was still.

Charlie said he lost track of me after Radcliffe. But now he's glad to know that I am a professor at MIT. Because, he said, he and I had been scientists together. We had done "experiments from the start."

Before I could ask what he meant, Charlie was talking about his scientific passions. Some, he said, were triggered by my birth. How does language begin? Is it innate? Could he make a groundbreaking contribution to child development? Was he perhaps the next Skinner? I felt a shiver, fearing what might be ahead, but Charlie seemed not to notice.

When I was a baby, Charlie explained, whenever my mother was not around, he used me as an experimental subject. I felt sick and was afraid to ask for details. I remember thinking that I must force myself. And so I did. "What experiments?"

I remember the moment when his story became too painful and I floated away from it, apart from the Sherry in the chair with the coffee cup on the table in front of her. I sat opposite my father and I could hardly breathe.

FINALLY I UNDERSTOOD why my mother left him. Why Charlie never dared a holiday card or birthday call. Later, when I told Mildred about my visit with Charlie, I didn't mention the experiments. I reassured my aunt that Charlie had done me no harm during our visit. But I asked her what she remembered about my mother's brief first marriage. She confided that very soon after the wedding, my mother was unhappy. Charlie was withdrawn and her new mother-in-law was intrusive and critical. Still, Mildred said, my mother chose her troubles with Charlie over the shame of a separation. No one in my family was divorced. Or knew anyone who had been divorced.

But then, one Saturday afternoon in late spring 1949, my mother called and asked Mildred to pick us up. We were living with Charlie in Bayside, Queens, and my mother wanted to leave. She named an intersection close to our home, near some shops. Mildred said that she and my grandmother drove right out and found us waiting on the curb, my mother holding me in her arms, our hastily packed clothes in shopping bags at her feet. The drive to my grandparents' apartment in Brooklyn was silent; no one asked any questions. Once home, my grandfather was happy to have us under his protection. When Charlie called after us, my grandfather got on the phone. My mother, he said, was getting a divorce.

As Charlie told me that afternoon: "That was the end of that."

. . .

OVER TIME, that meeting with Charlie set many things in motion: I let go of the father I'd tried so hard to find and reclaimed the mother I'd resented for keeping him from me. And something altogether unexpected: The encounter invested my academic work with deeper meaning. Charlie lived at the extreme of a dissociation of heart and mind. In listening to my father coolly describe the experiments he did on me as a young child, I experienced something I had already begun exploring in my research: how science and technology can make us forget what we know about life.

I've explored the human effects of science and technology since I arrived at MIT from Harvard in 1976 with a doctorate in sociology and psychology. My subject is the "inner history" of technology, how it changes our relationships, including our relationship with ourselves. Over the years at MIT, I have been able to see how easy it is for a fascination with technology to take well-intentioned people away from empathy and its simple human truths. So technologists become invested in the promise of electronic medical records and forget how important it is for physicians to make eye contact with patients during their meetings. Engineers become fixed on the idea of efficiency, and soon it seems like a good thing to prefer texting to face-to-face talk, because on screens we can discuss personal matters with less emotional vulnerability. Talking to and through machines makes face-to-face exchanges with people seem oddly stressful. And less necessary. These days, our technology treats us as though we were objects and we get in the habit of objectifying one another as bits of data, profiles viewed. But only shared vulnerability and human empathy allow us to truly understand one another.

There are plenty of good academic and philosophical reasons to investigate empathy as the defining characteristic of the human. Over the years, my commitment to this work evolved. I discovered a connection between my early family life and my professional interest that brought my purpose into focus. Not treating people as objects and trying to forestall technology's assault on empathy were personal for me.

My father's love of science and its theories made it easy for him to lose touch with the human needs of his wife and infant daughter. My mother kept secrets and spoke to me in a kind of code. Nothing was straightforward. From childhood, I had to figure out how to read her mind, to intuit the contours of her reality. If I developed empathy, at first, it wasn't so much a way to find connection as a survival strategy. My parents gave me burdens in childhood that I honed into gifts.

Star Trek popularized the idea of the "empath"—someone bred or groomed for empathy. As things turned out, and without design, mine was the education of an empath for a digital world.

When I was a child, my father's name was never spoken in our home, and I wasn't allowed to use my real name, our shared name. My first academic project was to study a French psychoanalyst who believed that your future was significantly determined by how your mother talked about your father's name. *Le nom du père.* Precisely. Without the name, I developed a passion for the tangible. I turned to objects stored away and tried to make sense of missing pieces. From a very young age, I saw myself as my life's detective.

"My mother was my first country, the first place I ever lived," the poet Nayyirah Waheed once wrote. And then one needs to build a home for oneself in another place, to learn to be oneself. That's the story I tell here, from an emotionally rich but insular postwar Brooklyn childhood until I was settled in my professional life. I had a sometimes painful path, but I was also fortunate, mentored and loved, present at many exciting crossroads. I was in Paris, Cambridge, and

Chicago in the late 1960s and early 1970s, times of extraordinary intellectual and political conversations, and at MIT in the mid-1970s, just at the start of the digital revolution. I was witness to the beginning of many worlds.

My grandmother was a practical woman. She said, "Do the best you can with what you have." She imagined a life of constraint. I have been given riches.

Part One

1948–1968

1.

Summer Palace/Winter Palace

Rockaway is a thin slice of oceanfront land, technically part of Queens, a peninsula you can reach by car from Brooklyn by crossing the Marine Parkway Bridge. It had been peppered with bungalow colonies since the late 1880s, a miracle of urban extravagance that New Yorkers of modest means enjoyed during the summers. In weekday Rockaway, the married women cooked, kept house, and minded the children, while the men and single women went to work in the city and took the subway home to Rockaway at night. That could mean a four-hour round trip. Those who stayed at home, including us children, were trained not to talk to the men when they returned until they took off their day clothes and went for an ocean swim. Then they—lords of their beachfront domains—showered, changed, and sat down to dinner with their families. In Rockaway, when we wanted entertainment, we sang to one another, listened to the radio, strolled on the boardwalk, and, once a week, watched fireworks. Everyone played cards.

My grandparents, Robert and Edith Bonowitz, and their daughters, Mildred and Harriet, had been going to Rockaway every summer since the 1930s. By the time I was born, in June 1948, the pilgrimage began from East Seventeenth Street in Brooklyn, between Church Avenue and Caton Avenue, just on the southern edge of Prospect Park's Parade Grounds, where we all lived together the rest of the time. The family joked that this one-bedroom rented apartment was our "winter palace" and the Rockaway bungalow was our "summer palace." From as early as I can remember, during winters in Brooklyn, we all yearned for Rockaway. Rockaway, where we could sit on our own porch. Rockaway, where, magically, we always had enough money to rent the very best bungalow, the one on the side of the court that was closest to the beach. In summer, the court was our world. Ten bungalows grouped together so that five of them faced the other five, concrete pavers in between, where children could play, adults could watch them, and teenagers could lie out in scanty bathing suits and admire themselves and one another.

My mother, Harriet Bonowitz, captured in her movie star look, 1946.

In a home movie filmed at Rockaway in 1939, my grandmother, Edith, is all dressed up and waiting for Rob (as he was known to his wife and brothers) to come home. He appears in a dark suit, white shirt, and tie. He walks briskly into Edgemere Court, on Beach Fiftieth Street, holding a briefcase. When he sees Edith, a great smile breaks out on his face. His dog, Beauty, a miniature Boston bull terrier, rushes to meet him. He pats her and together they go to greet my beaming grandmother. The camera follows Beauty, who is now leaping in joy.

After I was born, when my mother was released from the hospital, she went directly to Rockaway, where her parents and unmarried sister, Mildred, were already decamped to that same Edgemere Court. In the earliest photograph of us together, she's cradling me in a high-backed rocking chair.

Usually, my tall, voluptuous mother allowed herself to be photographed only in full makeup and when beautifully dressed, whether in a going-out ensemble or in shorts and a halter top. She was proud to be told that she resembled the movie star Ruth Hussey and had photographs taken that emphasized the resemblance, stark black-and-white glamour shots in which her dark-brown hair was lacquered into a sweeping pompadour.

First photo with my mother, Rockaway, June 1948.

But in this first photograph of us she's different. She's wearing a loose top bun and casual tee shirt. She looks full, just done with being pregnant, happy to be home with her family. I imagine her contentment with what she has achieved. She and the baby are healthy. And people fuss over her new daughter. Later she would tell me, "People stopped me in the street as I pushed you in your baby carriage and told me how beautiful you were." When I was only a year old, my grandfather had my picture taken by a professional photographer, who in turn submitted one of the photographs to a contest sponsored by a local newspaper. For my family, the fact that I appeared in a newspaper made it official: I was "the most beautiful baby in Brooklyn."

From the start, nothing was too good for this beautiful baby. My grandfather loved telling stories of how he indulged me, even before

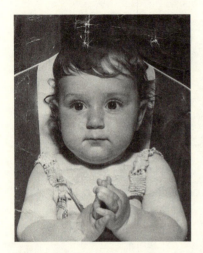

The photo of me that won "the most beautiful baby" contest. *The Long Island Star*, June 1949.

I arrived. The month before I was due to be born, he decided that he wanted me to have a baby carriage in the British pram style, in ebony black, the kind that sits high on large, spoked wheels with white rubber tires. Mildred was the only one in the family who owned or drove a car. So at my grandfather's request, she drove him to a baby-supply store in Far Rockaway, the closest "real" shopping town to the bungalows, where they special-ordered a pram through a catalog. Two weeks later it arrived. Perfec-

tion. The salesclerk took off the protective covering from the carriage and wheels and rolled the pram to my aunt's car, waiting at the curb. When the salesman began to arrange it in the trunk of the car, my grandfather saw that the wheels were no longer pristine. He refused it, saying he wanted another. This pram had been ruined. Mildred was mortified; my grandfather adamant. There was nothing to be done. The shop ordered a replacement carriage. Now, my grandfather was content. That first summer, he took me and the pram to his favorite bench on the Rockaway boardwalk where he read the newspapers and listened to the ball game.

As was Jewish tradition, both my first and middle names were in honor of deceased relatives. In my case, my grandfather would tell me, both of the names came from my mother's side of the family. I was named Sherry after my grandmother's brother Samuel and Roxanne after my grandfather's mother, Rachel. My father's family had no claim on me from the start.

My grandfather, Robert Bonowitz, carried this photo of the two of us in his wallet all his life.

I know little about my parents' courtship. I have tantalizing hints. Charlie and my aunt Mildred attended Brooklyn College at the same time in the 1930s. It could be that my aunt, two years older than my mother, knew Charlie from her college years and introduced them. My mother was twenty-nine when they were married in May 1947. I once found a photograph of her with a tall, mustached man with his arm casually draped around her shoulders. My grandmother told me that he had been my mother's boyfriend before Charlie. My mother had had her heart broken.

After I met Charlie, I learned that well before my birth, there was considerable animosity between the Bonowitzes and the Zimmermans. Charlie's parents gave my mother a hard time for not keeping a kosher home. Not raised in this tradition, she'd thought it would be enough for her to simply do what her mother had done and have a "kosher-style" home—no pork, no milk with meat. But these simplified rules didn't satisfy her stringent mother-in-law, who would visit, inspect my mother's cupboards, and find them wanting. My mother hoped that once she married Charlie, he would take her side, but he didn't. She also imagined that with a new baby Charlie's mother would have less sway. It would be natural for her own mother to have more of a role in her household. That's what happens when you have a baby.

Charlie had come out to Rockaway with my mother that first summer after I was born. But by the beginning of the following summer, my mother had left him. In all the years to come, I was never told why he was gone, only why I didn't see him: He had given up his right to visit because he hadn't been willing to pay child support. I understood that I should ask no further questions because I would get no further answers. When I returned to Rockaway during the summer of 1949, and for many years afterward, I was part of the Bonowitz family of five. My legal name, of course, was Sherry Zimmerman, but no one said the word "Zimmerman" in my presence. The first time I saw my actual name written out, I must have been about three, an early reader. It was part of an inscription in a children's alphabet book, buried deep in a cupboard over my grandparents' Brooklyn kitchen table. I hid the book in a corner of the cupboard, afraid that it would be thrown away. Soon after, when I was sent to a local nursery school, I saw my name again, this time on a list of the children in my class. It seemed unfamiliar. But I knew it was mine. In Rockaway and in our Brooklyn apartment building, things were simple: Everyone called me Sherry and understood that I belonged to the Bonowitzes.

My grandmother took care of me during the day and my mother went back to work as a bookkeeper. My aunt, too, worked in an office, writing English subtitles for Spanish-language films.

My Rockaway time was divided among reading alongside my

grandmother as she did her chores, accompanying her on her errands, and spending long hours with the pack of children who lived in the court and the few bungalows around it: We buried treasure, followed the Good Humor ice cream truck, got sunburns, and peeled off layers of our blistering skin. Every evening after dinner, we traveled in a pack to Essie's, a local sweetshop, and made decisions about penny candy and comic books. Once a week, I was given an allowance to make a purchase. In the end I always chose wax lips (I liked their soapy taste when I chewed them as gum) and an Archie and Veronica comic. Sometimes my mother would accompany us children on these expeditions and would stock up on her favorite Black Jack licorice chewing gum.

When my regal and stylish mother walked into a room, she was the center of attention. Yet she feared she was too tall to be considered feminine. She had a driver's license that gave her incorrect height (it listed her not as five foot eleven but as five foot eight) and also shaved a few years off her age, something she told me that certain ladies at the Department of Motor Vehicles would agree to do, understanding it was better if unmarried women over twenty-three were officially younger. When she married Charles Zimmerman in 1947, she took a year off her age on the marriage license, declaring herself twenty-eight. Six years later, when she married Milton Turkle, their marriage license had her at twenty-nine. When I found these documents, long after her death, I felt her presence, infuriating yet radiating confidence that any "reality" could be claimed as real.

My mother was much reassured about her height when she learned that the dancer Cyd Charisse, one of Fred Astaire's later partners, had to wear flat shoes to dance with Astaire—both of them were five foot eleven. Cyd Charisse became my mother's heroine. She admired everything about her, all the more so when she learned that just before

I was born, the dancer had left her successful show business career to marry the singer Tony Martin. My mother loved this story, not only because she would have been so happy to stay at home in a traditional marriage but also because Tony Martin was Jewish. We didn't know if Cyd Charisse had converted to Judaism, but my mother felt certain that the Charisse/Martin family observed the Jewish holidays because Tony Martin would want his children to grow up in a Jewish atmosphere.

The idea of Rosh Hashanah with Cyd Charisse and Tony Martin captured my mother's imagination. She thought about their home, comfortable, with glamour and dancing. My mother, winter and summer, would begin her day humming Frank Sinatra while she choreographed a fox-trot with me as her partner. My mother told me she relaxed by walking through the designer sections of department stores, not to buy but "just to see what's beautiful." When I was old enough to go on these trips, I learned that my mother was most relaxed looking at dance-ready cocktail furs and evening gowns.

I got a sense of the life my mother wanted from visiting my summer pediatrician, Dr. Dillon, whose office was on the Rockaway peninsula but in the wealthier neighborhood of Belle Harbor. While driving to these appointments, my mother took me as her confidante. She told me that she wanted to live in a house and not an apartment, to go on vacations in the Caribbean, and to buy dresses at Saks Fifth Avenue. She wanted a dining room where she could hold dinner parties, with someone to help her cook and clean up afterward. All of this, she said, came easily to the women of Belle Harbor.

From the earliest age, I heard dinner-table conversations about how my mother and aunt might find husbands who could provide this kind of life for them. It all seemed to center on sending them to the Catskills, which we could not afford. In those mythic "mountains," wealthier Jews ate and mated in ways we could not even imagine. Once this was mourned, there was a list of synagogue-sponsored dances to try. There were even synagogues in Belle Harbor. My mother went to Belle Harbor dances and came home flushed and happy.

I dreamed, even as a young child, that perhaps I could give my mother the life that her father and mine had been unable to provide. It seemed that you had to be a doctor or a lawyer or an accountant. It seemed to be about graduate school. Everyone said I was the smartest girl they had ever met. Surely I could do this. I observed Dr. Dillon closely. How intelligent was he *really*? If she had lived long enough, I am sure I would have bought my mother her dream home. But I know that getting these things from me is not what she really wanted.

MY GRANDMOTHER, Edith Bearman, was born in Hoboken, New Jersey, in 1897, the youngest of four children, one of whom, a frail son, died as a teenager. Her parents, Annie Newmark and Isaac Bearman, were from the area around Wolozin, in what is now Belarus. Both my Bearman and Bonowitz great-grandparents were part of a wave of Jewish immigration from Belarus in the second half of the nineteenth century, sparked by pogroms and forced conscription into the Russian army. Isaac arrived in America in 1882; by 1886 he was married and had opened a profitable dry-goods store. By the time my grandmother was ten, the family had a maid to help with cooking and housework.

Edith went to school until she was sixteen and then was sent off to a job selling gloves. My grandfather always envied that his wife had four more years of schooling than he did.

Sometimes I could get my grandmother to talk about her early life in Hoboken. What struck her most, she said, is that she did what her mother told her. And that her opinion of herself was what her mother told her she was. My grandmother, a devoted reader, had a fine-featured face and full-bosomed figure. But she never thought of herself as clever, and certainly not as pretty, because even as a child, she was nearsighted and wore spectacles, something her mother considered unattractive. So my elegant grandmother never thought she was much. She was vain only about her slender hands, with their beautiful almond-shaped nails. I once teased her about this as she gave herself her weekly manicure. She did not deflect the compliment but said: "My mother liked my hands. She said I could be a glove model."

As a young boy growing up on DeKalb Avenue in Brooklyn, my grandfather knew he was a good student, but after his father, Aaron, died when he was twelve, there was no question that he'd have to drop out of school to take care of his family. His mother had seven children, one who died in his teens and two who were sent to an orphanage because there was no money to keep them at home. My grandfather found a job as a bookbinder's apprentice and took responsibility for his mother and a younger brother and sister. When Rob was twenty-two, his mother introduced him to her best friend's daughter. An engagement was arranged between the shy, book-ish Edith and the handsome,

My grandmother, Edith Bonowitz, Rockaway, early 1940s.

streetwise Rob. They were married two years later, in 1915. He was twenty-four, she eighteen. This was the first time that my grandmother had done any cooking or housework. For the first month, knowing her ignorance, her mother sent someone over to help. And then she was on her own.

On the wall above their kitchen table in Brooklyn, my grandparents had a cupboard—as a child I didn't know that word and I called it the "memory closet," which has remained its name for me—in which they stored old photographs, books, and papers. As soon as I could reach it, I was given permission to poke around. That's where I first saw my name, Sherry Zimmerman, inscribed in the alphabet book. I also found bullets from World War I, a military dress cap, odd pieces of jewelry, and autograph albums from my mother and aunt's school days. And that's where I found what I considered my first treasure—an engagement photograph of my grandparents. The strict canons of early-twentieth-century photography could not hide how beautiful they were as a couple, how sexy. When I think of them as they were in their later life, having gone through so much disappointment and loss, I'm happy that I found this photograph. I remember that whenever I took it down and showed it to them, they always seemed surprised and embarrassed.

Early in their marriage, my grandfather lost his job as a bookbinder and had to move his young family, which by then included two young daughters, to Hoboken, where they lived over his father-in-law's dry goods store and he helped out during the day. My grandparents did not like to talk about this stage of their life. It's hard to imagine my proud grandfather not being the head of his own household. In 1925, still working for his father-in-law, Robert Bonowitz moved his wife and daughters, now seven and nine, to their own apartment in Brooklyn.

During the Depression, my great-grandfather lost the dry goods store in Hoboken; this left my grandfather without a job. After a long search, he found work as a security guard on the Brooklyn piers and then, during the war, at the Brooklyn Navy Yard. In this tough-guy role, my grandfather began to find himself. He liked using his heft. He gave the appearance of being fearless.

After the war, the Navy Yard laid him off. From my aunt I learned that my grandfather became depressed and, as she put it, he began to "raise his voice" to my grandmother. His daughters never fully forgave him for how he spoke to their mother then. My grandfather finally found work through my aunt Mildred. One day at lunch with coworkers, she heard of a job opening for an assistant manager at a Times Square movie theater. A background in security was not irrelevant.

As Mildred told this story, my grandfather almost didn't apply for the job because it had come to him through his daughter. But because the family was in crisis, he took it. And flourished in it. He held that job for the rest of his working life.

My grandfather's job required physical stamina and considerable bravery. He was respected by everybody from his employers to the theater regulars, who essentially lived at the movie house from when it opened at around 11:00 a.m. to closing in the early hours before dawn. My grandfather affectionately called them his "bums" but did not condescend to them. With a sixth-grade education, he knew that what separated him from them was the luck of having a steady job. So as long as they did not drink or take drugs in the theater, he let them sleep in the seats and wash up in the men's room.

We four Bonowitz women felt safe with him. We believed that if ever we were physically threatened, he would put his life on the line for us. In return, though, we pampered him and ignored his emotional carelessness with us, even his verbal abuse. When he raged at my grandmother over an overcooked egg or piece of meat or made fun of the tic under her left eye, we called him out but then simply left the room. When he lashed out at Mildred, calling her an old maid, we told him he was cruel but then, again, left the room. Inevitably, my mother calmed him down with flattery. Over the years, observing her taught me how to defer to him. To men.

If you shared a problem with my grandfather, one he couldn't solve on the spot, the only way he knew how to respond was with anger. Details that required balancing priorities—like paying bills—upset him. And although my mother, my aunt, and my grandfather were all bringing in salaries, everything about our financial lives required a delicate dance—shaving bits off the food budget to pay the heat, the electrical bills, and the phone company. My grandmother paid her bills at the bank, in person—and she spaced out these visits strategically to coincide with the times of the month when money was coming in.

She was also the master of stretching a dollar in the kitchen. Some weeks, we ate carefully prepared stews that featured fried doughy circles, called *mandlakh* or "soup mandels." Winter and summer, I helped my grandmother roll them out on a flat slab of floured wood. And then she let me cut them out with a thimble. The little thimble-sized dough circles were then fried in chicken fat, where they browned and puffed up. They were delicious, and they also expanded the stew without having to add more meat. Laughingly, my grandmother called what we were doing "Depression cooking." But we weren't supposed to talk about this around my grandfather.

My grandmother always had reason to be angry with my grandfather, but she also had a crush on him. It was obvious in little things, such as the way she took pride in his clothes. They were part of his allure, along with his obvious intelligence. In the summer, no matter how stifling the heat, my grandfather left for work in a suit and tie. In this family where none of us had many possessions, my grandfather had the most clothes. And the best clothes. Navy-blue and gray suits with pinstripes. Smooth cotton shirts with French cuffs. Silk ties. He let me help him with his cuff links. He bought his suits at a store called Wittes. My grandmother always accompanied him to pick out his suits, and she went to all of his fittings. I understood, even as a child, that my grandmother loved these trips. She told me that at Wittes, they served her coffee and little vanilla cookies while she waited outside the fitting room.

In Rockaway, long rope laundry lines stretched between the bungalows. My first job when we arrived at the start of the summer was to help my grandmother hang our lines. Nothing that belonged to my grandfather ever went out on a line. It was understood that it would not be appropriate for his private garments to be seen by strangers.

The women in our family bought our summer clothes at a storefront on Beach Sixty-sixth Street during our first Rockaway weekend. There was a large, open dressing room where we tried everything on over our bathing suits. Community conversation caught us up on a year of gossip—who had died, been married, had a baby or a cheating husband.

In contrast, my school shopping, done every year in late August, took place in an atmosphere of quiet concentration. My grandmother and I traveled by bus to Far Rockaway, had a list, and carried cash. Every item had to be inexpensive but sturdy enough to last a full year. There wasn't a lot of room for the softer side of things. But that's where my mother excelled. She'd sneak in a pearl necklace. A bouquet. These were gifts, delivered with explanations. The necklace was "costume," my mother said, but "you can still have style, even if you can't afford a real one." The flowers were white tulips. My birth flower, she explained, was honeysuckle, but that seemed too "southern." We would substitute white Dutch tulips.

.   .   .

My grandfather's shift at the theater ended around 4:00 a.m., and during the summer, he usually arrived in Rockaway before sunrise. But he was always up at eight thirty to have breakfast with me. My grandmother and I caught him up on family events and bungalow gossip. And he caught us up on what had happened at the theater. After breakfast, it was time for the two of us to get the newspapers. Always the *News* and *Mirror.* Sometimes the *New York Times* or the *Herald Tribune,* my favorites. I read them with him on the boardwalk and then, when my grandfather was done with them, brought them back to my bed. I couldn't understand the news stories. I asked my grandfather how I could catch up. Who were we at war with? What did I need to know? He seemed to avoid my questions but just said, "Keep reading." Perhaps he couldn't follow the stories either and was using this formula himself.

My grandfather, exactly as I remember him,
Rockaway, early 1950s.

My grandfather was always trying to teach me to play cards, but I refused to concentrate. When the cards came out, I ran to get my favorite pastime: a construction set called Block City. The kitchen table, winter and summer, was piled high with white plastic bricks and transparent ones, as luminous as sea glass. When it was time for dinner, we had to tear down our current project. But after dinner, I would build it back up in only a few minutes. Again and again, my grandfather asked how I could be so bad at cards but remember the plans for the many dozens of houses we built with Block City. It was a good question. Sorting it out has been a central theme of my professional life—the irreducible pluralism of intellectual styles.

Twice a week, my grandfather took me for a treat—a malted milkshake at the Fifty-fourth Street candy store. The malted machines were lined up in a row, heavy green metal with stainless steel trim. On malted days, my grandfather and I would sit side by side at the long, red Bakelite soda fountain. It was still morning, but my grandfather, who had gotten off work only a few hours before, always had a kind of jet lag. From his point of view, it was time to celebrate the end of a long workday. He always ordered a chocolate ice cream soda for himself and a chocolate malted for me.

On these malted days, as we waited for our drinks, I learned about life on the Lower East Side as it had been in the old days. The anti-Semitism of the streets. I learned about how hurt my grandfather was that one of his brothers had changed his name from Bonowitz to Bonner. My grandfather loved his brother. He didn't want to judge, but he didn't approve. Mostly, he was pained at what it took to get ahead in America.

We talked about Christmas trees. I had to promise that my home would never have a Christmas tree. That was an easy promise. Christmas trees had angels and five-pointed stars. I had learned that there were no Jewish angels and Jews had only six-pointed stars. I felt securely Jewish. But my grandfather had seen his brother peel off. He told me how during the war, so many had died for the right to be Jewish, to proudly show their Jewish symbols. Being Jewish was about standing up as a Jew, he said. "You can't just borrow all the Christian things because you think you'll enjoy them."

This may seem like a complicated conversation for a kindergarten-age child on a hot summer morning before 9:00 a.m. while waiting for a malted. It never seemed that way to me. This was how my family talked. During television commercials: why Joseph McCarthy needed to be stopped in order to save democracy. Over Rice Krispies at breakfast: ruminations about the Holocaust. While I was in the bath: how someone like Hitler could take power in the United States. No transitions.

I think this has given a characteristic cadence to my conversation. No matter what the occasion—I could be hosting a birthday party, I could be buying shoes with my daughter, I could be about to kiss my lover—I'm always one sentence away from bringing up democracy, religious freedom, the rights of minorities, all of these in danger.

By the time I came along at the end of the Second World War, ensuring the survival of the Jewish people had a feeling of urgency for my family, and they naturally wrote me into that story of survival. My destiny was to have Jewish children. The specific religious practices of my family-to-be wouldn't matter so much—since I was a woman, I would pass down the religion as a birthright. So my children would be, by Jewish law, Jewish children. But I had to take Christianity seriously. Manger scenes and Christmas trees are not seasonal delights. Crosses are not fashion accessories.

On one particular day at the candy store, my grandfather's soda was ready first. The icy drink had frosted the outside of the tall, fluted glass. The fresh whipped cream was a perfect triangle on top of the liquid.

My malted was in progress. The liquid was blended in a tall aluminum cylinder. You could drink what felt like an entire malted and still there was more. That sense of plenty reminded my grandfather of what he wanted for me. "Only marry a generous man," he said. "When I was courting your grandmother, I couldn't afford to take her to dinner. So I took her to the pushcarts. We went to two pushcarts, the pickles and the pretzels. She had one pickle. I ordered her another. And when she asked for one pretzel, I said, 'Take two.'"

That's what my grandfather wanted, that a sense of plenitude should reign. I could have enough for two. When I went shopping with my prudent grandmother and we stopped at a Chock full o'Nuts coffee shop for a date-nut sandwich with cream cheese, we split it.

Now the man preparing my malted milk faltered. The aluminum canister was moist and slipped in his hands. Some of the malted spilled onto the work counter. In a quick motion, the man curled his fingers into a scoop and swept the spilled malted into the glass. My grandfather roared: "You are not going to give that to my granddaughter! You are *not* going to give that to my granddaughter!" And he reached to grab the man behind the counter by the collar. I tugged at his arm, terrified. The store owner, in turn, pulled his clerk out of the way. Time stopped. "Fire the bum!" my grandfather yelled as he stormed out of the store, pushing me ahead.

Years later, I went to dinner with a man I loved very much. We were eating at a restaurant in Harvard Square. In my order of pad thai, there was a nail. Not a fingernail but a nail. I looked at my man expectantly. He suggested we leave. I agreed but I felt righteous, angry. Not at the restaurant owner or incompetent kitchen staff but at my man for not taking care of me. He suggested that we might contact the health department. So before we left, we took down all the information we would need: the time, the dish, the waiter, the chef, the owner. My man never called the health department, nor did I. I missed my grandfather's rage.

MY GRANDMOTHER'S DAILY routine in Rockaway was to get up, make breakfast for my aunt and mother before they left for work, and then sit down to breakfast with my grandfather and me. Afterward, she began her cleaning. It was important that the laundry be hung out on the lines by ten so that the clothes could be bleached by Clorox and the noontime sun. Cooking would begin in the afternoon.

I was never asked to help with cleaning or in the kitchen. I was told to read. Not just encouraged to read. Told. I clearly remember offering to help. And being told to read. Other children might do chores. I, in the tradition of a yeshiva boy, was set aside for study.

I was allowed to participate in my grandmother's domestic chores in only one way: I could accompany her when she went shopping. In Rockaway and Brooklyn, my grandmother took along a small piece of torn shopping bag paper on which she had written the day's list. At the fruit and vegetable store, my grandmother would smell, squeeze, and hold melons and peaches to her forehead and cheek. She was competing for the best against all the other ladies in the store, each with a slightly different technique of divination. On Sunday mornings, summer and winter, delicatessen shopping—for lox, whitefish, rugalach, and pickles from the barrel—was my mother's job. She pinned up her pajama legs and threw a coat over her bedclothes. My grandparents pretended to be scandalized, but we all knew they were only pretending. My mother would always come back laughing with a made-up story of having been (almost) discovered nearly naked in the delicatessen.

In terms of building my character, it seems so wrong that I was relieved of all household responsibilities. But very early in my life my family had decided that I was special. My aunt said that it was when I began to read as a toddler. And could ask for correct change at the grocery store when I was in nursery school. Later, my mother insisted I should not learn to type. Wherever I worked, someone else would have to be my secretary.

As I read and she cleaned, my grandmother would pause to help me with a word I didn't know or to read a favorite page or two in one of my books. On this program I learned how to read and write long before I went to school. I had a stack of Golden Books featuring beloved characters—Hopalong Cassidy, Sleeping Beauty, Cinderella— and a small, precious collection of "chapter books," harder to read but worth the effort: the Bobbsey Twins and books of fairy tales that came in colors (Blue, Grey, and Violet). Later, in Rockaway, sitting next to my grandmother while she cleaned, I would read the books from the *New York Times* bestseller list that my aunt brought home from the library. *The Devil's Advocate. Bonjour Tristesse. Marjorie Morningstar.* Of all these books I asked the same question: What was going on beyond Rockaway and Brooklyn?

Mildred provided books for the whole family, but she also took me to the library and got me my own card. In the division of child-rearing labor, she seemed tasked with culture and sports. Besides taking me to the theater and museums, Mildred taught me to roller-skate, to ice-skate, and to swim in the rough Rockaway sea. She dove under the breakers to the flat water beyond, and I followed her. This took considerable bravery for both of us because we were both nearsighted and swam without glasses or prescription goggles. If Mildred moved only a few feet away from me, I couldn't see her. We once admitted to each other that when we went out to a certain distance, neither of us could tell in which direction was the land except by listening for sounds—that's how bad our vision was. She made me promise not to tell my mother. And Mildred took me sledding, walking me up small hills in Prospect Park until I was not afraid of speed and steering.

My mother reserved special things for the two of us. On summer Sundays, we walked the boardwalk to where there were game parlors and food concessions. We would bring home the treats my mother said she had bought for her parents when she was a young girl: something she called a "takee" (I remember this as Chinese noodles fried in the shape of a cup and then filled with chow mein) and ice cream waffles. It was a lot of food on top of our delicatessen breakfast, but the food wasn't the point. Indeed, the ice cream waffles usually melted by the time we got home. The point was to bring back the foods of my mother's childhood. I felt part of history and told myself that someday I would have a daughter and we would bring my mother these same foods.

In winter, as soon as there was a forecast of snow, my mother and I walked together in Prospect Park, our tongues out to catch the new flakes. If she was at work when it started snowing, she would rush home as soon as she could. I'd wait for her in the lobby of our apartment building, all bundled up, with instructions not to go outside. My "first snow" always had to be with her. As soon as we got too cold on our snow walk, we went for iced sweets at the Savoy Diner on Church Avenue. My mother always had a black-and-white soda: chocolate syrup, seltzer, and vanilla ice cream. I always had a chocolate malted. If this meant we missed dinner, everyone understood.

I grew up with two deep convictions: Something was wrong with me because of my name. Four loving adults had made me the center of their lives.

MY GRANDMOTHER'S KITCHEN was "kosher style." This meant that if it crawled in the ocean, we didn't eat it. If it came from a pig, we didn't eat it—except if we were at a Chinese restaurant, then we could eat pork. If it was meat, we didn't have milk at the same meal if we were at home. I remain confused to this day as to whether it was okay to eat out and have a hamburger and a milkshake. I don't think I was told not to do that, but I wouldn't have tried.

For summer birthdays and anniversaries, we went out to celebrate with Chinese food in Far Rockaway. We always ordered the same thing: boneless spareribs, chicken chow mein with extra crispy noodles, and chicken fried rice. There was Chinese tea throughout the meal, sweetened by my grandmother "for the table." Going out to eat Chinese food was the only time I drank glasses of ice water, because our refrigerator at home had room for only one small tray of ice, and it was not used for everyday dining. Home ice was for medical emergencies.

In the Chinese restaurant, my grandmother was in charge of placing the order. And she liked everything with extra duck sauce, a sweet orange confection that I have since learned is altogether unknown in China but a central element of Jewish-Chinese gastronomy. Chinese food was the only "foreign" food that my family ate. Chinese restaurants were the only restaurants we went to when we "ate out."

In my family, the pork in Chinese restaurants marked the world "outside" of our home. Eating it said that *outside* we could still be Jewish while not obeying the rules we observed at home.

. . .

WHEN THE LONG, beloved summers ended, the five of us returned to Brooklyn. Our apartment building on East Seventeenth Street had a name, "Los Angeles," carved into its stone lintel. At some point I heard a neighbor say that Los Angeles was a city as far as one could get from Brooklyn and still be in the United States, a place where it was always warm and where movies were made. I thought this was wonderful and loved being associated with it.

Apartment 3E had three small rooms. You walked into a tiny foyer, with a hall closet on the right and the kitchen straight ahead. The foyer table held a Victrola and a pile of 78 rpm records. To the left of the foyer was the living room, where my mother taught me to dance. It had few furnishings: a foldout couch, where my mother and aunt slept; an armchair reserved for my grandfather; and a drop-leaf table that opened out for Thanksgiving, High Holiday, and Passover meals. There was a television, bought, I was told, so that I could watch "children's television"—puppet shows like *Kukla, Fran and Ollie* and *Howdy Doody*. I remember these but have more distinct memories of my family gathering to watch *The Goldbergs* every week, with its heroine, the matriarch Molly Goldberg, who we all agreed was not nearly as wise as our own Edith Bonowitz. To the Bonowitzes, it seemed a small miracle that a Jewish family, with heavy Yiddish accents, was the sympathetic subject of an American television program. My grandmother did not so much enjoy that program as rejoice in its existence. Television at our house was a medium you engaged with by commenting on the news, disagreeing with the politicians, and reviewing performances in real time. When, much later, I became engaged in debates about the dangerous "passivity" of television viewing, I knew that my own family hadn't gotten the memo.

Between the living room and the bedroom was a narrow corridor with my grandmother's prized possession: a wooden console radio on which the family had listened to Franklin Roosevelt during the war. When the television arrived, this radio was placed in the only spot available, the hall opposite the bathroom, a location with no electrical outlet. Whenever my grandmother passed the radio on her way to the bedroom or bathroom, she would pat it like an old friend. It might be decommissioned, but it had gotten her through hard times.

In the bedroom, I slept on a cot between my grandparents' twin beds. In that room, my grandparents, mother, and aunt shared one "lowboy" dresser. Each had one drawer. And each had space for a few personal objects on its surface. How did they choose these objects? My aunt had a watch; my mother had a pair of art-deco rhinestone earrings. My grandmother had pearl clip-ons that she wore every day. My grandfather's object wasn't on the dresser. It was a secret—a billy club, a black leather weapon, weighted with lead, from his days on the piers. He kept it under his bed in Brooklyn and Rockaway. He told me that he could kill someone with it—and would, to keep us safe.

The basic rule in our home was clear: Everyone not in our family was a stranger. The neighbors didn't come into our home and we didn't go into theirs. As a child in my grandmother's home, I learned to never fully relax around strangers. For one thing, they weren't family, so the very fact of them was a problem. And with them around, it was hard to avoid the evil eye, a constant threat because of the obvious envy of neighbors. My grandmother tried to ward it off the best she could, by frequently spitting on my forehead. This was an old-world superstition that my grandmother could not be talked out of. In her view, since I was pretty, neighbors would stare to try to cross my eyes. Since I was clever, they would stare in an effort to make me dull. Her protective spitting needed to happen within seconds. As a child, I found this whole procedure awkward. When I was in my twenties, I looked forward to it. I gave myself over to my grandmother's conviction that I was, at least momentarily, safe from all harm.

My grandparents' emotional lives seemed ruled by a fear of being singled out as Jews. The Bonowitzes felt connected to the Old World—but here we were in Brooklyn, with no one left in Wolozin, unmoored in an America about which my family, at least, never felt fully certain. The anti-Semitism of the 1930s had been hard on them. The hesitancy of America to enter World War II upset them every day, and for long after the war was over. The Roosevelts were their heroes, but at home we often discussed how the Roosevelts, too, had been brought up to be anti-Semitic. My grandparents struggled, often, with what at the time had seemed to them inexplicable: that the Roosevelts had not been willing to bomb the train lines that went to the concentration camps. My grandparents told me that they had made a strategic decision that America would not want to go to war if people felt that the country was doing it for the Jews, an explanation I remember being given during a bath. I was told that Winston Churchill, another family hero, was also a private anti-Semite. This was Bonowitz political reality: The people who had saved the Jews did not like the Jews. So to survive, Jews had to get people to do the right thing regardless of their private feelings. We had to change laws before we changed hearts and minds.

My grandmother saw America as a refuge, but it had its limits. She felt that everywhere she went, she was required to be vigilant. In the outside world, you had to keep your guard up. Your home was where you could relax. My family seemed to be afraid of being found out, even if they weren't sure for what. When the doorbell rang, everyone tensed.

Of course, the bell had to ring sometimes. An electrician had to fix some outlets. The icebox had to be taken away and a new refrigerator needed to be installed. The plumber had to work on a stopped-up sink or toilet. I remember the first time I was asked to please answer the door when a tradesperson came to the house. I was just about to turn five. My aunt and mother were at work. My grandfather put on a suit and sat in the bedroom. My grandmother was dressed up, sitting in the living room. Holding her pocketbook. I was sent to the door. Looking back, I think that, however irrationally, any stranger entering their apartment conjured their worst fears. They prepared by dressing.

I was given instructions: greet the stranger, walk him through what he needed to accomplish, make sure the work was done correctly, pay him in cash, tip him, thank him, and make sure to get a receipt. Later, when my mother remarried and I lived with her and her new husband, my grandparents would purposely schedule deliveries and repairs for times when they knew I'd be visiting their apartment. As a child, I was the "designated adult" who could best deal with the world outside. I dealt, but I, too, began to be afraid of strangers.

As the McCarthy era darkened around them, my grandparents were anxious. People needed their privacy. Every morning, my grandmother and I went downstairs to the mailboxes in the lobby of our apartment building. And almost every morning she would say, as if it had never come up before, "In America, no one can look at your mail. It's a federal offense. That's the beauty of this country." Sometimes she would repeat the phrase "It's a federal offense." She said it like an incantation. It was also a prayer. I came to understand that she was afraid for my aunt, who had made politically radical friends in college.

I think of how different things are for children today, who accommodate to the idea that their email and messages are shareable and unprotected. And I think of all the internet gurus who for so many years summed up their political positions about privacy and the Net by saying that "the way to deal is to just be good."

With that incantation "It's a federal offense," my grandmother went a long way toward making

My aunt, Mildred Bonowitz, posing on a Brooklyn rooftop, elegant and composed, 1940.

me a civil libertarian, a defender of individual rights, and a patriotic American citizen in the lobby of our Brooklyn apartment building.

AFTER BREAKFAST on Sunday morning, whether we were in Rockaway or Brooklyn, my mother and I snuck back to bed together. We shared a favorite literary hero, Hopalong Cassidy, a genteel cowboy, and I pretended that chapter books were difficult for me so that my mother would read me stories about him. I wonder who I thought I was fooling. Even at four, I invented short plays about Hopalong that incorporated characters from the Archie comics. On weekends in bed with my mother, I played all the parts, although from time to time, my mother liked playing Veronica. In one of our favorite plays (from my pen), Hopalong had a dude ranch that the Bobbsey Twins and Betty and Veronica and I could visit. My mother was always welcome there as well. In all versions of this play, on our last day at the ranch, Hopalong proposed to my mother.

Once, after I presented a Hopalong play, my mother grew serious. "I have a pact that I want to share with you. It's just for the two of us. No one else." I was excited but scared too. A pact sounded special. My mother said, very low: "Even when I am as old as Grandpa and as old as Grandma, I'll always love you." She looked into my eyes, repeated the pact, and asked me to say it back to her. We said it to each other every Sunday morning. I don't remember when we stopped.

2.

The Memory Closet

One spring night in 1953, just before I turned five, a strange man came to dinner at my grandparents' apartment. I wasn't told what to call him. Or why he was there. After dinner, my grandparents and aunt stayed in the kitchen and my mother took me into the living room with this man. She told me he was going to be my new father.

I was terrified. I still hadn't caught his name and now it seemed wrong to ask. The relevant details emerged: My mother said that soon her name was going to be Harriet Turkle. "And Sherry, since you and I are a team, you are going to be Sherry Turkle." And right there, she explained that there was a catch. At school, I still had to be Sherry Zimmerman. "It's just a technical thing. I'm taking care of it. It will go away. But everywhere except school, you will be Sherry Turkle. You can't let anyone know about Sherry Zimmerman." I didn't understand the instructions, but I didn't let on. I think I understood things this way: I had a new pretend father and needed the pretend name to stay in her family. The name Sherry Zimmerman had always been secret. Now it was really a secret.

And so it was. Although my name, legally, was Sherry Zimmerman, from the day my mother married Milton Turkle, in her mind and heart, I was Sherry Turkle. I did the best I could to keep up with her mind and heart.

That first meeting in my grandmother's kitchen was followed by outings with my mother and Milton, one of them to Beach Haven, a housing complex about a half hour's drive from my grandparents' apartment. This, my mother said, was where she, Milton, and I were going to live together, "as a family." Then she said that in our Beach Haven apartment there would be a special "dinette alcove" just to put a table and chairs. She explained how wonderful this would be: We could have company and not have to eat in the kitchen or put a table in the living room. Also, I would have my own bedroom.

I was skeptical. What about bagels and lox when we had Sunday-morning breakfast with my grandparents and aunt? What about our favorite TV shows that we all watched together—Sid Caesar, *The Goldbergs, Your Hit Parade*? At night, my grandparents took turns singing me to sleep. "You Are My Sunshine." "Too-Ra-Loo-Ra-Loo-Ral." "When Irish Eyes Are Smiling." And grandma hummed the best one: the song called "Serenade," the opening theme to *The Goldbergs*. What was going to happen to all of that?

My mother and Milton were married in August 1953. I moved with them to a bungalow on the other side of the Rockaway court from where my mother and I had been living with my grandparents. Now we were in Lafayette Court, where the bungalows were a bit larger than the Edgemere Court bungalows of my earliest years. They were separated by long, narrow side alleys. At the end of each alley was an outdoor shower, roughly built of wood, with no roof. It was

Me, age five, at the wedding reception of Harriet and Milton Turkle, Tavern on the Green, August 1953.

Harriet and Milton, bride and groom.

one of the great pleasures of Rockaway—to take a hot shower at night, under the stars.

On our first morning there, my mother was beautifully dressed in a floral cotton duster, makeup immaculate. Hair set and lacquered. I remember thinking, *Maybe this will be nice.* Right after orange juice and toast, my mother asked me to change into a bathing suit and follow her along the narrow alleyway toward our shower. She said: "This is good for you. This is what you have been missing by not growing up around brothers or a father from when you were little." This sounded like something from a book. Or from a conversation with Milton, who I had already learned had a tendency to talk in this declarative style. My mother opened the shower door. Milton was already in the shower, waiting for me, naked. I like to think that no one asked me to take off my bathing suit, but I don't remember. Whatever the reason, my mother put her five-year-old daughter in the shower with her new husband so that I could see what a man's genitals looked like. At that time, I knew that men had penises for when they had to pee, but I was unprepared for Milton's balls. I remember that they seemed to be as long as his penis and hung below it on his leg. I did not understand how looking at any of this would help me. When would it help me? Help me do what? I was frightened. I closed my eyes. Milton said, "Open your eyes." He put his hands on the side of my head and said, "You have to look. This is good for you." *This is good for you.* Those had been my mother's words. They were in this together.

I reached up for the lock. As I opened the door, my mother was standing outside the shower holding a towel to dry me off. I remember so clearly my mother's face, bright and smiling. For her, this was a special, happy occasion. Some kind of rite of passage. From what? To what? She must have seen my silent, tear-stained face. I don't remember any discussion about it. I don't think it ever happened again. It was as though it never happened.

I knew not to talk about the shower, but from the beginning, it shaped how I thought about Milton and my mother as "parents." They were trying to be different from the Bonowitzes, modern, and informed by books. I assumed that Milton or my mother had picked this idea up from some fashionable expert.

I didn't think this was going to be good for me. I liked living with the Bonowitzes, everything about it. The not-modern things about their life were comforting. I liked the early-morning walk that my grandfather called a "constitutional." My grandmother's fully set table for Friday-night dinner. Her household remedies. Saltwater gargles. Lemon and honey. A drop of ipecac on the tongue. Hot milk at bedtime. None of these things followed us to Beach Haven.

As I grew older, I thought more about what the shower had meant. It hadn't left me with sexual anxiety as much as what psychologists call hypervigilance, being oversensitive to your environment. The dictionary says that the purpose of the ever-watchful behavior is to "detect activity." That describes me. In any social situation, I am observant in ways that can make it hard to relax. But that same need to see what is going on (and remember how it is different from what was going on yesterday) has helped in my work. I notice things.

IN OUR NEW NEIGHBORHOOD of Beach Haven, Milton Turkle was presented as my biological father. "No one can know," said my mother, "that I was married before. No one can know that Milton is not your father." Of course, every day when I went to school, the name "Sherry Zimmerman" would be on the class list, and then I had to write this name on every worksheet. I had no choice but to answer to it. How could the Sherry Zimmerman in school disappear when I went home? I became gripped by a notion, part fantasy, part not, that I was invisible. For decades to come, I sometimes thought that if I didn't arrange my hair in its habitual style or wear full makeup, I would be unrecognizable.

As promised, our new apartment had an alcove for a dinette set. Our dinette table was oval, in an Empire style with gold-leaf decoration on the legs and six matching chairs. My mother loved this dinette set. I remember a few times that my mother had friends from Beach Haven to dinner in the alcove. At one party, I first served drinks and Ritz crackers topped with cream cheese and pimentos in the living room. And then I disappeared to a tray in my room while the guests had roast chicken with potatoes. There was ice cream and cookies for dessert. Later, my mother laughed with me when she realized that she had made so many "kosher mistakes." She hadn't thought of the cream cheese with the pimento as milk. The potatoes were buttered! The ice cream was milk, too, and there it was, right after the chicken. She was smiling. I think she must have been happy to be in this new marriage, where she didn't even have to be "kosher style."

In Beach Haven, my mother invited children and their mothers into our apartment. Considering the fortress world of the Bonowitz family, this, like her dinner parties, showed her desire for a different kind of life. But I entered this life with the anxieties of an undercover agent. When other children came for playdates, I was Sherry Turkle and dreaded being discovered a liar.

I looked forward to weekends when I could visit my grandparents and relax. Block City and constitutionals with my grandfather. Movies and the theater with my grandmother and aunt. Political conversation over meals. Talking back to the television when the news came on. My favorite thing was when my aunt and I went to the free

Sundays at the big New York museums and sat on a bench in a room with paintings. My aunt said it was allowed, and even encouraged, to talk softly in these rooms with the beautiful art.

On Brooklyn Saturdays with my grandmother, we would cover long distances, shopping and paying bills. We sometimes took trolley cars and buses, but mostly we went on foot. As we traveled, my grandmother talked to me about her daughters. Her stunning and charismatic Harriet had found a new man. Would her brilliant Mildred find work that was worthy of her? "Mildred," she said, was "ahead of her time." If Mildred were in her time, according to my grandmother, she would be running the companies where now she was only an office manager. But no man wanted Mildred. She was too smart. My grandmother did not say this at dinner-table discussions of how Mildred could find a husband. She admitted these things to me on our excursions.

My grandmother, on her favorite bench at the Prospect Park Parade grounds, early 1950s.

At first I thought that my grandmother was saying that I would have to choose between femininity and brains. But that wasn't the case. My grandmother knew that my mother had brains aplenty. My mother had skipped every other grade in grammar and middle school and raced through college with medals and awards. But she was also flirtatious and feminine. My aunt Mildred was quiet and serious. She led with her interests in books and ideas. My grandmother was saying that it wasn't who you were but what you let other people see.

What would I choose to hide and what would I allow to show? For as long as I could remember, I had been told I had special brains. But I was doing everything I could to model myself on my mother. How she danced and laughed. How she pulled up her hair. I dressed up in her open-toed silver sandals and her gray cloche hat with its sequined veil. Hers was the approval I sought.

From the start Milton and Harriet had money troubles. He was a civil servant who worked for the New York State Division of Employment. My mother wanted more children. And she wanted to move to a different apartment in Beach Haven, a more expensive one with a terrace. Milton's modest salary would not get her to that apartment. She did what was necessary; she took work into the house. Her job was to call a list of homeowners, encouraging them to buy aluminum siding from a company called Artcraft. If someone agreed to a home consultation with the Artcraft salesperson, she made money. She set up a little card table in the living room, where I did my homework quietly on the floor to keep her company. She said I was there "for solidarity."

I memorized my mother's Artcraft call and all the responses she was supposed to make if people hesitated, or asked for more information, or said they already had aluminum siding. I wanted to talk to customers. My mother loved the idea. She hated making calls and here I was, enthusiastic and probably good at it. But she was afraid it was illegal or that she would get into trouble. I was in first grade, only six years old; my voice would sound too young.

I was proud of her, but I gradually understood that she was ashamed of this work. She knew it made her father think less of Milton. She made it clear to me that I was never to discuss her Artcraft job.

To get my mother out of the aluminum-siding business, Milton began to work as a waiter at catered weekend bar mitzvahs and weddings. When Beach Haven acquaintances turned up as guests at some of the functions he worked at, my mother was upset. I sympathized with Milton. He had been told to keep this work a secret. But he had been given an impossible task.

WE MOVED TO the new apartment in Beach Haven—on a street called Murdock Court—just before I started third grade. By now, I had a new sister and brother, Susan and Bruce, born in 1954 and 1956. My mother was excited because her toddler and new baby could be put out in the "healthy air" on our gated terrace, just off the living room. And Murdock Court was farther away from my primary school, so we could have a circle of friends who would never have heard my Zimmerman name. Here, our family would be "one."

I liked being an older sister—especially the babysitting, reading, and birthday-party planning. But from the start, my mother showed me a special locked cabinet where I was to put away anything with the word "Zimmerman" so that Susan and Bruce would never see it. This was where I kept all my schoolbooks and papers. The first thing I did when I got home from school was to hide my things. I did my homework at school or in the kitchen when everyone else had gone to bed.

But when Susan was five, she found a notebook with the name "Sherry Zimmerman" written on the inside cover. Of course, Susan asked about it. I stood frozen in the hallway and watched our mother launch into a long story about the notebook belonging to "Sherry's friend." The notebook was in my handwriting and contained all the ideas for my third-grade Shakespeare project. Susan stared blankly ahead. She looked as though she didn't believe anything our mother was saying. I worried what this would do to Susan, to know her mother was lying to her, and considered telling her my version of the truth. But I was afraid. Our mother's lie had been so elaborate. I wondered why it was necessary. I came up with the idea that perhaps I would not be able to stay with my mother if the secret got out that I was not a true Turkle daughter.

That night, hot and headachy, I snuck into the kitchen searching for aspirin. I found it in a cabinet above the refrigerator. Now, with secret headaches, I gave myself something new to worry about.

My mother saw the Murdock Court apartment, with its terrace, as a social step up, but it had no dining alcove. Our oval dinette table had to be squeezed into a narrow kitchen where only two of its matching chairs could fit, one at each end. If more than two people wanted to sit at the table, there was only a narrow path to the stove or refrigerator. With my mother's kitchen in disarray, family meals were staggered, and there was no question of the dreamed-of dinner parties. Now my mother's reputation as a hostess depended on entertaining in the living room, where guests balanced canapés and drinks on their laps. My mother's specialty was a fresh pineapple that she cut into four quarters. Then she divided each quarter into easy-to-remove slices. Each slice had a toothpick inserted into it that held a marshmallow and a maraschino cherry.

Our new apartment was near the tree-lined Ocean Parkway, and my mother decreed that Milton and I would take Wednesday-night walks there. Milton, she explained to me, knew a lot about history and was a great reader. We would have a lot in common. My mother wanted a close-knit family. Now I think she was also trying to prepare me for an adoption hearing where I could testify that Milton and I had a good relationship.

Milton took our walks as an opportunity to unburden himself to third-grade me. He told me how disappointed he was in his professional achievements. He couldn't pass the tests that were required for advancement at the New York State Division of Employment. He said he felt intellectually inferior not only to me but to both my mother and my aunt. They had real college degrees. He had gotten his degree with the GI Bill. He didn't think it was the same thing. From our very first walk, I tried to change the subject from his feelings of inadequacy, but he just charged on.

I told my mother that I didn't want to go on any more Milton walks because I had too much weekday homework. She told me again that it would be good for me to be closer to Milton. Then the dreaded "We are all one family now." So, more walks. He told me he'd been discharged from the army for depression. He felt guilty for not serving in Korea. I didn't know how to stop this talk. I didn't know how to say what was wrong with it. My grandfather sang me lullabies and we talked about baseball. He stressed the importance of the High Holidays. And he explained that he had the highest admiration for Sammy Davis Jr. He thought he was America's most accomplished entertainer. This Milton talk was like nothing else.

During that same third-grade year, Milton decided that he wanted to participate in my education. I braced myself for the worst. He saw himself as an expert on Abraham Lincoln and decided he would give a lecture to my class on the occasion of Lincoln's birthday. Actually,

I'm no longer certain if it was Milton or my mother who first became fixed on this idea. All I know is that I was asked to propose it to my teacher. I was upset. No one else's father had lectured in any of my classes. I sensed that my parents were playing on my "smartest girl in the class" status, which I was trying to tone down in order to make friends. And his name was Milton *Turkle*. In that class I was Sherry *Zimmerman*! Could only I see that my task, as I understood it, to hide my difference from my family, was being made nearly impossible?

But my mother insisted. So I asked my teacher. And she asked the principal. Milton got permission to give a lecture on Abraham Lincoln.

Milton made regular trips to the library to fortify himself with more books on Abraham Lincoln. He prepared for hours every night at the dinette kitchen table. He asked for silence after seven. As I did my late-night homework, I watched him copying long passages from the Lincoln books onto yellow legal pads.

Finally the day arrived. Milton told an inspirational story of how Lincoln, having retired from politics, went back into public life when he saw slavery spreading into new territories. He saved the nation, freed the slaves, and was martyred. Milton read the lecture from a handwritten text and ended with Edwin Stanton's words at Lincoln's death: "Now he belongs to the ages." He delivered the line very dramatically, then looked up from his yellow pages, blinking, and the teacher signaled my class to applaud. His declamatory style took me by surprise, but I was relieved that nothing terrible had happened. Milton's speech was not pitched to third graders, but the real audience, my mother, was not in the room.

Milton was happy. My mother was ecstatic. She immediately went into an overdrive of ambition. Perhaps Milton had found his true vocation. Perhaps Milton should give lectures on Abraham Lincoln in all the Brooklyn schools. Of course, the lectures would begin by being unpaid, but it could be a kind of enrichment program. For a few days, she was the wife of a man who had achieved an independent success. Both my mother and Milton thought that the Abraham Lincoln lecture was a steady thing, nailed down as a family tradition. But the next year, my fourth-grade teacher said no. She said she had a carefully worked-out curriculum and it would not be possible to add an extra lecture. My mother did not take no for an answer. She wrote a letter to the principal, Dr. Levine, reminding him of this special learning opportunity and how well it had gone the year before.

Dr. Levine called me into his office. He commiserated with me as though I were the person being disappointed. I supposed, at the time, that this was how normal grown-ups would approach this. From the principal's point of view, a precocious child wanted to show off her father. So the *child* should be let down easy. I wanted everyone to think my family was normal, so I pretended that this was what was going on. I thanked the principal and said I understood. When I gave my mother the news, we were standing in the kitchen. She called in Milton so that we could tell him together. His mouth stiffened. He held on to the side of the oval dinette table. I saw something new. He did not need to be so diminished. I felt as though I had done this to him. I put myself in his place and wondered if he hated me.

More than sixty years have passed since the second Lincoln lecture that never was. Every year, on Lincoln's birthday, I feel anxious.

My mother owned a Brownie camera, but there was always a lot of talk about the expense of film and the cost of developing a photograph, which meant that a photograph, whether for the Turkles or for the Bonowitzes, was a big event. There was an unspoken understanding that each family member had a small allotment of photographs to be "spent" on them. When it was my turn to take a picture, I filled it with objects I considered special. In one birthday photograph, I am seated on my grandparents' damask couch. I am wearing my grandmother's white gloves and holding a small straw doll that Mildred had given me after a trip to Mexico and a porcelain doll she had brought home from France. I later realized that these were my first destinations abroad.

All of my special objects had their place in the memory closet at my grandparents' apartment. There, in a little leather box, I found a silver ring and matching bracelet from Thailand, a gift to my mother from her uncle Samuel Bearman, my grandmother's brother, the man

I was named after. He was my mother's idol when she was growing up. She told me he was handsome and had gone to pharmacy school at Columbia University. I imagined my mother wearing her uncle Sam's jewelry when she went out on dates as a single woman. My mother didn't talk about Charles Zimmerman. But she often told me how proud I should be to be named after Samuel Bearman, the Ivy League scholar.

Birthday photo, holding my object treasures, Brooklyn, June 1956.

I learned to push the kitchen table under the memory closet and then stand on the table to reach my treasures. I worked methodically, taking down and examining every book, every box. I was allowed to look at anything in the closet, from as early as I can remember, certainly from when I was three, but I was always to put it back. The closet seemed to me of infinite dimensions, infinite depth.

I can't remember a time when I didn't find something new in

the closet. Each object I found—every key ring or postcard—received the care and attention that my favorite heroine, the girl detective Nancy Drew, gave the clues she stumbled upon. In the closet, every high school notebook with its marginalia—some of it my mother's, some of it my aunt's—meant a possible new understanding of my history; every photo of my mother on a date or at a dance became a clue to my possible identity.

When I was very young, sometimes one of the adults in the family would come into the kitchen to watch me at work. When I began looking in the closet, I didn't know what I was looking for. I think they did. I was looking for the missing person. I was looking for a trace of my father. But they had been there before me and gotten rid of any bits and pieces he might have left—an address book, a business card, a random note. There were many torn photographs. Once, I found a photograph with the body still there and the face cut out. I never asked whose face it was; I knew. And I knew enough never to mention the photograph, for fear it might disappear. It was precious to me. The image had been attacked, but it contained so many missing puzzle pieces. What his hands looked like. That he wore lace-up shoes. That his pants were tweed.

FROM WHEN I was five to when I was eight, not often, perhaps three or four times, I saw Charlie, rare episodes cloaked in secrecy. Milton would drive me to my aunt Mildred, and Mildred would drive me to some meet-up with Charlie. To see a dance performance. To take a walk in the park. I remember, much later, someone saying, "He never takes her to anyplace where he has to spend any money." Charlie never bought me food, but he brought his own refreshments to our meetings. I was careful not to mention if I ate something that Charlie brought to a meeting. Apparently this, too, was very bad.

My mother had a two-part plan: first to end these court-mandated visits. Then for Milton to legally adopt me. As she saw it, that's how we would get rid of the stink of my name. I remember no conversation about this at the time, just that one day, when I was eight, I was kept home on a school day and my mother told me we were going to court. I didn't know what that meant.

Milton drove us to downtown Brooklyn. He sat upright in the driver's seat, peering forward through eyeglasses that didn't seem to give him a good view of the road. At the courthouse we entered a small room that was empty, save for Charlie, who sat with a lawyer on one side of the room. I sat with my mother and Milton on the other side. We also had a lawyer.

Roller skating in Beach Haven. I broke my arm skating before a visit with my father, 1950s.

So that the grown-ups could talk, an older woman wearing so much powder that her face was white as fresh snow took me to a still smaller room adjacent to the courtroom. After a while, the powdery woman led me back to the courtroom and I was told to sit in a chair to the right of the judge, who asked me, without preface, "Do you love your father?" I said nothing. I didn't really know Charlie; I just pined for him. Once, when he took me to a dance performance when I was six, I had just broken my right arm while roller-skating. At the recital,

Charlie sat to my right. When it came time to clap, he had raised his right arm so that I could clap by striking his right hand with my left. I thought that was brilliant. Was that love? I glanced toward my mother. She was staring straight ahead. The judge spoke again. Same question: "Do you love your father?"

No one else had ever named Charles Zimmerman as my "father." Everyone else just called him Charlie. When the judge said "your father," I immediately felt warmth toward him. "Your father." It sounded hopeful. As though I had one. I called Milton "Daddy." I wouldn't have dared call him "Milton." But I arranged my mind so that the word "Daddy" meant nothing to me. The judge gestured to Charlie. This time he got an answer.

"Yes," I said.

"So go over and kiss your father," the judge instructed me.

I stood up, walked toward Charlie, and kissed him on the cheek. Now, from a different vantage point in the room, I tried to meet my mother's eyes, but she still stared straight ahead. For weeks afterward, she didn't speak to me. I had given the wrong answer. Her only punishment, ever, was silence. I was in agony.

The day had consequences. The judge said I would have more "visitations" with my father. But they, too, turned out to be infrequent. On the few occasions that I remember meeting with Charlie after this court date, he took me to Prospect Park.

Charlie's Prospect Park had a lake and grand arches. I had never seen it before. My grandparents lived near the Parade Grounds bordering Caton Avenue. That and the little hill where my aunt took me sledding were the only Prospect Park I knew. The visits with Charlie were usually on a weekend when I was sleeping over with my grandparents, so Mildred drove me to see him. She and I didn't talk much in the car. When we arrived, there were no handshakes between

Mildred and Charlie. My aunt kept it simple: She told Charlie when she would pick me up.

I think we had three hours. During one visit I remember vividly, my father rented a rowboat on Prospect Park Lake. I had never been in a rowboat before. He asked if I would like to take an oar, and we sat side by side. Then he asked if I would like to row by myself, and I wanted to say, *No, please row with me,* but I didn't dare say no to anything he asked. So I said yes and rowed alone, and then he took over again. I remember the pain of disappointing him. He told me to make the oars "stand up like soldiers" when they hit the water, and I couldn't do it, not even once. When we returned to land, my father spread out a picnic blanket and took a thermos from a knapsack.

My father's thermos was tall, wrapped in tan leather. It was filled with something cold and icy. "This drink is healthy," he said. "You need to drink healthy things." He explained that it was a malted—not a chocolate malted, the only kind I'd ever known, but a cantaloupe malted. He poured the orange liquid from the leather thermos into a stainless-steel cap. It was thick and pungent. I didn't know if I liked it. But the sun was strong, the grass soft. I wondered if this was permitted.

I WOKE UP every morning with fantasies of escape. I thought I would pack a lunch and leave.

If you are a little girl yearning for a change, fairy tales are waiting for you. Snow White, Sleeping Beauty, the Beast's Beauty all end up in new lives, the lives intended for them. "Cinderella," the blueprint story for transformation of circumstance, makes this aspect of the narrative explicit: Cinderella is not where she should be. I had a suitor once, a famous philosopher, who had been born in Brooklyn in modest

circumstances—in fact, similar to mine—who told me that throughout his childhood, he believed that he had been switched at birth in
the hospital nursery for another, a prince or the son of a wealthy busi-
nessman. How else to explain his talents? His beauty? His elegance?
He did not belong with his parents and, in a sense, did not recognize
them. He felt entitled to his transformation to Ivy League professor,
international star. I didn't have anything like the detail of his fantasy,
but I understood it.

With no information, I could fantasize who Charlie *really* was. I
knew he wasn't a literal prince. He clearly had some flaw that was
never shared with me. But his true identity was unknown. He could
have qualities that made me special.

When I was seven years old, Mildred took me to see a film version
of the Cinderella story that has remained with me all my life: *The
Glass Slipper*. My aunt and I loved this movie and talked about it end-
lessly. What drew my attention right away was that at their first
meeting, Madame Toquet, the story's stand-in for a fairy godmother,
talks to the heroine, Ella, not about the magic of sorcerers but about
the transformative power of intelligence, self-reliance, and words. Madame Toquet has favorite words: "pickle relish," "apple dumplings,"
"windowsill." As we watched the movie, my aunt memorized them on
the spot. She cultivated this ability as a theatergoer who knows she
will see a performance only once. She helped to cultivate it in me.
Sometimes, when I would go to my aunt with a problem, Mildred
would say: "Pickle relish, apple dumplings, windowsill." I understood
this as an invitation to conversation.

I lived in my reveries and played the original cast recordings of
Broadway shows that Mildred collected. Like *The Glass Slipper*, my
favorites—*My Fair Lady, Gigi*—had a spirited young woman achiev-
ing her dreams through becoming her better self. A tutor could help.

There was Ella's Madame Toquet, Eliza's Henry Higgins, and Gigi's aunt Alicia.

In Rockaway, when I was eight and recuperating from appendicitis, my grandmother took my desire to understand how the world beyond Brooklyn worked and turned it into a game. I was given the task of planning a family trip. She found a book of states' chambers of commerce and departments of tourism. She taught me how to compose a formal letter of inquiry and provided stationery, envelopes, and stamps. I began to write away for itineraries, maps, and hotel information all around the country. The status of this trip always lived between reality and dream. None of the trips I planned actually took place. But all of that writing away for information and receiving piles of mail in return expanded my world. The post office was mine. People all across the United States were willing to tell me things I wanted to know.

I thought of my grandmother's lessons when, in junior high, I got it into my head that since John F. Kennedy had gone to Harvard, I wanted to go to Harvard. I assembled my best form letters and composed a short note to Harvard, asking for admissions information. The admissions office wrote right back. The letter said that Harvard did not consider undergraduate women, but the office put me in touch with Radcliffe College. This felt like a significant advance. Harvard University had answered my mail.

I still remember the "Introduction to Radcliffe" catalog that arrived at Murdock Court. It had words, of course, but what I remember most are its photographs, featuring intense young women studying, drinking coffee, and talking. I was struck by this one: A girl reads a book in a French café in Harvard Square, a curtain of long, dark hair almost hiding her face. The post office had not failed me. I was going to Radcliffe.

. . .

DESPITE MY TOTAL lack of musicality or dramatic talent, for several years my mother was convinced that I would become a nightclub singer. Only because it's what she wanted to do. So for my tenth birthday, going to a local Brooklyn supper club—called the Elegante— was my designated treat. When the chanteuse came onstage, my mother nudged me to pay close attention. I knew she hoped the performance would inspire me to a life on the stage. I remember feeling immune to her exertions.

I was armed with a powerful idea: To be good at a job, you had to love the objects associated with that job. I found this idea in a book that Milton had brought home from work, *How to Choose the Right Job for You*. The book explained that if you love hammers, wood, and tools, think about being a carpenter. If you enjoy tidying things up in files, think about office work. In other words, imagine yourself with the *objects* of your craft. My mother relaxed by walking through the fur and evening gown departments at downtown department stores. It was natural that she should think about being a nightclub singer. I loved fountain pens and beautifully bound notebooks. I could see myself as a writer, like Jo March in *Little Women*.

That we owned a book about career choices was unusual—we had so few books at home. Milton had his biography of Abraham Lincoln. I cherished an illustrated edition of *Cinderella*, and my grandmother had bought me *Little Women* and the twenty-four-volume Funk & Wagnalls encyclopedia—the volumes were released once every two weeks at her local A&P supermarket. Our largest collection of books was my stash of Nancy Drew mystery stories—my half of the pile of books, tied up in neat parcels, that my best friend, Helene, and I had found in the incinerator room of our apartment building. This was the way books got passed from family to family in our building; most of the families in the building did not know one another but had similar backgrounds and incomes—they were Jewish and worked as civil servants, for the post office, as waiters in delicatessens, struggling to be in the middle class. We knew a family where the husband was an accountant, and we viewed them with awe. These families did not have extra cash to buy books for their children. My grandmother's gift of *Little Women* and the encyclopedias was a special treat. When it came to books, we all used the public library. There were two public libraries near Murdock Court, one a half hour's walk, a larger one a short bus ride away. So for Helene and me, finding a pile of Nancy Drews was dizzying. There were nineteen volumes. Helene had made the discovery and summoned me to the incinerator room, so she got to keep ten and I got to keep nine.

In order to solve her mysteries, Nancy was often called upon to decode an object: a brass-bound trunk, an old clock, a pair of twisted candles. Some of the objects had hidden compartments or secret drawers that would suddenly open. I searched my neighborhood for mysterious objects to decipher. One stool at the soda fountain was a different height from the others. It could be hiding a secret compartment. One fall Helene and I put on our Brownie scout uniforms and roller skates and pretended that we were Nancy Drew Girl Scouts, deputized by the FBI. We asked neighbors to tell us about any suspicious activity. My mother was mortified. I told her I would stop, but I promised myself that I would find mysterious objects outside of Brooklyn.

I WAS TOLD EARLY on in school that a record had been opened on me. It was called a permanent record, that is, it allowed no erasures.

It would stay with me long enough to determine whether I got into college and where I got into college. This, I was made to understand, would determine all the rest.

One of the large themes in my studies of online life is how the early internet provided an opportunity for what the Harvard psychoanalyst Erik Erikson called a "psychosocial moratorium," particularly important to identity development in adolescence. Online, people (and not just young people) had an opportunity to try out a range of identities and roles, to play at being more assertive than they could be in real life, to play at being more flirtatious, more uninhibited, a different age, a different gender.

Erikson stressed that adolescence does its job of identity confirmation best if everyone is allowed to "try on" different selves, to get a sense of what "fits" them best in an atmosphere where they are not judged. Making space for this moratorium means that false starts and mistakes are not counted against you. It's a "time-out."

When I first read Erikson as a college freshman, I began to think about my own experiences growing up. I'd been allowed my dreams, certainly, but I'd had a life without a moratorium. Instead, I had been terrorized by the idea of a permanent record.

On my fifth-grade report card, Mrs. Malinow gave me a failing grade in behavior for talking in class with my friend Carol. I loved Carol because she was smart and witty and introduced me to *MAD* magazine. More than this, her parents were divorced, and she was allowed to talk about it with anyone. She invited me to her home for dinner and I was shocked when the subject of divorce came up. I was invited a second time and it came up again. I spent as much time as I could at Carol's apartment. I was on a campaign to see how other people lived and decided that when I had a family, I would run it like Carol's family. No secrets.

When Carol and I got to school, our animated conversations spilled over into official "put your heads down on the desk" rest times. When I got that first failing grade, Mrs. Malinow stressed that it was on my permanent record. I still remember my walk home from school that day. I was ruined. My mother made me promise to stay away from Carol. Forever. I've missed her ever since.

IT WAS AROUND THAT TIME, when I was in fifth grade, that my mother had her first breast cancer operation. I remember the day of my mother's surgery because it was the day of the PS 216 spring spelling bee. I had a good shot at winning, but my mother wasn't coming to the spelling bee, and my grandparents were at our apartment, but they weren't coming either. I was told my mother was having minor surgery and Milton was with her. My grandparents were there to watch over me, Susan, and Bruce. My grandparents always got dressed up when they left their apartment, but I remember thinking that on this day, they were dressed formally, as though it were a Jewish holiday. My grandfather was in a suit and tie and my grandmother in a soft gray dress with a rhinestone pin at the collar. They sat at opposite ends of our odd dinette table, my grandmother at the far end. That put her chair right under our telephone, which was attached to the wall.

I must have won the spelling bee, because I came home feeling triumphant. When I walked into the apartment, my grandparents were where I had left them in the kitchen, my grandmother still at her post near the phone. In response to my high spirits, my grandfather said, "Ignorance is bliss," and my grandmother shot him a look to keep quiet. I shut right up because I must be in ignorance of something bad. Something was wrong with my mother.

I think of this moment often because it had to be the first time I was given a clue that my mother was ill, and I chose to not pay attention. Or rather, I paid close attention and did what the grown-ups signaled they wanted from me: to pretend not to notice what was happening. I knew I could receive no comfort, because no one would admit that anything sad had happened. It was a very particular loneliness: knowing that people around you were also sad but that you couldn't be sad together.

I later learned that there were several surgeries. There was radiation and steroids. For one treatment, I was sent on a Girl Scout trip. For another, my aunt took me to Colonial Williamsburg. My mother had considered an experimental hormone regimen that would have radically changed her secondary sexual characteristics. My mother turned this down and my aunt supported her decision. After my mother died, Mildred shared this with me in tears, asking if she did the right thing in encouraging my mother to reject this treatment. I reassured Mildred that their instincts had been right. My mother knew that was not her path.

It must have been in the aftermath of my mother's surgery that Milton took me for a walk on Ocean Parkway and told me he didn't want me spending so many weekends with my grandparents. Summers in Rockaway should be enough. Now he was working steady "jobs" as a waiter and I should keep my mother company, spend more time with my sister and brother, and help my mother take care of them. But he wanted to be reasonable, he said. What games did I play at my grandparents' home? Board games? He might get some of these games for our apartment. What did my grandparents have?

I tried to think. I could not tell him about the memory closet. I could not tell him about the photograph of Charlie with his head cut out of the picture. I told him another story—that I played with fabrics and liked to make curtains, sometimes costumes. I didn't say that when I draped the fabric, I imagined myself in dramas in which an older character, sometimes a mentor or a teacher, would in the end reveal himself as my father. Milton said that perhaps we could get some yards of cloth for Murdock Court. Could I be happy playing with fabric here at home? I mumbled something about trying.

3.

An Unsentimental Education

At my elementary school, PS 216, there had been the Jewish kids from Beach Haven and the Italian kids who lived on the streets closer to Avenue X, lined with pizzerias and bakeries. I envied the Italian kids. They lived in proper houses (not just apartments), and during the holiday season, their houses had Christmas lights; they seemed so much more a part of America.

Mark Twain Junior High School was only a twenty-minute drive from PS 216, but it was a different world, just blocks from the Coney Island boardwalk. By 1960, Coney Island was dying. It still had the parachute jump, the Wonder Wheel, and freak shows. It still had bumper cars and strip clubs. But everything seemed on borrowed time, as though it was already about nostalgia.

At school, some students wore the same clothes all week, and cafeteria hot lunch was their main meal of the day. Mark Twain also had children from a gated community called Sea Gate. For the first time, I had friends whose life was a struggle and others whose fathers were doctors and lawyers, the first people I knew who wanted to grow up and be like their parents.

In September 1960, the presidential election campaign was in full swing. All my friends and I wished we were twenty-one so that we could vote for John F. Kennedy. Of course, we girls also wanted to be Jackie Kennedy. In my seventh-grade class assembly, I got to play her. My grandmother had bought me a small Singer sewing machine to make Rockaway curtains and doll clothes, and we used it to make my costume: a navy-blue pencil skirt and a pink bouclé jacket. I borrowed a pillbox hat from my aunt and a fake-pearl choker and matching earrings from my grandmother. My mother gave me an Elizabeth Arden tube of coral lipstick.

And since that was my only makeup, I decided at the last minute to improvise and use the lipstick as eyeshadow as well, which gave my Jackie an alarming, vampiric appearance. My lines in the play were these, repeated several times, "Oh, John, you will make a wonderful president. I will love being First Lady." I remembered my lines on the day of performance and I remember them still. I thought of them in 1976 when I realized that Seymour Papert, the charismatic mathematician I was dating and eventually married, was the author of programming languages used around the world. I didn't just feel proud of him; I felt a curious sense of relaxation, as in, "Now I can stop trying so hard. I can be Mrs. Papert. I can bask in his reflected glory." And then I had to stop myself, as though stepping away from a toasty fire on a snowy day.

In junior high, Kennedy fever struck me hard. I read all his campaign literature and handed out leaflets in the supermarket. The indelible lessons of my campaigning: The young will inherit the earth. The clever will inherit the country. Stand up for civil rights. Try to marry well, but try to do something on your own. Jackie Kennedy's allure came from the unmistakable impression that she could, *if she wanted*, do something on her own.

IN ELEMENTARY SCHOOL, my teachers had seemed to follow their passions, perhaps because our classes were tracked, and my advanced classes quickly covered the basic material. My third-grade teacher, Mrs. Dome, loved Shakespeare and thought elementary-school children should love him too. For many months of third grade, it was pretty much all Shakespeare, all the time. When we came to a scene that referred to sex, Mrs. Dome simply said, "You'll understand that later; you don't need to understand all of Shakespeare now," and we breezed right by. When I consider elementary school, I think that permission to not understand was its greatest gift. Later in life, I would come to a rough patch, say, in French social theory, and if I was understanding something but not much, I would say to myself: *This is only the beginning. This isn't your last chance to read Derrida. Keep at it.*

In seventh grade, things changed. I was in a "special progress" class that brought together thirty gifted students and had us do three years of junior high in two. At the beginning of every class, we were given a soft-sided yellow book—it was called a "review book"—and it contained the state of New York's expectations for us in that class. The teachers had to teach us from that book and test us on what was in that book. Everything had to be memorized.

In the review-book system, if you had strong general intelligence and a good memory, you could get perfect grades on all the tests across all subjects. That meant that I ended up being valedictorian in junior high. And again in high school. I won according to the rules, but something didn't seem fair. There were much better mathematicians; much better science students. I worried that what I excelled in was memorizing review books. I felt fraudulent, for all my hard work.

But my life as a reader was taking me in another direction. On weekend nights when Milton worked as a waiter, I took babysitting jobs for a young couple who lived in the apartment next to ours and who had a living room lined with bookshelves. I taught myself to speed-read in order to get through as many of their books as possible. It was during babysitting that I first read *Pride and Prejudice*. My previous heroines—Jo March, Gigi, Eliza Doolittle—all seemed like paper dolls next to the passionate, articulate Elizabeth Bennet. Elizabeth Bennet was not where she should be. And she did not waste her time before she got to that new place. She did not become vulgar when surrounded by coarseness. While waiting, she cultivated herself.

AT THIRTEEN, if you were invited to a boy's bar mitzvah, you went to services on Saturday morning and then to a party, usually that night.

Being a bar mitzvah guest was expensive, and in seventh grade, I was invited to about eleven. I needed to buy a present and something appropriate to wear to services. I needed a real party dress and kitten-heeled party shoes. I shopped for all of these things with my grandmother; they were my grandfather's "treat." My bar mitzvah dress was velvet-embossed rayon in a light sage green. It had a deep neck, a cinched waist, and a wide bouffant skirt. It came from Mays discount department store in downtown Brooklyn. It was my first serious piece of clothing. But the first time I wore it, one of my girlfriends told me that the boys were making fun of me. When they danced with me, they could see down the front of my dress. I ran to the ladies' room, sobbing. An older woman found me there and offered to call my mother. My mother called my aunt. Mildred arrived with my grandmother. They brought needle and thread, sewing scissors, safety pins, and my aunt's embroidered evening shrug from Saks.

My grandmother sat in an overstuffed armchair and talked softly to me. The problem was not as bad as I thought, but we certainly would take the dress to the tailor. For now, she could pin the shoulders so that the dress lay closer to my body. She did not try to talk me out of my anguish. She explained that when I tried on the dress in the store, I had been standing up very straight and she had not seen the problem. She said that we could go home now, but that if I wanted to stay at the party a bit longer, I could wear Mildred's beaded shrug over the dress. It would be pretty. But she and Mildred would wait outside in the car. Whenever I wanted to leave, they would be there. I don't remember how much more of the evening I got through. I remember how soothing it was for an adult in my family to acknowledge my reality.

I found services awesome. So many members of these old Brooklyn shuls were Holocaust survivors. Or, as in the case of my family, they had lost whatever extended family they had in Eastern Europe. These bar mitzvahs celebrated that another generation of Jews was alive. Somehow we children understood this. No matter what our individual relationships with our parents or how distant we felt from them, we knew what we meant to them. We were a miracle, including us girls who didn't know the prayers, who were there to wear petal frocks, gossip during services, and someday have babies with the boys—we were all part of the miracle.

When we first got to Beach Haven, I was placed in Jewish Sunday school taught by Rabbi Israel Wagner. Rabbi Wagner was already a star rabbinical student in the Ukraine when the war broke out, engaged to the daughter of the rabbi of the city of Buchach. During the war, both hid from the Nazis and survived. After the war, they found each other in a displaced-persons camp and married in Salzburg, Austria. They traveled first to Bolivia, then to Los Angeles, and finally Rabbi Wagner was asked to minister to the spiritual needs of the residents of a new housing complex built in Brooklyn in 1951. This was Beach Haven. Rabbi Wagner began to hold services and teach Sunday school in the basement of one of the Beach Haven buildings. As I was growing up, a permanent synagogue was being built for the community.

I loved Sunday school and I loved Rabbi Wagner. He believed that his personal survival had been a miracle, and he believed in the miracle of the survival of the Jewish people. He had faith that a democratic Israel with the ability to turn the desert into a garden would inspire the world.

As Israeli politics turned more conservative, he comforted me by asking me to be empathic: When people are under daily siege, he said, they are overwhelmed by fear for themselves and their families instead of what is good for the country. They can lose their moral compass. It was just this, the frailty of people under pressure, that made Israel such an existential necessity for Rabbi Wagner. Tyrants often use anti-Semitism as a shortcut to fascism, he said. Jews are and will always be the other. Jews need a place to go. As a survivor of the camps, he felt this viscerally.

Jews, the rabbi explained to his round-eyed charges in the basement, lived in a kind of silence about their experience of persecution. Because if you confront gentiles about their crimes against Jews, these gentiles will turn on you. This was not a good thing, he said, but as a survivor, he understood it. You could not live a life among gentiles if you made them feel guilty every day.

But there were other reasons to avoid talking about the camps. Even as it might make gentiles feel guilty, it made Jews feel ashamed. As though we had done something wrong, something to deserve the Holocaust. We had not fought hard enough. We had allowed Hitler's rules against Jews to happen, one after another, one incursion on Jewish life after another. Of course, the gentiles had allowed this as well, but the burden of protecting Jews fell ultimately on Jews. We had allowed laws to be passed that had turned Jews into criminals. And then we had allowed ourselves to be rounded up like animals. That was Rabbi Wagner's phrase: "We had allowed ourselves." "We had allowed ourselves."

Rabbi Wagner explained that Jewish men from Europe felt that they had allowed the Holocaust to happen to their families. On a rational level, political events had overtaken them. The police had come for them. But on an emotional level, they had packed small bags and comforted their families as they were put on trains to the camps. Most of their wives and children had perished. But some of these men had survived and were now living with new families, here in Beach Haven. They had a special kind of anguish. They needed a special kind of comfort.

It was a lot to take in, but I wanted to keep listening. I wanted to go beyond Sunday school to more intensive study in Hebrew school and to attend Sabbath and holiday services. I brought this idea to my mother. She said she would think about it, but we never talked about it again. In the many days and then weeks and months of not talking about it, I figured out why my request was being ignored. Sunday school, one day a week, had not been expensive. Perhaps it had been free. Hebrew school cost money. I'd violated one of my mother's taboos. We didn't talk about things we couldn't afford.

My mother was never explicit about what we could not discuss. It made her feel close that I should know *without words* what was off limits. It made me anxious; I would assume that something was a reasonable topic for conversation, only to find it taboo. In my work, I have been called intuitive. Growing up, this was a bitter necessity.

I once met Rabbi Wagner on the street when I was pulling my sled in the snow. I was perhaps nine. We had already moved to Murdock Court. He told me that he missed me, that he had enjoyed teaching me in Sunday school. I said, "I can't come to classes. I've been traveling." In my mind, saying anything else put me on the road to betraying my mother. But no nine-year-old from Beach Haven was "traveling." He looked at me uncomprehendingly and moved on. I was ashamed to be caught in a lie and from then on tried to avoid him.

I learned what would upset my mother (sleepaway camp—it costs money—don't mention it; Hebrew school—it costs money—don't mention it again) and tried to work around these. Gradually, I became determined that when it came to the one thing I really cared about, going away to college, I would act on my own. I would not treat going away to college as something my parents had to give me. I did research: If you were first in your high school class, you could be poor and go to the best Ivy League school. By the time I was in junior high school, I knew about Radcliffe scholarships and loan programs. I knew about on-campus jobs.

In Sunday school, Rabbi Wagner specifically made the point that money should never stand between a Jew and prayer on the High Holidays—Yom Kippur, the Day of Atonement, and Rosh Hashanah, the New Year. Yet at many American synagogues, members *are* asked to pay to reserve seating for services on these special days, and my parents thought that not buying tickets would label our family as a charity case. Because we didn't have the money to buy High Holiday tickets, we usually celebrated by getting all dressed up and standing on the synagogue steps to say hello to neighbors before driving off to have a holiday meal with my grandparents. It was implied that we had tickets "elsewhere," with my mother's family. I followed my family's customs but sometimes, early in the morning, I would sneak into Beach Haven services and stand in the back of the sanctuary because I loved to watch Rabbi Wagner pray. All of this was upsetting to me because I knew that our not having tickets was upsetting to my mother. I felt her shame as though it were my own.

But more than anything else, I wanted to pray with my mother. I knew I couldn't get her into the Beach Haven Jewish Center because of the "we don't have money for tickets" problem. So when I was ten years old, I asked her if she would take me to Temple Beth Emeth on Church Avenue, just a few blocks from my grandparents' apartment. There, I said, no one knew us. If anyone asked us about tickets, we could just say we were visiting relatives and smile. And while Rabbi Wagner's services were in Hebrew, Beth Emeth was a Reform temple. Services were in English. She might feel more at home. To my delight, she agreed. So that year, my mother and I walked together to Temple Beth Emeth and took balcony seats. But before we even sat down, she warned me that we would move for anyone who told us they had a right to our seats. I presented her with Rabbi Wagner's pitch. No synagogue should turn away a Jew on the High Holidays. She shrugged. She knew the real world. We hadn't paid money. We didn't belong.

That day at Beth Emeth, no one came to claim our seats, but my mother was unhappy and we left early. I blamed myself. We never went again; I tried to get better at reading her mind.

. . .

EARLY IN THE fall of ninth grade, I was called into the office of my school guidance counselor, Mr. Friedlander. He told me that something important had happened. I was terrified. He went on. The school had received a legal notice that I was no longer Sherry Zimmerman. I was Sherry Turkle. Tomorrow, my homeroom teacher would make an announcement to my class, but now, if I wanted to, I could go home. My mother could come and pick me up. I remember thinking that this protocol was pretty much the same as what had happened to a girl who had gotten her period at school and had bled through her clothes. I felt I was being treated as though something shameful had occurred. Mr. Friedlander also said that I could have a special counselor, a woman if I liked, to get me through this special time. Now I thought that this was perhaps like the shame of getting pregnant. But however awkward this time with Mr. Friedlander, I knew this was my mother's triumph.

And there she was, beaming. Picking me up to take me home. Of course, we couldn't talk about this at home because my half sister and half brother couldn't know that anything had happened. But in the car, my mother was crying, hugging me at the red lights. Once we were home, my mother composed herself and reminded me not to say anything to anyone about what had happened, because in our family and to our friends nothing *had* happened. My name had always been Sherry Turkle. I said nothing. It was not the time to tell her that for me, this story had been crazy for nine years and it was crazy now. I did not have the confidence to tell her my fear: Perhaps it had made me crazy. I knew it was not a good thing that I sometimes imagined myself invisible.

I had lived in terror of slipping up. Once, at Girl Scouts,
just after I had "flown up"
from being a Brownie to be an
Intermediate Scout, I introduced myself at the first troop
meeting as Sherry Zimmer-
man. At the time, my mother,
beautiful in her tight green
skirt, starched white blouse,
and green scout sash, was my
troop leader. When I said the
word "Zimmerman," the room
darkened. I had forgotten that

My mother as Girl Scout Troop Leader,
Beach Haven Jewish Center, 1961.

here I could only be a Turkle. I didn't know how to correct my error.
We walked home in silence. My mother did not speak to me for a
week. I did not so much feel punished as I felt that my mother did not
know what to say. I had outed her in front of her Girl Scout troop, and
she didn't know what to do.

THERE HAD BEEN MUSIC at my grandparents' home in Brooklyn.
There was the music that my mother and I danced to—our favorites,
"Blue Tango," Benny Goodman, and many cha-chas. There was Mario
Lanza singing opera, piles of show tunes, and Burl Ives singing children's songs. Once we moved to Beach Haven, there was no music at
all. Milton told me that it gave him headaches. My mother said nothing. So I listened to music in my room on a transistor radio that I put
next to my ear. When I turned thirteen, however, my mother objected

to Milton's rule. A teenage girl needed music. Milton modified the house rules. He would allow what we still called a "record player" in my room. As soon as she heard this news, my grandmother went to Macy's and bought me a small blue "hi-fi." And every time I had a sleepover weekend with my grandparents, she and I went to the music department at Macy's on Flatbush Avenue and she let me choose a record. My first LP, in 1961, was Dion's *Runaround Sue*. And then Jerome Kern's greatest hits, and the original cast recording of *Gigi*, all of these played until the grooves wore down. I listened for hours to Richard Chamberlain singing "Love Me Tender" and the theme song to *Dr. Kildare*. I imagined being in love. I imagined being loved. But I imagined all of this very softly. Because all music annoyed Milton.

Corrine, a friend from Mark Twain, lived in a small house in Coney Island. She invited me for a weekend sleepover and I learned that she played music in her room all the time. Even her parents played music—in their living room! Her family cooked dinner together and talked as they all pitched in. My grandmother hadn't taught her daughters to cook, because she wanted them to have maids just as her mother had. An immigrant dream gone amiss. At our house, my mother might broil something in the toaster oven. Or reheat something frozen on the stove. She worked silently and didn't want company. For me, the gift of friendship was seeing how other people lived.

I asked if, please, during the summer after ninth grade, I could invite a friend to visit me in Rockaway. For a sleepover. I was invited to sleepovers with other girls' families. I wanted to return these invitations. Only now can I appreciate the pain this caused my family. At the time, I didn't understand their insecurity. Above all, they feared exposure. They didn't know if how they ate, what they ate, how they talked were okay. Somehow I was given permission for a Rockaway sleepover.

My mother said that my friend could sleep with me on the living room daybed.

So I invited a Mark Twain classmate, Susan, to Rockaway. It was everything I had imagined. Susan showed me how to section my hair geometrically before putting it in rollers and to use beer as a setting gel. We bought teasing combs at the five-and-dime and worked on putting our hair up in French twists. We practiced walking in high heels—we didn't own any real ones yet, but she had a Salvation Army pair for practice. We told each other secrets. I had real secrets—I didn't tell those, of course, but came up with the kind of secrets she wanted, like who was my crush. We made a tent with our light summer blankets, turned on flashlights, and listened to Ricky Nelson sing "Travelin' Man" on the radio.

I remember Susan's departure. I think her older brother picked her up, and I was so happy that no one in my family had to be inconvenienced by my sleepover. I kissed her good-bye. I thought the visit was a great success. I was unprepared to come into the kitchen and find my mother stone-faced.

"What's the matter?"

"We can discuss it later."

"What's the matter?"

"I'm not sure that this is the kind of friend who will be a good influence on you."

My mother, in her typical way, thought I understood the problem without her having to name it. Usually she was right. This time I had to cross-examine her. My friend Susan had not brought a house gift. She had not brought any of her own money. So when we went out for ice cream, she had not offered to buy it for us, a gesture to her hosts. This showed her to be someone who was not raised in a good family.

I defended my friend. This was so unfair! No one had taught me these house-gift rules. Susan's family might be financially struggling. How unfair to accuse her of not being willing to treat us to ice cream. And then I understood: In my mother's mind, my intelligence was to be used to associate us with our betters. Susan would not suit. My mother saw us as a team. I was ashamed of our team.

SHORTLY AFTER STARTING at Lincoln High School, a school of more than five thousand students, a school so large that we had to attend in shifts, I met with a college guidance counselor to plan my schedule. If Radcliffe was my dream, she said, I had to be number one in my high school class. "But you have always been number one," she smiled. "That shouldn't be so hard."

Fortunately, many of my teachers would not let the Lincoln experience be purely transactional. Elaine Spielberg taught me to read poetry; Mark Lewis helped me channel my interest in politics into a love for history. Before Bernard Goldhirsch's yearlong literature class, "Heritage," I read to find heroines whose paths I could follow. "Heritage" turned me into a reader for ideas. And it remains a model for how I teach. Design a course that's just over the heads of your students, but not if they stand on their toes. In the first semester, we began with the tradition of the Old Testament. We ultimately read Genesis, Revelation, and the book of Job. We read George Bernard Shaw's *Androcles and the Lion*, which makes a case for a gentle, peaceful Christianity whose values predated the crucifixion. A group of students at Trinity School in Manhattan was putting on a production of the medieval work *The Play of Daniel*, and Mr. Goldhirsch took our whole class to see it. The day after that field trip, Mr. Goldhirsch says, he was cornered by another teacher and accused of doing a terrible thing to Lincoln's

Jewish children: "What Hitler couldn't finish, you did." Jewish children did not need to be challenged by images of seductive Christianity.

During the second "Heritage" unit, I had trouble reading the *Iliad* and the *Odyssey*. I tried reading them aloud. I took to mapping out the stories and time lines. By the time we got to the classical plays, I had charts across my bedroom wall made of sheets of construction paper and Scotch tape that traced the Greek families in their expanding circles of deception, illegitimacy, abandonment, and illicit love.

The charts were soothing. My secret father, the competition between my aunt and mother, between Milton and my grandfather for position of "man in the family," the fight over me to the point of cutting me into bits—the Greeks had seen worse than this.

I WAS OF THE SPUTNIK GENERATION. My talents were clearly in the humanities, but my college counselor wanted me to dot every *i*. During my junior year of high school, I was convinced that what my college application needed was evidence of my seriousness as a *science* student. So I applied for a scholarship to spend a summer at a National Science Foundation program in biology at Syracuse University. There I made friends who were having a high school experience very different from anything I knew at Lincoln. I met kids talking about proms, sororities, and dance parties that went on until three in the morning. Sometimes, they said, their parties lasted all night and they had breakfast together. And the students at Syracuse sang folk songs. Here, at least, I could catch up.

I made two close friends, Elaine, who lived on Staten Island, and Chris, who lived in rural Pennsylvania. During fall semester, Chris invited Elaine and me to a festive weekend at her high school, just before Christmas break. In Pennsylvania, we would stay at Chris's house and get to know her family. Best of all, Chris would find both of us dates for the whole weekend, including a senior-class brunch and a big dance. I had never been to such events. And this would be my first experience of being in a home with a Christmas tree.

I was moved by my mother's willingness to let me go on this trip. She wanted me to venture into the larger world, in part so I could tell her about it, and in part to be more prepared for what was to come. But she also wanted me to have some of the pleasurable experiences (like high school dances and parties and dates) that I was not having at Lincoln, where my life was focused on academic success. The first boy who had kissed me, Jay, on the Rockaway boardwalk, told me I had a reputation "as some kind of genius" and so I was not for him. As a genius, I was not invited to parties. I had a few awkward dates. But my mother told me I was beautiful. She wanted me to see myself as desirable. In Pennsylvania, I could just be accepted as a pretty girl. When I got home and my mother asked me how it had gone, I knew that her real question was whether, in those two days, I had romantically connected with a non-Jewish man.

By SENIOR YEAR, I was editor of the high school newspaper, the *Lincoln Log*, and had a monthly column called "A Spot of Sherry." I wrote one about the performance pressures on college-bound students. This rat race, which we think of as a recent invention, was in full force in Brooklyn more than fifty years ago. We were told our rankings down to several decimal points. We knew how to "college count" not only our grades but the number and the quality of our extracurricular activities. In the column, I described being a Lincoln teenager as being something close to a mechanized object. Of course, I was writing about myself. Above all else, I was trying to be an object that Radcliffe could love.

Once a month, I was responsible for getting the paper to Eastern Printers, near the DeKalb Avenue subway station on the D train. I brought the layout of the newspaper exactly as it would be printed, with each headline letter counted out correctly to be typeset as it would be on the page, because each letter had a point value and took up a certain amount of space. I felt adult. When I took those subway rides, I believed that my brains and determination would get me out of Brooklyn, but when I looked around me I saw a world run by men. I remember finding this natural but somehow feeling undeterred. I had driving personal ambition and planned to achieve something for myself. On the *Log*, something clicked. Whatever my job in the future, I knew that I would always be writing and editing—my work, my students' work, my colleagues' work.

During my senior year, I visited all the colleges I considered attending. Mildred drove me to Pembroke, the sister school to Brown University. I went to Wellesley on my own. I don't remember the interview at all, but I have a clear memory of the early-morning train from New York to Boston and then a bus to Wellesley. On that cold January dawn, I had been in Beach Haven. By midafternoon, I was beside a frozen, magical lake in a land called Welles-

On the terrace of Murdock Court, wearing my "college interview outfit," fall 1964.

ley. Girls, seemingly without care, floated through campus buildings that looked like the interiors for an English romance. Fireplaces. Carved balusters. I was close.

My mother and I wanted to visit Radcliffe together. We took the train to Boston on a Friday afternoon in February, after school. We had a room at the Sheraton Commander in Cambridge, a lovely hotel, walking distance from the college. Susan and Bruce were having a sleepover with Mildred so that my mother and I could have this time.

Our interview was with Dean Kathleen Elliott, in the late morning on Saturday. My mother had bought a new suit at A&S in downtown Brooklyn. It was elegant, double-breasted, royal blue. She was wearing high heels, a tight girdle, and stockings. Gold clip-on earrings. She had just had her hair done.

My mother had her hair done once a week at her favorite salon, called Don's. Don washed her hair, then moistened it with setting lotion. This accomplished, he set it on large, bristly rollers and put her under a dome-shaped hair dryer. When the curlers were taken out, her hair was back-combed to stand out straight from her head, then sprayed to create more body. Thus fortified, my mother's hair was patted and combed into a shining helmet and secured in place with more spray. At night, the precise waves of the bouffant were secured with metal clips at my mother's temples and all along the back of her head, standing guard like steel soldiers in a row.

At the interview, we were told by Dean Elliott's secretary that first we would have a brief chat together with Dean Elliott, and then I would speak with Dean Elliott alone. As my mother preceded me into Dean Elliott's office, I saw, in her hair, the steely glint of a hair clip.

I suppose the interview went well. I was accepted at Radcliffe. But walking back to the hotel, in all of my insecurity, I caused my mother, who wanted nothing more than to share in this moment of aspiration

74

and promise, the greatest pain. I told her that she had forgotten to take out one of her hair clips before seeing the dean. She could say nothing. I was accusing her of betraying me, of betraying us, of showing us to be who we were.

If in life you could get just one do-over, that is the moment for which I'd want mine.

THE RADCLIFFE ADMISSIONS envelope was thick with hope. In the first year, Radcliffe offered me a scholarship, a loan, and a library job. There was about five hundred dollars a year left for my parents to pay. I held my breath. My mother told me not to worry about it. I didn't ask her how she would manage. I allowed my mother to give me my dream. I said that I would help by taking a summer job, and I found one right away, as a counselor at a sleepaway camp, Camp Woodstock, in upstate New York.

I was made the assistant drama counselor. I had one qualification: I knew the story and the songs (words and melody) to almost every popular musical comedy produced in the postwar years. In this job I was useful, always busy, and never challenged. This gave me mental space for my true preoccupations: my crushes on four boy counselors.

Now that I was away from my identity as the smartest girl in high school, I felt free to stare at boys. And I felt free to stare at the woman whom I imagined I should become before I got to Radcliffe: my fellow counselor, the cool, self-possessed Leslie.

Leslie was the first woman I knew who was more or less my age whom I saw as beautiful, sexual, and interesting. When I first saw Leslie, she explained to the group that had formed around her that for some reason, her clothes had gotten lost. Or was it that on the way to camp she had lost her luggage? Or had she gotten into a quarrel with a rival who had stolen her luggage? In any case, she had no clothes and so, no matter, she had borrowed a few things, just a few things, from the male head counselor to get her through the summer.

And so there she was, wearing men's cutoff jeans, tied with rope around her tiny waist, and a white T-shirt. A soft gray cardigan was wrapped around her shoulders. Exquisite. I learned only fragments of Leslie's story. They came in bits and pieces, like elements of myth. She might have lived in Greenwich Village. She might have been in an Andy Warhol movie. She might have been an actress. Here's what was verifiable: She could play the guitar. She wore Fred Braun sandals. She carried a notebook and pencil with her wherever she went. She had a worn leather pocketbook that looked like a saddlebag. As soon as the summer was over, I tried to adopt as many of Leslie's habits as I possibly could. I began by carrying a notebook and pencil everywhere. I couldn't afford the pocketbook, but I put it on my to-do list. Later I would buy imitations of her sandals at Touraine's department store in Harvard Square.

I don't think I ever had a conversation alone with Leslie. I wouldn't have known what to say. I tried to be on the edge of groups where I could hear her speaking. I wanted to learn something very concrete from Leslie: how to be a whole person. I knew Leslie could not teach me that. But I thought observation would help.

As I worked on copying Leslie's authenticity, I was taken aback when the head counselor at Camp Woodstock told me it would be best if no one at camp knew I was going to Radcliffe. I was so accustomed to lying about who I was that this strange idea seemed perfectly natural. He suggested I tell people I was on my way to Brooklyn College—better for making friends and fitting in, since all the other counselors were going to city colleges or to New York state schools. I spent the summer of 1965 trying to stick to that story. When I was found out (and of course I was found out—by a counselor who really was going to Brooklyn College), my behavior seemed weird and condescending to the other counselors. It taught me this: The most insecure people often seem like the most obnoxious ones.

I was focused on finally leaving home. But I had tried to take what I most admired: my aunt's intelligence and integrity; my grandmother's empathy and resourcefulness; my grandfather's tenacity. As for my mother, I wanted her capacity for joy in small things, the energy she brought to every moment.

But when I considered what I had accomplished, I was ashamed of my achievement because of how much I thought my effort showed.

4.

Dépaysement

Milton and my mother drove me up to Radcliffe, Milton hunched over the wheel, my mother beside him in the front seat. I was traveling light. My clothes had been sent ahead in a red leatherette suitcase that Milton's sister Ruth bought me as a graduation present. The suitcase was ugly; I thought it called attention to itself. I had wanted to get rid of the red suitcase without insulting Ruth, but I didn't know how. Instead, it had gone to Radcliffe as my first representative.

We stayed at a run-down hotel in downtown Boston, the three of us in a room, my mother and Milton in a double bed, me on a cot. I had my hair dryer with me, a round turbine attached to a large pink plastic bonnet that distributed hot air over twenty-four wire mesh curlers. It had its own leatherette travel case. The next morning, as I arranged myself under it, I created myself as a bouffant Sherry who would match my out-of-place red suitcase.

We drove to Cambridge with a street map that the hotel gave us. We had to get from Boston past Harvard Square to Radcliffe Yard. Milton got lost. We were worried that we were going to be late for the welcoming party at North House, where I had been assigned to live. I reminded myself that being late was not going to keep me from Radcliffe. I had reached escape velocity.

Radcliffe Quadrangle was charming, elegant. Dorm after dorm, the buildings looked like jewels from the early twentieth century. Mine, Holmes Hall, in North House, just off the main quad, struck me as box-like and grim. I put these thoughts aside. I was at Radcliffe.

I was sure that we three had never made small talk on a lawn over lemonade and cookies. I hoped that my mother did not notice that we were dressed all wrong for the occasion. My mother and I were wearing "afternoon" fall dresses from Abraham & Straus, pantyhose, and high heels, dressed to stand on the steps of the Beach Haven Jewish Center on the High Holidays. We were dressing up for a fancier life. But I wasn't in a fancier life. I was in a different life.

We stood out in a sea of chinos, linen, and cardigans thrown over sleeveless cotton shifts. A tall, poised girl wore a taupe corduroy suit with suede kitten heels; another, quiet, with a persuasive, resonant voice, wore an embroidered peasant blouse and short denim skirt over bare legs. My first impressions of my classmates centered less on their conversation than on the ones who seemed to have effortless style. I imagined that it reflected composure and self-knowledge.

Soon after the house master's speech, my mother and I were alone in my new room. Now I wanted her to leave before she realized that when we packed me up for Radcliffe, we didn't think of including any personal objects that could warm this cold, institutional space.

Families up and down my hall were busy helping their daughters arrange small items of furniture from home—a bedside table, a writing desk. They were unpacking trunks with rugs, paintings, bedspreads, mirrors. I wondered if these were the sorts of things you brought to college if you had a home with extra things.

We stared at the room across the hall, where a comforter and a collection of throw pillows and framed photographs had just been taken from a large trunk. The room's occupant was arranging personal stationery and a portable typewriter on her Radcliffe-issued desk. My mother seemed exhausted. She opened her handbag and searched for her coin purse. I understood that she was looking for a twenty-dollar bill so that I could go shopping for some things to put in my room. I stopped her. I sat down on the bed next to her. Her lacquered hair made it hard to get my cheek next to her face.

I felt ill-prepared for what lay ahead. I told her it would be fine.

"One of the girls will lend you a typewriter?"

"Yeah, I bet that's how it works. And I think the college has some you can borrow."

"What about a bedspread?"

"Don't worry. There's a Woolworth's in Harvard Square. I will get everything there."

"And throw pillows."

"And throw pillows."

I walked my mother to the door of Holmes and to the car, where Milton waited, tight-lipped. I did not want to let her go. I should have found my way to a better start. For me. For her.

For years afterward, I tried to learn a way of being that would make me at ease in the world without blaming myself for what I didn't know along the way. How to hold a fork. How to write an academic paper. How to order in a restaurant. My second goal was to find a way for my family to participate without feeling diminished.

. . .

NORTH HOUSE, which included Holmes Hall and two other dorms, was built in the 1950s. These newer buildings were not trying to be anything other than useful college dormitories. The women of North House did not do a scientific study, but this was our understanding: We were disproportionately girls from public schools, Jewish and Black scholarship students. Girls who were from families that had never attended Radcliffe before. It seemed to us that if we were in a less lovely dorm, this discrimination was not intentional but "by default." If your mother or aunt or a classmate at your private school had been to Radcliffe, you would have asked to be in one of the older and more beautiful dorms of South and East Houses: Cabot, Bertram, Eliot, Barnard, Whitman, Briggs. If you went to a private school and several of you were going to Radcliffe, it made sense for you to ask to room in Cabot together. You knew it was cozy and had a beautiful library. If you were new to the whole scene, you didn't know to ask for anything in particular, and you were put into the newer and less lovely North House. That is the charitable explanation. I've been in conversations where less charitable explanations were offered, but the charitable one makes a lot of sense to me. On my housing application I was asked if I had a house or dorm preference. Was there anyone with whom I wanted to live? I answered no to all these questions.

The theory seemed to hold up during a garden party held during freshman week for all of the students on scholarships, most of whom lived in North House. Years later, at a Radcliffe twenty-fifth reunion, I was approached by several other women who attended that garden party. They asked me a question that had not occurred to me at the time. Why did the scholarship students need a party of their own?

Did the college want us to recognize one another? From that party, I knew who else could not afford to pay for Radcliffe. I knew who else was from a public high school. And I met most of the Jewish and Black students in my class.

But I had been glad to attend this party. I had survived a rough obstacle course to make it to Radcliffe, and I wanted to see if it was possible to have navigated that path with more grace than I had mustered. I met women whom I admired because I thought they wore their efforts more lightly.

It was at that event that it first struck me, happily, that I was with peers with whom I felt no sense of competition. As far as I understood, at Harvard, everyone chose their courses and did their best. Good graduate schools and professional schools accepted plenty of Harvard and Radcliffe seniors. If I saw a bottleneck ahead, it came from being a professional *woman*, and I would fight this battle alongside my Radcliffe sisters, whom I already heard talking about careers in fields that had been traditionally dominated by men. Some classmates spoke about becoming Harvard professors, even though Harvard at that point had no tenured women faculty. I heard conversations about going to Harvard Law, Business, and Medical Schools. The Harvard undergraduate library, Lamont, in Harvard Yard, was closed to all of us as women, but the world, strangely, seemed open.

At the first welcoming freshman assemblies, Radcliffe told us that it was almost impossible to flunk out. Now that we were here, everything would be done to help us succeed. I wasn't going to be competing with these women. I hoped they could be friends. But there were limitations on what kind of friend I could be. I felt compelled to stay at a distance so people wouldn't see things about me I wasn't ready for them to see.

I couldn't make decisions. I was still haunted by my experience in the courtroom when the judge asked me if I loved my father. Nothing good had come of that "yes." But saying no seemed a horrible thing as well. I developed a symptom. Freshman fall, I couldn't settle on what classes to take.

Looking back, I have compassion for the girl I was. She needed to change. She had the wrong temperament for her talents. At the time, she embarrassed me.

HARVARD BEING HARVARD, I wasn't accepted into the one course I *knew* I wanted to take, a freshman seminar on American politics and society. The teacher, Martin Peretz, held admission interviews at his office in Kirkland House during freshman week. Kirkland was one of the "river" residences, where male undergraduates lived after a first year of living in Harvard Yard. At the time, Peretz, a Government and Social Studies tutor, was known for his radical views, his glamorous social circle, and his charisma. I had never heard of him. I'd never heard of anybody.

Kirkland House was an intimidating jumble of Harvard things: entryways and common rooms, fireplaces and libraries. Finally, I was with a small group of students, all men, waiting outside Mr. Peretz's office. He invited me in, a compact, energetic man with a red beard and auburn hair. I liked his coiled-up energy immediately. He asked me about any activities that might be relevant to my participation in his seminar. I told him that I had been the editor of my high school's newspaper and its social science magazine. This seemed to be a wrong track. Mr. Peretz tried to get me onto his track: Had I worked on a political campaign? What quarterlies did I subscribe to?

My only work experience was as a babysitter and camp drama counselor. I had never worked on a campaign and did not know what a quarterly was. From the context, I understood it must be a kind of magazine. My only subscriptions had been birthday presents: *Calling All Girls* for two years, starting when I was ten, and then, in my sophomore year of high school, *Seventeen*. I didn't know the names of any quarterlies, but I knew enough to stay silent on the topic.

Then Peretz asked what questions I would bring to an analysis of an apathetic polity. And where these questions came from, either theoretically or from my personal experience. This question intrigued me, but I wasn't sure what a polity was. I had grown up surrounded by Holocaust survivors who wanted their children to put all thoughts of politics out of their minds. They believed that thinking about the Old Country would get in the way of living their dream of America. I thought political apathy might be a kind of posttraumatic stress. The traumatized want to be invisible and, most of all, they want their children to be invisible. I was thinking all of this, but it was too late. I couldn't collect myself. None of these ideas were available to me in words. The interview was over.

I started to walk home and realized almost immediately that I had to pee. The only place in Harvard Yard where I knew of a women's restroom was in the basement of Memorial Church. There was a small Radcliffe reading room there. Nearly doubled up in pain, I made my way from the glories of Kirkland House to the dark church basement. Not an auspicious beginning. No style. No quarterlies. Bouffant hair. Between classes, I would be reading in a basement.

I decided to buy something for my room. The Fogg Art Museum sold prints of its collection. I bought a reproduction of a Picasso line drawing of a mother cradling a child in her arms. I had it mounted on a light-gray mat. I had my first object. Then I got a haircut at a salon in Harvard Square from an Italian gentleman—I remember only that his name began with *G*. As I recall, it cost thirty-five dollars, so expensive that I had to cut back on book buying during the first semester and read in the library. The idea of this haircut, G explained, was that you tossed your hair rather than setting it. I put away my bouffant rollers.

But I did want to know about quarterlies. I did want to be in conversations about political engagement and apathy. I was ready to learn. Unfortunately, this took place in a sexist environment that every Radcliffe student had to navigate. Only men could be nominated to be Harvard Junior Fellows or for most of the Harvard Prizes given at graduation, prizes to study at Oxford or Cambridge for a year, to travel, to explore. What strikes me most, looking back, is that I found this natural. I did not challenge these constraints or rail against their injustice. I just felt lucky to be there.

When psychological experiments—posted on the bulletin boards of William James Hall, where I took introductory courses—would specify that only male subjects were being asked to participate, I saw that as natural as well. When I asked why only men were being studied, I was told that the experiments used "baseline" numbers collected on soldiers; thus, future experimentation had to continue on men. That also sounded right.

I find it helpful to think about those days because it reminds me how sexism, like racism and authoritarianism, can seem invisible when it is the familiar. Harvard professors seemed to me the authorities on how to do experiments. And they were telling me that this was how experiments were done. This was the expected. The expected is invisible. To see your own culture, you have to make the natural unfamiliar.

In my time at Harvard, much of its structural sexism was overturned. The university opened up the undergraduate library and its other facilities, including the Harvard housing system, to women. And so many other invisible things were finally visible to me, so many "natural" things became unnatural. I had been trained to expect my university to be sexist, but I also expected to see mostly white families on television. I was brought up to expect men to work and women to stay home if they could. With some exceptions, for I knew of distinguished exceptions, I expected politicians, professors, lawyers, and doctors to be men. When I first went out into the job market in summer 1966, I expected that women and people of color would have less opportunity than white men.

As an undergraduate, I studied the notion of *dépaysement*, literally "decountrifying," making yourself a stranger in your environment in order to see it more clearly. I loved this idea from my anthropology courses because it spoke to me personally. I *lived* the idea of my world becoming strange to me. Everything that seemed natural during that first week at Harvard, the palatial men's accommodations and the women's meager lot, taking Harvard classes but not being able to read in its undergraduate library, that I had to walk to the basement of Memorial Church in order to find a bathroom, all of these natural things would soon seem odd. And then intolerable.

ONE MORNING at breakfast during freshman fall, just before the final deadline for course selections, I summoned my courage and asked a senior for advice. She told me that until I knew my interests, the safest thing to do was to "go with the classics." These were the courses that were the best known and got the highest student ratings. Exhausted, I let my schedule fall into place with what you could describe as Harvard's "greatest hits." I studied epic poetry, the history of art from the cave paintings to Picasso, and a course that, despite its banal title, most opened my mind to its possibilities. This was "Social Sciences 2: Western Thought and Institutions."

Samuel Beer, a professor of government, taught Social Sciences 2 from 1946 to 1978. Beer once said that from year to year, he would switch up a lecture or change some of the jokes he told in class, but its basic structure remained intact for thirty-two years. You would never know this from his classroom style, which was to rush into class, fling his briefcase on a desk, and begin to pace as though there were an urgent problem. The behavior of the English lords after the Norman invasion needed to be explained, and it would be best to get it settled now.

In class, we read about a historical event from the perspectives of historians with different points of view. Then we read a social theorist whose ideas offered a prism for thinking about this event. The first unit in Social Sciences 2 was the narrative of British history from the Norman invasion in 1066 through the 1215 signing of the Magna Carta. There were details, dates, and lots of British topography to learn, but what thrilled me was Beer's use of the German sociologist Max Weber's writings to describe how the Magna Carta "routinized charisma." William the Conqueror had been a charismatic ruler. But by the time of the Magna Carta, you didn't need that kind of leader anymore. Now you had the law.

The course had a message: *Use concrete events to think about large ideas. Use large ideas to think about concrete events.* The best learning follows from looking at specific events through competing theoretical prisms, although some will work better than others. This meant that you didn't have to be a Marxist to think that certain of Marx's ideas were well suited for understanding key historical moments. So no matter what your politics, put Marx in your tool kit. Not to criticize him but to use him. The same went for Freud. Read theorists *con-*

structively. Because you weren't swearing allegiance to any theorist, you should read all of them for their *best* ideas.

I came of age as an academic in the sixties and seventies, during a tsunami of ideology. When I presented papers and submitted them for publication, I would be asked to choose between strands of Marxism and schools of psychoanalytic thought. Through my education and professional life, I have been sustained by Sam Beer. Use the theory that is most useful for sorting through a time, a place, a new set of materials. Expand your intellectual tool kit. Be theoretically promiscuous. In more academic language, practice theoretical pluralism.

THERE ARE SO MANY HARVARDS for undergraduates—academic Harvard, athletic Harvard, drama-production Harvard, musical Harvard, literary Harvard, journalism Harvard. In each of them, things are done to a standard of professional excellence. Indeed, at Harvard, students have to compete to participate in most academic and extracurricular activities—this is known as the system of "comps" (competitions) and it persists to this day. It has a cost. Because you can't participate without competing (that's what I was doing when I "tried out" for my freshman seminar at Kirkland House), students are encouraged to participate where they can excel. I had always led with my academic gifts. When, as a Harvard freshman, I wanted to step out of my comfort zone, that turned out to be not so easy.

I wanted to be in a play. I had no reason to think I was a good actress. Or any kind of actress at all. But one crisp fall day, I saw a notice in the *Crimson*, the Harvard newspaper, that for the next three nights there would be tryouts for a new play at the Loeb Drama Center. On the first night of auditions, dressed in my best skirt and blouse, the same one I had worn for Lincoln High School yearbook photograph day, I walked to the Loeb theater, on Brattle Street, and found my way to a rehearsal room. It was filled with young men and women, most in jeans and T-shirts, none of whom I had ever seen before. But they seemed to know one another. Some of the women wore leotards and tights with scarf skirts wrapped around their waists, as though they had just come from dance class. Most had brought scenes to read for their auditions. Of course, I didn't have anything prepared, so the person in charge gave me some lines to read from the new play. She was very kind. I was to look at the scene for fifteen minutes, and then she and I would read it together. I did what I was told and then I left.

The Loeb was halfway between Harvard Square and where I lived in Radcliffe Yard. Instead of going home, I walked to Harvard Square and went to Elsie's, a sandwich shop where I ordered its famous Roast Beef Special—thin-sliced roast beef, onion slices, German mustard, and Russian dressing on a bulky roll. From eavesdropping at the Loeb, I learned that as a novice, if I wanted to do something with theater, I should start by volunteering to work in the props department at the main stage or try out for a small part in a house production. Also from eavesdropping, I learned that many of the actors in that room had been in the theater all their lives; some had already studied at Juilliard or the Royal Academy in London. Harvard had chosen me because I had academic promise. Harvard had chosen these students because they had theatrical promise. During my time at Harvard, Lindsay Crouse, Tommy Lee Jones, and John Lithgow were all appearing at the Loeb theater.

There on a counter stool at Elsie's, I got into a new frame of mind. I loved Social Sciences 2. And notebooks and fountain pens. And typing out my papers, editing them, and retyping them. I was happiest in the Holmes Hall basement study room, working on my papers late at night. Somebody told me that if I loved Social Sciences 2, I should try to be a social studies major. It gave me something to think about. Martin Peretz was the head tutor of social studies, the same Martin Peretz who had asked me if I read quarterlies but who had also asked me the wonderful question about political apathy that had gotten me thinking for weeks. Now that I had a bit more confidence, being asked those kinds of questions might be just right for me. What Harvard could do best was give me an opportunity to become what I was best at. I was going to go all in on that.

MY MOTHER PRAYED I would have a Jewish roommate. I just wanted a friend. Neither of us got our wish. During my freshman year at Radcliffe, I was given the most glamorous member of our class as a roommate. She was California beautiful and blond, and her name was Mary Lou.

This was fall 1965. There was no Facebook. But there was a real book, printed on paper, with the faces of the Radcliffe freshman class, a name and photograph for each of us (along with our home address before attending Radcliffe), and our dorm assignments.

In those days, calls came into a central dorm line and were routed to a phone at the end of the hall. That was called being "buzzed." If you weren't in your room, you got a message. Mary Lou was buzzed perhaps ten times a night. She was a lovely person, but she could not share her popularity or good fortune with me. I was attractive in my genre, but Mary Lou was playing at a different level. She went out with Harvard students who came from elite prep schools and belonged to final clubs (selective all-male social groups), and with business school students. It was understood that I wouldn't belong among them. I don't remember being pursued by any "Harvard men" who were not Jewish and from New York. Perhaps a first date but no more.

Mary Lou's dresses were from "the Villager," a designer I had not heard of until coming to Radcliffe. In the spring of freshman year, I ate only yogurt flavored with instant coffee for two weeks so that I could fit into her size-six clothes, and she let me wear one of her Villager dresses, black cotton printed with little red strawberries, with a pin-tucked bodice. I loved that dress so much. When it was time to return it, I handed it back to her, grateful for the experience. Only then did it occur to me that my behavior was all wrong. I should have first had the dress dry-cleaned. I was so ashamed that I could not bring myself to apologize.

I don't talk when my vulnerability feels like too much to bear. When, years later, I met internet users who told me about the pleasures of hiding behind screens, I understood what they were trying to say.

GROWING UP, I had shopped only for categories of things. "Winter coat." "White blouse." When I shopped for college, my mother changed the rules. She decided I needed inexpensive "fashion" shoes to go with date "outfits." My grandmother found a kelly-green wool dress with white wool trim, a copy of an André Courrèges design. On my mother's instructions, she bought it with short white boots, also Courrèges look-alikes at a sale table at Mays, the same discount store in downtown Brooklyn where I had bought my bar mitzvah dress. I wore this ensemble once, during freshman fall, on my way to a date with a Harvard graduate student. My thinking was that perhaps someone older and more sophisticated might like the Courrèges. I was supposed to meet my date for dinner at the Wursthaus, a German delicatessen in Harvard Square. But after just three blocks, I looked down at those white boots, already starting to shred on the cobblestones, turned around, and walked back to my dorm. When I got to the front desk, the "bell desk" of Holmes Hall, I called the Harvard house where the man lived and left a message for him, canceling our date.

I got to my room; Mary Lou was out. I stripped down. I knew from watching the girls in the bathroom that even my underpants were wrong. They were the same cotton white briefs that my aunt and grandmother wore. We bought them in packs of five at the Lamston five-and-dime store next to the Church Avenue subway station. I was sobbing. I could not get naked enough. I put the dress and boots in a paper bag and stuffed it in the bottom of my closet. Two weeks later, I would throw all of it away in a trash bin on Massachusetts Avenue.

In fall 1965, the air in Radcliffe Quad resembled that breathed by Mary McCarthy's Vassar coeds in *The Group*. Men were allowed in our rooms for a few hours a week. These hours were called "parietals." The word itself sounded obscene. Parietals.

On weekends, you had to be checked back into your dorm by 11 p.m. You could get special permission for a later check-in if you had a reason to be out— for example, you worked on the Harvard Crimson and were filing a story on deadline. You could ask for an overnight pass if you were going off campus and could say where you would be (designated events such as a football weekend at Yale). In this system, sex was transgressive. It was happening all the time, but like birth control, it was illegal.

At North House, formal socializing with Harvard students took place when your dorm held a "jolly-up," a dance to which Harvard students were invited. As I recall, there was one at the beginning of each term. My experience of the jolly-up was that men looked over my shoulder to check out other women while they were taking my name and dorm number. It wasn't as bad as it sounds because you could see that it was also happening to other women. During the first jolly-up, I went down to a basement bathroom to throw some cold water on my face and collect myself. Did I have to do this unpleasant thing? There, in a side hall, I found a small group of laughing, Black students. I think they had a portable radio. They were holding their own party. I could feel the sting of the need to retreat from what Radcliffe had on offer.

My grandparents were Roosevelt democrats, but felt that the burdens of Jews were enough for them to carry. As a child, my only contact with Black people was a woman who cleaned our house in the fall, before we came home from Rockaway, and in the spring, before the Passover holidays. My grandparents did not befriend her. Mildred did.

When I started high school, Mildred took me to Wednesday night Brooklyn College lectures on civil rights and gave me James Baldwin to read. I copied over quotes from his writing: "People are trapped in history and history is trapped in them." "Once you find yourself in another civilization, you're forced to examine your own." At Radcliffe, I realized how much these words had meant to me.

I trudged back to the joyless jolly-up. An attractive boy asked me to dance and made a joke about the famous "jelly-ups" at Radcliffe. I was embarrassed not to get the joke. Defeated, I left the party.

If the jolly-ups were my window into what was not fun about the social customs of Radcliffe, wait-ons were just the opposite. At North House, Radcliffe students served each other meals. The kitchen staff was wonderful. Some were older Irish women who had worked at Radcliffe all their lives. Family-hungry, I befriended them as much as they would allow themselves to be befriended, which wasn't very much. Several times a week, students had sherry in the living room, and then we waited on each other for proper sit-down meals. This chore was given in rotation; everyone pitched in. The kitchen staff taught us how to set a table, to fold napkins, to put the dessert spoon above the place setting. And then we learned to serve. (Approach from the left; remove from the right.) Radcliffe called all of this instruction, "gracious living," and everyone made gentle fun of it. We used the same phrase ironically when we were served afternoon tea. But I was only pretending to make fun. I wanted to learn all of this: how to serve before-dinner drinks, where to put a dessert spoon. And I loved feeling, just for those brief times, that I was part of a group of equals.

I wanted that feeling, but there were moments that made me aware of how much I was seen as an outsider. In spring of freshman year, there was a series of thefts in Holmes Hall. Someone was stealing small bills, anything that was left in sight, not locked up. There was an investigation. An all-dorm meeting. The house masters explained that the person who was doing this needed help. She should come to them and seek help.

We were told that the mystery of who was stealing the money was never solved, but I was shocked to overhear in a lunch conversation a hint that several people thought it was me. I didn't have close friends, but why would people see me as a thief? I approached Lynne, a tall, studious blonde, and I asked her this question point-blank. I trusted her. Like me, she was quiet. Unlike me, she had a roommate with whom she was close, so she never seemed isolated.

Lynne was forthright. In Holmes Hall you needed coins for the pay phone and the Coke machine. Lynne said that I was the person who most often asked other people for change. I thought that might be right. When I was lonely, asking for change was a way to have a quick visit. I could see that it might have been irritating, unwelcome. And perhaps I did it more than I thought.

I waited for more evidence of my being a criminal. There was none. Lynne described the group thinking: I was someone who was so isolated that she needed excuses to come into other girls' rooms to feel a part of things. Perhaps I would take their stuff as another way to feel connected. My eyes smarted. Lynne said she had no reason to think I had ever stolen anything. But she thought I should know how I was coming off.

I remember Lynne's low, steady voice and the dirty blond wood of the Holmes Hall furniture. She didn't think I was a thief. She thought I was lonely and didn't know how to make friends.

I didn't sputter or defend myself. I was able to put myself in the place of all those girls in the middle of their conversations when I came looking for change. I could imagine their annoyance. And I could put myself in Lynne's place. She was brave. I thanked her.

Lynne said she would have been happy to talk if I had just knocked on her door and asked to chat. I told her I would have been afraid to do that because she seemed so close with her roommate and I knew she had a famous dad. I thought her life must be so different from mine. She shrugged. "It doesn't matter about my famous dad." Something in me settled down. Lynne taught me something about empathy. It's not just listening. She stayed with me, she made sure I took something positive from our conversation. I talked about the review books and how they made me feel that I hadn't learned the real thing. I think she talked about the ups and downs of growing up with a well-known parent.

I didn't talk about Sherry Zimmerman. Or my adoption. I didn't begin a new life in the sunlight. But I had taken a risk in reaching out to another person, and she hadn't let me down. I knew I would try again. I realized how much I wanted to talk to other people. I wanted to hear their stories. I had heard too little of life.

Not surprisingly, Mary Lou had requested a different roommate for sophomore year. And I wanted to leave Holmes. I longed for a fresh start.

My conversation with the housing dean was brief. She said there was one single room available, but it was in Bertram Hall, South House. That was fine with me. South House sounded like the opposite of North House. It might be good luck.

IN THOSE DAYS, fancy department stores hired "girls" from the Seven Sisters schools (each a sister of an Ivy "brother") to form a panel of experts (a "college board") who could help newly accepted freshmen buy their college wardrobes. I wanted to fit in better when I moved to my new dorm, and I thought a job in fashion would help. Despite my imagined future as a social theorist, I considered the position of Radcliffe representative to the Saks Fifth Avenue College Board my dream summer job.

I was honest at the job interview. I said that I loved Radcliffe and I admired my roommate's beautiful clothes. I myself did not shop at Saks, but I wanted to learn about the kinds of clothes that were sold there. My favorite designer? I didn't have one. But I had borrowed my roommate's Villager dresses whenever I could. I got the job. No other Radcliffe students had applied.

Until the official opening of the Saks College Board, we were all assigned to departments on Saks's busy first floor. I was put in fine leather gloves, a surprisingly hectic place in early summer.

My grandmother's one job before she married my grandfather had been selling gloves. Now I felt a new solidarity. She was surprised that I was so proud of doing what she had done. And I felt a different kind of connection to my aunt and mother. My grandmother called us her "working girls."

The store hummed like a city, with a secret inner life. What I liked best was the system of pneumatic tubes that took each written order and the client's money away in a canister and returned it with the client's change and a receipt. The short delay between sending off a canister and getting one back gave you time to talk to your customers if they wished, but more usually to the other salespeople who were waiting for their canisters to return.

While waiting at the pneumatic tubes, I learned the pleasures of a certain kind of small talk: that you should put Vicks VapoRub on your tongue if you had a sore throat; that the Russian Tea Room was ideal for a serious second date; that the best place to get your eyebrows tweezed was at the Elizabeth Arden Red Door salon. I cannot say if what I learned at the pneumatic tubes was good advice. What I can say is that I took all of it. On Red Door tweezing day, an older man took charge of me, thinned my virgin eyebrows, and moved along to makeup advice: Under no circumstances should I wear pink lipstick, pink blush, or blue eye shadow. These things were only for my mother. When I showed up at the dinner table with brown lipstick, my grandmother was alarmed.

Then, after two weeks on the main sales floor wearing the Saks sales uniform of a navy or black skirt and a white blouse, came our metamorphosis: Each college board member would now wear a camel-and-navy plaid skirt and a navy sweater vest. Easy to identify, we would work in a special department and be assigned to women whose college destinations were in the cities where our schools were located.

For Boston, there was just me and a glamorous red-haired Wellesley student who, unlike me, had actually gone to Harvard final club parties and football games and tailgate parties and knew what to wear to these events. Of course, no one wore anything like the skirt-and-vest outfits we were dressed in.

Halfway through the summer, a dress appeared in the college department at Saks, an A-line wool knit with cap sleeves, closely fitted at the bust, with diagonal stripes of purple, blue, and pink. I think it cost fifty-five dollars. I had a 30 percent discount at Saks, but this dress was still more expensive than anything I owned. Close to a week's salary. I loved this dress and feared that it would sell out in my size. One day, as work was ending, I saw the red-haired Wellesley girl change into the dress on her way to a dinner date in the city. Now there was only one dress left in my size. I bought it immediately. When I modeled the dress for my mother the next day and told her I had bought it with money intended for fall textbooks, she shrugged. She reminded me that her favorite scene in *Gone with the Wind* was at the end, when Scarlett O'Hara declares that she will think about her troubles tomorrow. The dress was amazing, she said. In the fall, perhaps I could work some extra hours in the college library. I took this as permission, absolution. The next week at breakfast, I found a ten-dollar bill under my plate. My mother, sitting opposite me, laughed and said she was paying off my dress "on time."

I have a photograph of me in the dress the following spring, the spring of my sophomore year, posing in it just before a date. My hair is blown out straight; G in Harvard Square would have been proud. I am trying to look as sexy as the dress but I don't know how, so I look quite vacant, but you can see the effort. I wore this dress for fifteen years, the

last three, when it was thread-
bare, only around the house or
to go to the corner store. It reminded me of my life, my brief
life, as a college student so care-
free that she could vamp around
in her room, wearing a dress her
mother had loved.

Vamping in the special dress from
Saks Fifth Avenue, Bertram Hall,
April 1967.

DURING MY Saks College
Board summer, I dated a pre-
med Harvard freshman whom
I met on the Eastern Airlines
shuttle from New York to Bos-
ton after freshman-year spring break. Bob was holding a copy of *The
Great Gatsby* and asked me if I had read it. When I said no, he showed
up at Bertram Hall the next day with a copy.

On one of our first New York summer dates, Bob told me to dress
in cocktail attire. He planned for us to crash a send-off party for one of
the big ocean liners. Bob had done his research: In 1966, ocean liners
departed from port without security. So if there was a farewell party in
a stateroom, two well-dressed young people could walk right in. I wore
a slinky lace dress borrowed from one of my colleagues at the college
board, and sure enough, Bob and I were allowed onto the boat. The
parties we crashed that night were not Gatsby level, less lobster and
caviar than cheese and crackers, but we had accomplished the essential:
Bob got us on the boat, he had wineglasses placed in our hands, and we
were striking up conversations with strangers on their way to Paris.

When I told Mildred about crashing the boat launch, she laughed and said, "Marry him." I knew what she was trying to say. It wasn't about Bob but about choosing a life of invention.

After our Friday-night New York dates, Bob and I would stay over at his family's apartment in Riverdale, something sanctioned by my mother because this was a chaperoned, practical sleepover—and we returned to Rockaway the following morning.

But I never wanted to go home. I wanted to stay in Riverdale. Bob's father was a physician, handsome and literary; his mother, beautiful, sophisticated. They seemed devoted to each other and to Bob. If I got up early, I could have coffee with Bob's parents and pretend that I was their daughter. I could pretend that I lived in their apartment, with rooms lined with bookshelves and art on the walls and magazines piled high. Once, Bob's family invited me to a party and I met Mark Strand, then a young poet just starting his career. He was a family friend. I was overwhelmed. Imagining myself as a daughter distracted me from the son. Looking back, I see that the intensity of my fantasies made me feel disloyal to my mother. I pulled away from Bob and then regretted it. But not before he gave me a glimpse of what a partnership might be like.

I remember this scene: My mother, hair in a teased bouffant stiff with lacquer, in shorts and a high-necked, long-sleeved white blouse, sat in a large green rocking chair in Lafayette Court. The rocking chairs usually stayed on our porch in the shade, but my mother loved the sun and during the day would bring chairs into the middle of the court, paved in square, concrete slabs. Bob sat in another rocking chair, opposite hers, listening intently.

She had lost her voice that year—from an attack of shingles, she said—and she didn't want her raspy voice to interfere with her teaching. By summer 1966, my mother was a "regular substitute" teacher at Lincoln, the same Lincoln where I had gone to high school. She explained that she had hired an electrician to make her a portable microphone for when she was in class. She wanted to be able to wear the electronics and amplification gear on a belt around her waist. But technology had failed her. She ended up with something that had to sit on a desk and had a long cord to a microphone. Could Bob help her invent a better design? My mother picked up a pencil and started to sketch the contraption she had in mind. I watched admiringly. I was proud of my resilient mother and delighted by my boyfriend's warmth toward her.

I remember not feeling concerned about my mother's having "shingles." Or about her having lost her voice. In the years since, I have imagined this scene so many times. Sitting in the sun, she seemed relaxed. From her point of view, I was loved by this good man, this Jewish, Harvard doctor-to-be. Perhaps she let her guard down. She had accomplished her goal of keeping her illness from me so that I would go away to Radcliffe and achieve my dream. Perhaps she behaved like someone who was trying not to keep a secret but to share one. I didn't give her an opening and she didn't insist.

5.

Twelfth Night

In Holmes Hall, my Radcliffe classmates and I had waited on one another at meals. In Bertram Hall, we ate all of our meals cafeteria-style in Barnard Hall, in the South House dining room. Almost all the foods at the steam tables were new to me. Jell-O with fruit mixed in. Jell-O with vegetables, a food that some of my class-mates called "salad." Tapioca pudding. Chili. Green vegetables other than peas and string beans. Spaghetti with white sauce. Grits. I had my first cheeseburger. And made the step to bacon and eggs. For this, I used my grandmother's "I am eating pork in a Chinese restaurant" rule, counting the South House dining room as "eating out."

In Holmes, it had been hard for me to connect. In Bertram Hall, the warmth of the physical space made it easier. My room had a win-dow seat; on the second-floor landing there was a place to step out of a window onto a little balcony. You could have a private moment in the sun or night air. The classically shaped rooms, the soft wood floors, the moldings and fireplaces felt burnished and inviting. This remains the aesthetic of spaces that make me feel at ease. It's Bertram Hall space. It seemed built for conversation. I learned the wisdom of what Winston Churchill said about buildings: We build them and then they make and shape us.

I APPLIED TO SOCIAL STUDIES, where Martin Peretz was head tutor, but this time things went well. I was even assigned to his sophomore tutorial, where I was encouraged to call him "Marty." I couldn't bring myself to do that until midway through graduate school, so I tried to avoid addressing him directly. He cotaught with Paul Robinson, whose specialty was the relationship of intellectual history to writing about culture. This class exploded with conversation. Peretz and Robinson weren't afraid to disagree. And certainly encouraged it in class discussion. Since we were reading the most controversial thinkers of European intellectual history—Marx, Weber, Durkheim, and Freud—there was plenty to disagree about. As in Social Sciences 2, I got the message that the best thinking comes from an attitude of intellectual pluralism. Social Studies 10 was Harvard's greatest gift to me. In the years to come, I would often lose my way in how to chart my career. When this happened, I summoned the experience of Social Studies 10. Not because it suggested any specific direction but because it offered this: Try to do the work that brings out the best in you.

I say this to my students: *You are at university to understand your gifts and what you love to do.* If you are lucky, they will be the same thing. If not, let's talk and see if we can increase the overlap. If you relish your work, you will not have a disappointing career. When failures come, and they come to everyone, you will have loved the work itself.

. . .

CONFIRMED IN MY IDENTITY as a student, I decided to try out for another play.

Now I understood that I should aim for something more modest than the Loeb main stage. I auditioned for a production of *Twelfth Night* at Leverett House and got a supporting part as Maria, the maid.

My grandmother and mother called to say that they wanted to come up to Boston to see me. They called together, giggling on the line. I was touched. They had attended my every school performance from the time I was in nursery school. I warned them that I wasn't the star here, and the play, well, *Marat/Sade*, set in the asylum of Charenton, had been produced on Broadway the previous fall, and since then, setting plays in asylums had been the rage in college productions. My *Twelfth Night* was set in an asylum, and even though I was in it, I didn't quite understand why. "No matter," my mother said; she and Grandma already had their bus tickets. On Saturday afternoon, I met them at the station, and we took a taxi to their hotel, a Holiday Inn on Massachusetts Avenue, minutes from my dorm. It was icy-deep winter. My mother looked as she had the summer before, her face a little puffy—she said that she had been taking cortisone shots to combat the hoarseness brought on by her shingles. But she and my grandmother were in high spirits. We walked in a line, with me in the center, laughing at our vanity that we were all wearing high-heeled boots despite the weather. That night, I assembled a group of classmates for an early dinner in Harvard Square and invited my new friend Nancy Lipton, who was in my Social Studies 10 tutorial. Nancy, from Teaneck, New Jersey, was city-wise, but had the social confidence of someone who had gone to the kind of high school where friends hung out and went to parties. At the time, I inferred this from the fact that she wore distinctive white eyeliner and knew how to drive—not entirely relevant data. We argued ideas together, wrote papers together. We were not ashamed that we thought of ourselves as aspiring social theorists. It was so pretentious, yes, but that is what we were, right? She had strong opinions but understood how to listen. She had strong opinions, but never seemed to judge me. I wanted to learn from her. I was confident that Nancy would know just how to reassure my family.

Before dinner, there was a moment in Bertram Hall that still gives me comfort. I introduced my mother and grandmother to the girls who were sitting around the bell desk. I knew how much it would please my mother if I introduced my grandmother first.

"Rachel, this is my grandmother, Edith Bonowitz. Grandma, this is Rachel. Rachel, this is my mother, Harriet Turkle. Mommy, this is Rachel."

I hoped that this small gesture would be some compensation for the moment of the hair clip and the hurt I knew I had inflicted then. At the play, my mother and grandmother clapped, laughed, and seemed to have fun.

On Sunday morning, before their bus, I took them out to brunch, and we shared the foods that we never ate in our Brooklyn life. Cheese omelets. Real waffles with strawberries, not frozen from the toaster. Pancakes. We didn't eat bacon. For my grandmother, a Chinese restaurant was the only place for pork.

They told me I was wonderful in the play. And how nice it was that the lead, Viola, was played by a Jewish girl. And then my mother told me how happy she was with how I had introduced her mother to my friends. She had been proud for Grandma. And she was proud of my lovely manners. I belonged in this beautiful Bertram Hall.

. . .

IN SOPHOMORE YEAR, I went home for Christmas with a lot of homework. Most vexing was trying to understand *Capital*, which I read in the Avenue X public library.

One night during that vacation, Nancy and I made a special date in the city. We thought we might have crushes on the same young man. We laughed about that. But we spent more time on our social studies reading. She, too, was working her way through *Capital*. We discussed it over dinner—that helped a bit—and went on to see two arty movies in a row. Then we slept over at her grandmother's apartment in the city.

Perhaps it was the solidity of my friendship with Nancy that emboldened me for the first time to resist, deliberately, my mother's way of shaping our relationship. One night just before Christmas, we sat down to dinner, just the two of us, late. Susan and Bruce were asleep. Milton was at a waitering job.

My mother said, "I have a favor to ask you. I know you are taking a course about France. Right?"

"Yeah."

"Well, I am too. It's a sociology course for my teaching credits. It's about French youth as seen through their cinema. I have to write a paper, but I don't feel up to it. I've missed a lot of classes with my shingles problem. Could you help me with the paper?"

I was annoyed and let it show. "Let me look at the assignment. I'll see." I don't think my mother understood why I was upset. She was asking me something she knew was not difficult for me. And it was clearly important to her, because my hesitation did not deter her.

I began work on the paper. My mother had secondary sources she had to read, written by people described on her syllabus as "French youth sociologists" who had opined on *Les parapluies de Cherbourg*. These critics *were* tough to understand. Their work was opaque and jargon-filled. My mother's job was to say in twelve pages whether she agreed with them or not. I sat at that familiar dinette table in our kitchen, with its odd lack of space for chairs, and began writing my mother's paper. She made coffee. As she relaxed, it became clear that my mother had tried to do this assignment without me. She had asked for Mildred's help, but the unreadable French cultural theorists had broken her confidence. "But perhaps," said my mother, "Mildred might have some ideas now." Suddenly, Mildred was there, at the door with cheesecake.

In the movie, young lovers are separated by the Algerian war. They end up not happily united but oddly coupled to others. Mildred, my mother, and I decided that the film showed something about the dislocations of normal feelings and connections after the war. Something like that. It was a lovely moment, three brainy Brooklyn Bonowitz women, turning their cross-generational firepower on the pretentious French cultural critics. But I couldn't enjoy it. I started writing the essay, got about eight pages in, and promised to finish when I got back to school.

Back at Radcliffe, I put off the assignment. I knew I was going to finish my mother's paper, but I wanted to make her feel bad for asking me. I think I was trying to act out my side of what should have been a conversation about other things. I had allowed her to live through me. But my interests were getting more political; it would no longer be a question of only telling her things that would please her. Now I would have to invent a parallel life. And I felt growing resentment about why I knew so much about Milton's insecurities and nothing about my own father.

I know that we had a phone conversation about her paper in which I was testy. I think I said a curt good-bye. After the call, I went to the Bertram Hall bell desk and looked at the other girls drinking coffee and eating cinnamon toast. Right behind the bell desk were a large kitchen and adjacent dining room, relics of the days when students were served meals in the dorm. Now the kitchen was stocked, oddly, erratically, with white bread, cinnamon, sugar, and butter. When the shipments of white bread came in, there would be binges of making cinnamon toast. The day I had my quarrel with my mother was a cinnamon-toast day. Did any of these girls eating cinnamon toast have mothers who were asking them to do papers for them? I didn't have a way to calibrate what was being asked of me. Was it outrageous or a small thing? Mothers ask all kinds of things from daughters.

A letter came in the mail from Mildred. She rarely wrote to me. I didn't so much read this letter as let my eyes pass over it. I didn't allow it to communicate anything except that I should help my mother with her essay.

Looking at the letter today, this paragraph was the essence.

> *Your mother has asked you something that she really should not be asking. But consider that she is a very brave woman. Remember last summer when she lost her voice and found a way to soldier on, teaching and preparing her courses, and just putting whatever was going on with her voice out of her mind. She wants to do everything for you to succeed at school and be happy and have the life you deserve. So, be gentle with her. She takes criticism from you very hard.*

In other words: Your mother is ill. She is bravely fighting her illness. Her medications make it hard for her to focus. She can no longer keep up with the things that let her function in her life—like keeping her teaching job at Lincoln, for which she needs to take these night credits. So she is turning to you, for whom writing a paper about the plight of French youth is not so big a deal. Don't embarrass her. Do this out of love. She doesn't have a lot of time.

That was what I refused to read. When we don't want to know the truth, we don't hear the truth spoken to us.

I hastily finished the paper and mailed it to my mother. We never discussed it. Nor did we ever talk about my anger. And I didn't have a follow-up conversation with my aunt about her letter.

Later, after my mother died, I tormented myself about all of this. My aunt comforted me by telling me how often my mother spoke of her visit to Cambridge to see me in *Twelfth Night*. Knowing my mother was dying, my aunt had encouraged the visit, no matter how small my part, no matter how bad the play. My mother had loved the trip.

HARVARD STUDENT AGENCY's Flight S-1 was legendary. S-1 was a round-trip flight to Paris for $199 that left from New York the day after Harvard's last final exam and returned to New York just before fall registration in September. It left you in Europe for over three months. I worked all spring semester to save money for that flight, and for the rest, I imagined I would try to do Europe on $5 a day. I might have to tutor English along the way.

My family did not resist my plan, and this should have been a sure sign that something was the matter. By summer 1967, my mother did not want me to observe her at close range. That summer, my brother went to sleepaway camp and my sister stayed with my grandparents so that my mother and Milton could take a ten-day cruise to the Bahamas, their first real vacation. Later, one of my mother's close friends, who had accompanied my parents on this cruise, said that she knew that my mother was ill, but my mother would not let anything keep her from this trip. On board the ship, my mother's breast lesions opened and began to weep fluid. "Harriet went to the infirmary and asked for a large bandage and hospital tape. She covered up what she didn't want to see. She had a black dress that showed a bit of cleavage and she bought a scarf to hide the tape. She didn't even go to the ship's doctor. She knew there wasn't anything more to do. Your mother was my hero."

I knew two other Radcliffe students on S-1: Nancy from Social Studies 10 and Susan, a Bertram classmate from California. Toward the end of spring semester, Susan asked if she could come to Brooklyn

after she flew in from San Francisco on the day of the flight. The request made me feel like a member of the tribe of girls who had an easy relationship with one another's homes, with one another's families.

When Susan arrived, my mother served bagels and lox and a pound cake. She made coffee. The three of us crowded around the dinette table. Almost immediately, Susan told me she had left San Francisco in a hurry and had not had time to go to the bank. Would it be okay if she borrowed a thousand dollars from

My mother on her cruise to the Bahamas, August 1967, the summer before she died.

my parents to get traveler's checks? Her mother would put a check in the mail that evening to reimburse them. Her tone was matter-of-fact.

When Susan made her casual request, I should have said, "I'm so sorry. That's not possible." With no further comment. Instead, I tried to be as nonchalant as she. I said, "Let's ask my mom." I set my mother up. She could only tell Susan, "I'll look into it." But then she had to take me aside, and I could see that, of course, there was nothing to look into.

Eyes lowered, bright spots on her cheeks, my mother spoke to me slowly, as though she were imparting new information: "We don't have that much money in the bank, Sherry." She was protecting herself from the truth, that I had known this and put her in this position. That I had created a situation where she had to say this to me out loud. In the moment, I wondered if I had perhaps indulged a fantasy—since I was in the tribe of girls who could drop by one another's homes to wait for a flight to Europe, I was now in the tribe of girls who could make such requests of their parents.

I thought of all the years that I never applied for camp scholarships in order to spare my mother the pain of talking about money. But now I had allowed myself a casual cruelty. It was up to me to tell Susan that we could not loan her the money. Susan shrugged. "No matter. My parents will wire the money to the American Express office in Paris." Her face was blank. Her request had had no malice. I don't think it had occurred to her that we might not have a thousand dollars in the bank.

My aunt drove us to Kennedy Airport for the departure of S-1. I sat with my grandmother and mother in the backseat, and we held hands all the way. I promised to send a telegram as soon as I landed in Paris. I felt the emotional cost of my adventure. Three months away was a long time. Mildred said something about maybe coming to Europe to check up on me. I wanted to say to my mother: *I wish it could be you.*

NANCY'S FATHER WAS an international oil consultant, the kind of person who had been to Paris many times. He had given Nancy the perfect bon voyage present: two nights at a lovely hotel when she landed.

So for our first two nights in Europe, Nancy and I shared a double at the Hotel Madame. Each bed had a duvet, the first time I had seen such a thing. In the morning, we had Parisian breakfast in a little dining room off the center hall: orange juice, croissants, French bread, butter, and jam. And then: tea, hot cocoa, or coffee—black or with steaming-hot milk.

On our first day in Paris, Nancy and I saw the Eiffel Tower. We walked on the Champs-Élysées. And we looked for a cheaper hotel. A group of students we knew were staying at the Hotel Pierwige, 51, boulevard Saint-Germain. A single room was ten francs a night, or about two dollars, breakfast included. This was for a room without a bath or shower. For fifty centimes you got a few minutes under a spray. But even this cheaper hotel came equipped with the puffy duvets and endless French breakfasts.

The plan—for Nancy, Susan, and me—was to stay a week in Paris and then hitchhike through Brittany. I didn't know anything about traveling in France and was grateful for this plan, suggested by Nancy and her worldly father.

Summer 1967 was a magical time to be in Europe. Students with knapsacks had descended on the Continent, so all travel had the feeling of a giant, moving party. And Europe itself had not yet gone through the final convulsions of modernization. Local cultures were still alive. When you visited something old, you were visiting a shored-up version of the old thing, not its restoration as a safer and more amusing version of itself. I saw the authentic rather than the rebuilt or enhanced. The authentic is often boring because it doesn't explain itself to you. It doesn't have instructions etched into it or sign posted. It's often dusty, dull, and chipped away. What it has going for it is, quite simply: It is. I saw Europe without the patina of restoration and tidying up.

We arrived in Quimper, walked into town, and found a hotel. No reservations, no calling ahead. We showed our passports and paid for inexpensive rooms. We had even better breakfasts than the ones in Paris because we ate fresh butter and eggs, something I had never experienced. For lunch we had *galettes*, the buckwheat crepes of the region.

We made it to Saint-Malo, had a visit to Mont-Saint-Michel, and then it was time for Nancy to travel on to her summer job in London. Susan and I made our way back to Paris, where I was enrolled in a French history and culture class at the Sorbonne. My mother had wanted me to take Spanish as my language in high school because it was a "practical" language for a New Yorker and it was what she had studied. I hadn't bothered to argue with her; I wasn't even considering it. *The Glass Slipper* and *Gigi* were French Cinderella stories. I took five years of junior high and high school French to prepare for the moment that was upon me—I was going to a lecture, in French, at the Sorbonne.

FOR SO LONG, I had imagined this and other Paris moments. I wanted to see myself reading great French literature in the Luxembourg Gardens. I wanted to see myself with a French boyfriend, having conversations in French.

At the Luxembourg Gardens, I paid for a small, hard chair and settled into memorizing "Le Lac" by Lamartine. But my back hurt, I got headaches in the sun, and I became weary of self-dramatization. I went to Shakespeare and Company, a legendary bookstore for English speakers, and bought Virginia Woolf's *Mrs. Dalloway* and *To the Lighthouse*. I moved to the cool banquettes of indoor cafés. My French fantasy had had a slight change of program.

The obligatory French romance proceeded apace. A nice-looking engineering student, Matteo, asked me out for a coffee while I was still staring at my Lamartine. His parents were Algerian refugees, French Italians who had lived for generations outside France but had returned as the war heated up. Matteo and his family lived in Drancy, a suburb outside Paris. From Matteo, I learned that Drancy had been an internment camp for 62,000 of the 75,000 Jews deported from France during the war, most of them to Auschwitz. The French police, working in liaison with occupying Nazi officials, had played the lead role in rounding up and deporting these unfortunates, who had trusted the promise of the French Republic: *Liberté, Egalité, Fraternité*. In 1967 the French did not discuss such

With my boyfriend Matteo, from Drancy and the Luxembourg Gardens, Paris, June 1967.

things, but Matteo told me the whole story, because if you lived in Drancy, it was part of your life.

After I visited Drancy, I became fascinated by how the French, for the most part, denied their role in the Holocaust. I remembered Rabbi Wagner's warning to my Sunday-school class about talking too much about the war years. At Drancy I could hear his voice from over a decade before: You could not live a life among gentiles if you made them feel guilty every day. At eighteen it seemed to me that in France, anti-Semitism was a taboo topic because people feared that speaking about it could make it return. If Jews said they were angry, people would be angry at Jews.

IN THE LOBBY of the Pierwige, being a college student provided an instant membership in a club of itinerants, many of whom were using Paris as a jumping-off point for European travel. Or for a trip to Versailles, or Chartres, or the cinematheque. In that lobby I learned that Elaine—my friend from the National Science Foundation summer in Syracuse, my companion to visit the "real America" in Pennsylvania—was in Paris. I cut short my lectures at the Sorbonne, and we set off by train to explore "the Continent." Elaine even had a friend of a friend whose father owned a villa near Capri. This was the world I had read about in my girlhood. I would go where Aunt March took Amy in *Little Women*. A nineteenth-century grand tour.

Actually, I think I was also trying to retrace the steps of the heroines of a book I read in the Avenue X Public Library when I was a high school junior—*Our Hearts Were Young and Gay* by Cornelia Otis Skinner and Emily Kimbrough. In that book, two recent Bryn Mawr graduates go on a trip to Europe in 1923. They had only to show up in Paris and suitors would arrive to take them dancing. They had only to show up in London and family friends would arrive to take them to the chicest clubs.

It didn't happen quite that way, but I did have a crush on a boy in Rome and a visit from a relative. My aunt made a plan to come to London at the end of the summer, and I figured out how to take a boat train from Paris to visit her. In London, I could stay with her in her proper hotel room, a respite from the student hostels and the one- and two-star hotels of the rest of the summer. When Mildred arrived and I moved into her modest room—only then did I realize how much I wanted her to take care of me.

My aunt and I ate roast beef at Simpson's, something she had done on her first trip to London in 1953 and was eager to share with me. We had afternoon tea as our main meal almost every day. We saw Muriel Spark's *The Prime of Miss Jean Brodie* and Eugène Ionesco's *Rhinoceros*, both plays about the rise of fascism. I talked to her about Social Sciences 2, where the seduction of fascism had been a theme during the second semester. During times of insecurity, the Frankfurt-born psychoanalyst Erich Fromm asked, do people try to eliminate uncertainty by looking for an authoritarian leader to tell them what to think and how to act? These conversations in London, late into the night, eating room-service tea and toast, reminded me that all my life, Mildred had been there, talking to me.

While in London, I ran into a Harvard classmate who told me he had found a cheap flight from London to Israel and another that would get him back to Paris in time to pick up the S-1 Harvard flight to New York. Would I like to join this Israel side trip? It was leaving the following week. I brought the idea to Mildred, who immediately of-fered to buy me a ticket.

When I stepped off the El Al flight, my reaction was instinctive: I kissed the ground. I was born in 1948, the year of Israel's founding as a state. I thought of it as the refuge for the Jews no one else had wanted, even after the horrors of the Holocaust. The place for the people who had managed to survive places like Drancy.

Within days of arriving, I was on a bus tour with twenty other college students seeing classic "first visit" things: The Dead Sea. Jerusalem. Masada. In my other travels, I had fallen in love with cities, objects, language, food, vistas. What I remember of those weeks in Israel was the experience of being on a bus with Jewish college students from all over the world who all felt we had come home.

6.

Taxis

Before I returned to Bertram Hall for my junior year, a big box from Macy's was on my grandmother's kitchen table. My grandfather and aunt were smiling. My grandfather said: "This is from Mama! This is from Mama," his pet name for my grandmother. My grandmother was beaming. This was her present: a Smith Corona portable electric typewriter in the most beautiful colors, a light and a darker taupe. From the beginning of my junior year, I wrote every college paper on it. I wrote my senior thesis on it. Then I wrote every graduate school essay on it. I brought it to Paris when I was researching my dissertation on French psychoanalysis and used it with a voltage converter.

Everything about the typewriter pleased and still pleases me. Its touch is firm; you hit a key, and the machine gives you feedback that work has been done. Its touch is light; effort never strains. It hums while you think. It's heavy enough to not slide around when I put it on a coffee table and sit cross-legged on a couch and start to write. Its ribbon is easily accessible, and this is a good thing, because sometimes, to avoid confusion, I use one color for what my interview subjects say and a different color for my own thoughts. I still turn to it when writer's block strikes. And sometimes just for a different writing experience. My grandmother's typewriter asks me to compose a sentence before I begin to type. It brings back the pleasures of the deliberate and the familiar.

It was at the taupe Smith Corona that I began to seriously think about the idea of *evocative objects*, objects that carry meaning far beyond their instrumental value. When I began to use the Smith Corona, I felt the full force of my grandmother's love. When, after two years at Radcliffe, I had talked with her about waiting in line for the public-use typewriters and borrowing typewriters that belonged to other girls, she had gone to the Macy's department where I had shopped with her since childhood. The same department where she bought me my first record player, my first album, and my own copy of *Little Women*. I could feel her wanting me to succeed and not knowing what she could do. And then her pleasure when she found that it was in her power to help.

IN OCTOBER 1967, Harvard students protested the recruiting activities of an officer of the Dow Chemical Company, as Dow was making napalm, and napalm was being used against civilian populations in Vietnam. The intensity of the confrontation sparked a demand for a group where students and faculty could discuss such issues together. Much to the students' surprise, the administration came back with a concrete proposal: a Student-Faculty Advisory Committee (SFAC) that would make policy recommendations. The administration would nominate sixteen faculty members who would meet with twenty-three elected students. Each Harvard house would elect a representative, as would each of the four Radcliffe houses. I decided to run, and when South House voted me its representative, it meant more to me than any other Harvard accolade.

The professors appointed to SFAC were among the most vocal across the political spectrum on the Harvard faculty: Oscar Handlin on the right; Stanley Hoffmann and Erik Erikson, moderates; Martin Peretz and Barrington Moore on the left.

When SFAC, after much deliberation, asked Harvard to cancel an upcoming return visit by a Dow recruiter, our recommendation didn't go to the administration, as we expected, but to a regular faculty meeting that voted it down. SFAC faced a crisis. If anything we proposed could be blocked by the faculty, the administration might never see our work at all. We had no independent power and no place in any decision-making chain. Created with great fanfare, our committee seemed reduced to political theater. But for me, it was an education. I saw how institutions find ways to defer what they don't want to deal with. And I watched my faculty mentors try to persuade colleagues who did not agree with them. When they advanced arguments that didn't win over new support, they backtracked and came at the problem from a different angle—early lessons in how to participate in the public square.

DURING THE FALL of my junior year, I took a lecture course on modern Jewish history. Professor Yosef Yerushalmi, handsome and intense, stood in front of a classroom in Sever Hall considering Judaism's particular alchemy of memory, history, and identity. I was mesmerized. Yerushalmi would consider an idea, build up what seemed to be a sturdy edifice to support it, and then cast it away and make a fresh start in a new direction. I was not indifferent to the subject matter or his personal charisma, but that's not what I found most compelling. I wanted to be able to think like that. In retrospect, I suppose he was borrowing from the Talmudic method I might have learned if I had gone to Hebrew school.

Harvard had offered me this experience of wanting to think like my professors several times before—there were Samuel Beer's lectures in Social Sciences 2 when I was a freshman and, when I was a sophomore, Social Studies 10 and Stanley Hoffmann's course on French society and politics. In the first semester of my junior year, I studied the history of industrial society in a social studies tutorial with the political scientist George Ross, and what I learned about structural inequality made me so angry that I thought of going into public advocacy law or politics, not because I thought I would be good at either, just because I was so fired up. I saw the connection between what I was learning in class and what we were debating in SFAC. That junior fall I marched on the Pentagon to protest the Vietnam War. I was not yet confident, but I was no longer thinking about my permanent record. I was imagining myself in the world of stumbling and trying again. I was finally in college.

Just before I left for winter break, I received an invitation to Marty Peretz's holiday party, a glamorous invitation for any social studies student. At the party, held at the beautiful Cambridge home of Marty and his wife, Anne Peretz, I met another social studies student who admitted he also felt lucky to be invited: a senior named Rick. He was from Scarsdale. He took my number and said he would call during the break.

Over Thanksgiving, my mother had seemed weaker—she said it was a flare-up of her shingles. I looked forward to spending time with her over the long vacation. I had a paper due for my course on Jewish history, so I spent much of it at the Forty-second Street library in Manhattan, reading up on anti-Semitism in early French socialist thought. I got there early but was home by five to spend the evening with my mother.

She told me that in early December she had caught pneumonia. Now, as she recuperated, she was sleeping in my sister's room, my former bedroom. At night, my mother and I lay in my childhood bed, propped up with pillows, drinking homemade chicken soup that my grandmother brought over for reheating, watching TV movies that repeated in a loop until the early-morning hours. I curled up with my mother as I would with a lover. Spoons. My mother would doze off a bit at ten and then wake up at midnight and again at two and ask me what had happened in the movie. I would catch her up.

I finally decided to talk to my aunt about this on-and-off sleep pattern, which was not getting better. I called Mildred from a pay phone at the Forty-second Street library so I would have privacy. And I called her at work so that she would have privacy as well. When I reached her, Mildred said she was in a meeting, and she quickly called me back. She said, "It's the medicine she takes. She's sleeping from the medicine. It puts her to sleep at odd hours and then she can't sleep at regular hours. Don't worry about it. Just go back to school. It's nice that you had such a long vacation to be with her."

Rick called as he had promised, and when he came to pick me up in Brooklyn, my mother, too weak to leave her room to greet him, called out jauntily from her bedroom, "Have fun!" Our romance took off immediately. Rick had a ready smile and a willingness to talk unself-consciously about social studies things we were both trying to understand: Antonio Gramsci, Herbert Marcuse, and Marx's *Eighteenth Brumaire*. We learned about existentialism together. Rick was also handsome and a former wrestler and enthusiastically introduced me to jogging, which at the time I considered an esoteric practice. I no longer felt disloyal when I enjoyed Rick's Scarsdale kitchen, with its books and magazines and loving parents having coffee together. In January 1968, most of this was in the future. But by the time I returned to Radcliffe, I was hoping that Rick saw me as his girlfriend.

Days after winter break, there was a letter from my mother, attached to her Brooklyn College take-home exam on marriage and family research in the United States. "Daddy picked this up for me last nite. Am wondering if you can help me on it. . . . Please, if you can't, forget it. I'll understand. I love you dear and hope that my wishes for you come true real soon. Come home real soon. Mom." I began to make up answers to the questions she had checked. I called her and, without preface, said that I had some ideas to help with the test questions. She began to take notes. I remember thinking that when I next saw her, I would find a new, gentler way to talk to her about these requests.

But her letter, too, seemed a new kind of request. This exam was made up of general-knowledge questions that, under other circumstances, my adroit mother could waltz through unprepared. ("What should you say to an unmarried couple contemplating having a child?") In her letter she said that she couldn't make her thoughts "jibe."

On January 10, I was coming out of the coffee shop in Radcliffe's Hilles Library when one of the freshmen in Bertram Hall approached me. My aunt Mildred had called the dorm. She said that my mother was in Brooklyn Hospital and I should come home. There was no way to reach my aunt; she was at the hospital. My instructions were simply to go home. And to go immediately to the hospital. Within hours, I was in its dark entry. My eyes adjusted to find the check-in desk for visitors.

It was January, but the hall was parched with dry New York radia-
tor heat. Why wasn't there more light? When I told the receptionist
my name, I was given a pass and I signed a logbook. The nineteenth-
century building was run down. Some corridors were paneled in dark
mahogany, but large sections were painted over with greenish paint.
The moldings were ornate, but sometimes they ended abruptly where
large pieces had fallen off.

I had the sense of arriving too late.

Outside there was snow, treacherous ice; the plane I took from
Boston to New York had been twice delayed to de-ice the wings, and
then again to clear the runway. I was wet when I got to the hospital,
damp from sweat and rain when I saw my aunt and grandmother in a
smoking lounge at the end of a corridor. I went to greet them. Quick
kiss, not much talk: plane, ice, flight, snow. They looked ashen, but I
thought, *Of course they do; my mother is in the hospital. I wasn't around
for the shingles hospitalization. This is the second hospitalization in less
than a year. This is awful for them.* I kissed them again. "I want to go
see Mommy," I said. They nodded. "Of course. Go see Mommy."
Now, in the dark corridor outside her door, I shivered in the oppres-
sive heat.

My mother was sharing a room. Her roommate had a curtain
drawn around her. It made a curve, a strange ellipsoid shape, like a
cocoon. My mother lay flat in her bed, hooked up to an IV line; a
young doctor was whispering to her, smiling. He was just leaving; her
eyes were almost closed. I thought dully that, just as over the break,
it must be the medication that was putting her to sleep. Was she in
pain? My mother saw me hesitate at the door to her room, waved
away some tubing, and gave me a kiss when I approached. "Sherry,
Sherry. Baby." She was not upset. I kissed her and said that I would
be back in a flash, I just want to say hi to Grandma and Mildred.

Another kiss. The way to the lounge was down a long corridor. I passed a nursing station. Behind it there was a glass enclosure with the young doctor who had been whispering to my mother. I gestured to the doctor; I was surprised that he immediately came out of his glass place.

I introduced myself. "I am Harriet Turkle's daughter, come home from Boston." The question on my mind was how long my mother would be in the hospital.

"How long?" I asked.

He said: "About ten days, maybe two weeks."

"Why so long?" I asked.

An odd, trapped look crossed his face. He realized that I didn't know. Was he the one who was supposed to tell me? "No," he said, "she only has two weeks. I thought you knew." I realized the unacceptable: I did know. I looked up; my grandmother and aunt were far away, looking at me, squinting behind their glasses.

LOOKING BACK, it is hard to believe that I got to this point without knowing anything of my mother's cancer. She was committed to hiding it from me, but still, there were moments when something was revealed. Over ten years, child to nineteen-year-old woman, I showed little curiosity, although when it came to anything other than my mother's health, I was curious about everything. Or rather, I was brought up not to ask about matters that I knew from the start were shrouded in silence.

In 1959, that day of my fifth-grade spelling bee, my mother had had a radical mastectomy of the left breast. I'm not surprised that I didn't notice anything different about my mother's body, at least not at first. In my family, women's bodies were hidden. My grandmother,

mother, and aunt dressed and bathed in private. My aunt wore a bathing suit and swam in the ocean. My grandmother never went near the water. Nor did my mother, except to stand at its edge. She said it wasn't good for her lacquered hair. I only half believed this story. All my life I assumed that women who felt themselves too large did not like to expose themselves this way. So I have memories of my grandmother, corseted, in her crisp summer housedresses, and my mother, resplendent in pedal pushers, a long-sleeved blouse, earrings, and full makeup, sitting in chairs, watching us children on the Rockaway beach.

My mother dressed a certain way that I now think of as camouflage. Long-sleeved blouses. High-necked blouses. Suits with jackets that buttoned up close to the neck. And I think she learned to hold herself just so, even when we embraced. There was something characteristic, a way of leaning in with her face, holding my face in her hands.

My mother, like her mother, was so large-bosomed, she never was without undergarments. So by the winter holiday vacation when she and I watched movies in bed together, I did not find it unusual that my mother would be dressed in stylish pajamas and wearing a bra underneath to have her figure look its best as she essentially "received" family and friends at her bedside.

Something else colors my effort to reconstruct my not knowing during all those years. The more I have analyzed what I *should* have known, given the data before me, the more I believe that what I knew most of all was that I was not supposed to know about my mother's body. I understood it was taboo. In this sense, our empathic connection worked.

And when I made that one call to my aunt, during that last winter vacation, to ask why my mother was sleeping so much, Mildred said she was in a meeting and had to call me back. She returned my call within minutes, reassured me, and told me to go back to school. I think now that Mildred took those few minutes to get in touch with my mother. Did she finally want to tell me the truth? My mother said no. We all had instructions to behave as though my mother were not ill. My special instructions were to repress what I suspected.

Later, I blamed myself for what I knew without knowing. I blamed my family for not giving me the opportunity to say good-bye to my mother. I blamed my mother for not letting me say good-bye, not even in those last weeks, when we lay in bed, watching bad movies, drinking chicken soup, eating popcorn, and chewing the licorice gum she loved. As time went on, I saw things differently. Our intimacy on those nights was how she wanted to be with me if those were our last moments. We ate her favorite foods, prepared by her mother. We watched romantic movies that referred back to a lifetime of watching romantic movies together.

As for blaming my family, I had one talk with my grandmother that ended all that. It was just after her seven days of ritual mourning were over, and I walked with her as she did her chores on a snowy February day. We passed our family drugstore, Church Pharmacy, and she stopped to look wistfully at its window display. This, my grandmother said, was where she had bought special vitamins for my mother. The pharmacist would make them up for her in high doses. She described how she regularly clipped stories out of magazines and brought them to my mother's doctor, "ideas that might help Harriet." Vitamin cures. Blood transfusions. Avocados. Something from Paris. For ten years she had only one thought: to keep Harriet alive. When I asked my grandmother, "Why not tell me so I could have helped?" her face softened. "Knowing you were where you should be was Harriet's consolation. She felt she had accomplished that, no matter what.

I would never have taken that away from her." And that was the end of my blaming other people.

AFTER I LEARNED THE TRUTH, my life in the hospital began. It lasted seventeen days. My mother knew that I should be in school. She understood what my presence meant. But she did not suggest I return to Cambridge. She had never spoken to me about her cancer. We didn't talk about it now.

At Brooklyn Hospital, visiting hours didn't officially begin until one, but our family was allowed in early. I resented this special status because it meant that there was no hope.

So, a 9:00 A.M. arrival. My mother was usually sleeping. My grandmother arrived at nine thirty. My aunt came after spending the morning at work. Her boss was letting her work half days. My mother was too weak to walk, but one day she was helped to a chair by the window so that she could wave to Susan and Bruce, thirteen and eleven. I stood with them below, trying to help them count the windows up and to the right so they could find her fluttering hand. No one had told them that our mother was dying or gravely ill. They still thought that she was recuperating from pneumonia. I told Milton that he must prepare them. He wouldn't talk about it. I knew this was wrong, but I didn't feel that I could defy him. He was their father.

Sometimes my aunt drove my grandfather to the hospital, but he was not able to stay more than a short time without losing his composure. My grandmother was stoic, but my grandfather couldn't control his tears, and he didn't want his daughter to see this. Watching my grandparents with my mother was almost more than I could bear.

Brooklyn Hospital is a short walk from the DeKalb Avenue subway station. I'd been riding to that station all my life. To shop with my grandmother at A&S or Mays discount department store. To go to the printer for the *Lincoln Log*. I'd always liked getting off at DeKalb Avenue because my mother told me that after college, when she took her first full-time job, this was her station. I liked to think of my young mother, strong and beautiful, emerging from the subway, excited to be part of the adult, working life of the world. But from the very first day after I learned that my mother was dying, I could not face a subway ride. I walked out of Murdock Court and hailed a taxi. On that first day riding to the hospital, I knew I was spending money I didn't have, but I thought, *It's just one day.* Then I took a taxi on the second day. I could not bear the thought that someone might touch me.

I was assaulted on the subway when I was thirteen, returning home from my grandparents' on a Sunday evening. First I took the subway from Church Avenue Station, and then there was a bus ride from Sheepshead Bay to a few blocks from our home. I was wearing green checked polyester slacks. The subway was crowded, and I was standing, holding on to a pole. I felt pressure on the crack of my backside. I thought someone was touching me and I tried to move away. I sensed a man behind me, but I couldn't be sure. My pants felt wet. Warm. Then, something cold. A knife? I was confused. Had I urinated? I knew it wasn't my period. I reached behind me and my hand was pushed away. And then all of a sudden, the train stopped and emptied out. I was standing in the middle of the car with no one around me. Again I reached around. My pants had been slit down the crack of my buttocks. I didn't have a sweater or a coat. I sat down to hide the tear. When the train reached my stop, I walked home. It was dark, and I thought I was less likely to be seen walking than in the bright light of a bus. When I took off the pants, the cut was blade sharp. And my panties, also slit, were wet with what I thought must be semen. I hid the pants and the panties. I told no one. I had very few clothes. I would be asked about these pants if they just disappeared. I was terrified. I thought all of this was my fault. I never told anyone. I threw the pants away the next time I went to the Sheepshead Bay subway station. I told my mother I had gained weight and the pants had split. She said I should ask my grandmother to mend them on her machine the next time I visited. Miraculously, my mother then seemed to forget about the pants, but for months I worried that she would inquire about their repair.

Now, faced with the prospect of taking this same subway line to the hospital, all of this came flooding back. All the years growing up in New York, I had thought of this on every subway ride, but since I never had any choice, I had always let it come to me, felt a bit sick, and then proceeded, cautious, anxious. But on these visits to Brooklyn Hospital, I could not make myself go underground. I did not want to be in crowds. I wanted to be taken care of, and there was no one taking care of me. I could think of only one thing. I would not put myself at risk of being touched on the subway.

ONLY A FEW BLOCKS from Brooklyn Hospital is Junior's restaurant, famous for its cheesecake. Most days, there was nothing I could do for my mother but sit beside her bed as she napped, but one day, she was alert and said she wanted cheesecake. She asked me for her pocketbook.

She took out forty dollars, for us, a very large sum. My grandmother was in the room, and my mother told me to buy all three of us cheesecake, and also, while I was out, she wanted me to buy myself a new handbag at A&S, the department store that is only a few blocks from Brooklyn Hospital. She said that the one I brought home with me from college looked old. I had never owned a leather bag, so I knew that my mother wasn't even thinking of that. I went to the main floor of A&S and bought a vinyl luggage-colored bag, something in the spirit of Leslie's bohemian style. And we all had cheesecake together.

The next day, when I arrived at the hospital, my mother was agitated. She had just remembered an errand I must run. Now, immediately. She explained that during the fall semester she took a course at Brooklyn College to keep up her certification as a full-time substitute teacher. She had a required student/teacher meeting scheduled for later that very morning. Obviously, she was not able to attend this meeting, but she had no way of reaching the instructor. The meeting was important because this was a two-semester course. She explained that at this meeting, the instructor would return her first-semester exam and give her a paper topic for spring semester. I must go in her stead. I must not say she was ill but that she had had an accident. I must get his exam feedback and her paper topic. I'd know what to do. She needed the credits. She could not afford to lose these credits.

I did as she said. I went to Brooklyn College and met with my mother's instructor in a course on educational psychology. I didn't tell him the made-up story about my mother having been in an accident. I simply said that my mother was not feeling well. I had a superstitious moment. If my mother was not ruling out that she was coming back for the second semester, why should I? The instructor said he was sorry that my mother was ill; she was a very nice lady. I held back the desire to ask him about my mother. Did he know her, this nice lady? I just said "Thank you" and took back her final exam. On the back of my mother's exam book he had written out a suggested paper topic for the following semester. This was a different exam than the one for which I'd offered on-the-phone tips. I know she passed the course, but I remember nothing else. I returned to the hospital to find my mother sleeping. She never asked about the exam, her grade, or her assigned paper.

In the days that followed, my mother slept most of the time. I noticed for the first time that my mother, who dyed her hair almost black, had gray hair. It had been more than six weeks since she had gone to the hairdresser, and her face was framed in a halo of light. Her nails, always lacquered bright red, were ragged. One day, I asked her if she wanted me to give her a manicure. She shrugged, as though to say, *It doesn't matter now,* and grabbed at her gown where her left breast, the missing breast, should be. After her mastectomy, she did not have a breast reconstruction. She had worn a bra with a form in it; she had worn it, even to bed, for nine years. I had not figured any of this out. Now, in the hospital, for the first time, I saw her without her bra, with one side of her chest flattened.

When she asked me to get her purse for cheesecake money, I opened her hospital closet and I saw the clothes she wore to the hospital. Later, while she slept, I examined them. Brown slacks, one of her modest long-sleeved white cotton blouses from A&S, a pair of flat shoes. In a travel bag, there were many changes of panties and her bra, white, 38DD, with very wide straps. The left cup had a pocket into which a foam prosthetic had been inserted and sewn in. I was surprised at how soft it was. I noticed that the right cup, too, was lined with foam, so that the feel of the two breasts, once the bra was on, might be similar. That night I went home to Murdock Court and found my mother's collection of bras, black and white and nude colored, each with its own form sewn in. Each ready to wear. All of these garments, my mother's secrets. Hidden in her closet under a sleek wool coat with a large mink collar.

When I asked my mother if she wanted a manicure and in answer she grabbed at her chest, her gesture, clawing at herself, was rough. I felt that she was trying to say something, even then, so late. That she'd had a hard time. It had been hard not having her breast. It had been hard not being able to complain, hard, perhaps, not having my comfort. I imagined all these things she did not say and now never would.

It was then that my mother closed her eyes and turned away from me. A lifelong regret: I did not claim a few moments right then, to tell her I was sorry that I had not known what was happening to her. That I had not been a greater comfort. Or had I been exactly the kind of comfort she wanted?

My absence was, after all, what she asked for. For her, it was what made things normal. I was at Radcliffe, not preoccupied with her.

The next day, my mother's lungs were filled with fluid. She had already had a lung tap, which led to a lengthy infection. This time, her doctor said that he would rather not cause her the discomfort and risks of another. He suggested that we just make her more comfortable.

I was not in the room when my mother died. When I was allowed in, my mother's IV line had been removed. Her arms

This captures my bond with my mother, but I won't look at Milton, who is taking the photo, Lafayette Court, 1953.

were under fresh cotton blankets. Her face was washed and her head on a clean pillow. I had never seen a dead person before. I heard myself crying out, "I love you. I love you. I love you." That was what came out. I heard the sounds. The part of me that was listening thought, *At least you have that. This is what came out of you when your mother died.*

My grandparents left the hospital with my aunt. It was decided that I would go home with Milton. Susan and Bruce needed to be told. They were having dessert in our small kitchen. They had been staying with neighbors and were brought back to our apartment when Milton called from the hospital. Milton was distraught. Sweating. Without preface, he faced his two children and said: "Your mother passed away this afternoon." I remember Susan's cry and Bruce's silence.

TRADITIONALLY, JEWS ARE not embalmed. Burial follows quickly upon death. Milton decided to depart from these conventions. He instructed the funeral home that my mother be cosmetically enhanced and that there be a "chapel" evening, during which friends and family could assemble with my mother's body on view. At the time, Milton said that this would make it easier for Susan and Bruce. That seeing their mother dead would help them cope with the fact that her death had really happened. When he explained what was going to happen, he took on a didactic tone. The tone of someone who knew the literature. My aunt, acid, called this his "amateur psychologist" voice. I said that this seemed like a bad idea. Milton then moved to another reason for an open casket. He said, "I want people to see what I have lost." This seemed more honest. His wife was young. Forty-nine. Harriet's beauty and youth would win him sympathy.

At the chapel, a new and more forceful Milton was in evidence. He wanted Susan and Bruce to look at my mother. The funeral home had applied heavy pancake makeup, two dots of rouge, and a smear of lipstick that looked like a wound. I recoiled.

Milton took charge of his children and I sat quietly in the corner with my grandparents and aunt. They were stoic. As Milton circulated, talking about his loss, my aunt watched with contempt. "He's looking for pity." Walking young children around a funeral home and talking about your pain was indeed the opposite of Bonowitz.

My mother was buried the next day. Milton, Susan, and Bruce sat shiva, the Jewish ritual of mourning, at Murdock Court; Mildred and my grandparents at 51 East Seventeenth Street. I shuttled between them. I expected that sometime in the next few days, Susan and Bruce would visit their grandparents and aunt. But Milton did not want his children to leave his side at Murdock Court. My grandparents became increasingly upset, and I felt responsible for their misery. I begged Milton to let his children see their grandparents. He refused. I can only think that for years, Milton felt that my grandfather did not accept him as an equal. Now, in Milton's moment of grief, he did not want to do the right thing.

Finally, Milton allowed Mildred to drive Susan and Bruce to their grandparents' apartment. But the damage was done. There were my stepfather and his children. There were my grandparents and aunt. My mother had held things together. But perhaps it had always been this way, the Turkles and the Bonowitzes.

7.

Mourning

I began to go through my mother's things, looking for something that she might have written, a note or letter in which she talked about her illness. I was haunted by all I had not done for her. What I had not seen. What I must have known and denied.

The only thing I found was an exchange of letters between my mother and a Catholic psychic in Mexico, a connection that had been set up by my mother's friend Frieda. Frieda worked in the theater, helping to dress the actors. When she visited, she always brought a bag of costume jewelry from which my mother and I could each choose a piece.

The psychic had given my mother some prayers to say, printed on a small piece of fabric, a fabric you might use to polish your spectacles. In the letter to my mother, there is some mention of a rosary—I searched for the beads but never found them. The psychic said that she and her community were praying for my mother and told her to continue with prayer even when discouraged.

I found this beginning of a letter from my mother to the psychic, written on a kitchen pad.

Dear Maria,

Thank you for your letter. Frieda has visited and told me that you have written her as well. I have used the beads and your prayers. But they are not working. I am getting weaker. I have places on my chest where the skin is opening.

The letter ends there. At first, I was shocked. A psychic. Rosary beads. Nuns in a Mexican convent. Over weeks, I saw things differently.

My mother didn't have anyone to talk to. She had kept me out of the picture. She understood that her mother was losing a child. There were limits to what she could ask. Perhaps she had been afraid to talk freely to Mildred for fear that her sister would call me home from school. Milton seemed on the edge of a breakdown.

And although she understood the gravity of her condition, my mother had made it clear to her family and her doctors that she wanted everyone to emphasize hope. So my mother was surrounded by a version of the truth that she knew wasn't true. Keeping it up silenced everyone around her. In the end, it silenced her. The psychic allowed her to speak.

I went back to Radcliffe for the second semester, although I arrived a few weeks late. My friends in Bertram Hall and Social Studies were warm and solicitous. I went to SFAC meetings and tried to feel part of things. Although I fell behind in my reading, I got on a schedule of commuting from Cambridge to Brooklyn because Milton said that weekend visits would help him cope. Only a few weeks into this program, he and I went on one of our Ocean Parkway walks and he surprised me with the directness of his speech: "I need you to take over for your mother. That is the place of the eldest daughter. I cannot go on without your help."

Flat out, just like that. He wanted me to leave Radcliffe and take care of Susan and Bruce. I could enroll at Brooklyn College, or, he said, "You are so smart, you can always go back later and get a degree." What was essential was that I had to live at home. He said that his request was reasonable. It was how things would have been done "in the Old Country."

I knew better than to point out that we weren't in the Old Country. This was about more than helping Milton with his children. Right then, he began to talk to me as though I were someone who owed him emotional support. He told me that he must explain what he had lost and why he could not go on alone. I told him that he should not talk to me about his most personal feelings, but I made the same mistake I had made as a child: I did not walk away.

Milton told me that he had been discharged from the army because of depression. I'd heard this story since childhood. Now Milton added that he had been sexually impotent, and an army psychiatrist had declared him too depressed to serve. He wanted me to know that he had done "the honorable thing." He told my mother all about this before they were married. He said, "She saved me."

As Milton told his story, I remember taking a moment to marvel at my mother's magical thinking. How far it had taken her. She had fulfilled this man through a sixteen-year marriage, two children, and nine years of her ravaging disease. And now he had no idea who he was without her.

I threw everything at him, everything that might make him understand that I was not coming home. My mother hid her illness from me so that I would go to Radcliffe. Continuing my education there would do the greatest honor to her memory: "I will find you help, professional help. I'll work. I'll take more time with my graduate education if you are short of money. But I will not move back home."

Then, suddenly, Milton brightened. He had another idea, as though he might have anticipated this outcome. "In the Old Country, the unmarried sister of a woman who had children married the widower." I was incredulous. He was going to ask Mildred to marry him.

I begged him not to do this. I told him that this proposal would damage his relationship with my aunt and grandparents, relationships that were in the best interests of his children. These were their loving family. Milton's mood blackened. He did not want to hear this. He liked the idea of marrying Harriet's sister. I wondered if he was drunk.

Milton grabbed my shoulders, insisting I face him. My mind flashed to the shower in Rockaway. I had always blamed my mother. I saw her as the more powerful figure in their relationship. But now, as Milton grabbed my shoulders, I blamed him. I told him again that I was not coming home and not leaving school. He said I was not behaving as a daughter should and he no longer considered me his daughter. He wanted me out, right then.

I had only a small valise. I packed the clothes I had brought home from school that weekend. I was leaving behind my notebooks from grade school through my sophomore year of college; the scripts I had written for school plays; the speeches I wrote when I was class valedictorian.

Milton was already throwing some of my papers into the trash. I reached out for my third-grade report on Shakespeare.

I was losing my home after losing my mother, and yet I felt released. Milton had tried to be my father, but all I felt was obligation. He had always been annoyed that I was too much on the Bonowitz team. Now I could tell myself that I owed him nothing. But what did this mean for my responsibility to care for Susan and Bruce? Even at nineteen, I could see things I had access to that they, here in Brooklyn, hardly knew about. I had always imagined that I would be, to some extent, a mentor to them. But now not only did Milton want me out of his house, he wanted me away from "his" children.

I can't remember returning to 29 Murdock Court until after Milton died almost twenty years later. Even if there was a visit that has slipped from memory, Milton had achieved his goal of exiling me from that family. From the time of my mother's death our relationship was cordial but distant. In 1987, I returned to Murdock Court to sit shiva for Milton with Susan and Bruce. They had learned I was their half-sister only two years before. Milton told them in a moment of pique, when I did not thank him in the acknowledgments of *The Second Self*, my first book that reached a wide audience. He kept my mother's secret until I wounded his pride.

In Milton's frustration on that Ocean Parkway walk, he said he would do whatever he could to prevent me from continuing at Radcliffe. I had so much else on my mind that I didn't dwell on this. But he did, in fact, have some power. The parents of scholarship students had to file something called the "parents' confidential statement." If you had a certain amount of money, you had to contribute to your daughter's education. My scholarship depended on my parents' declaration of their *lack* of money. Milton said that he would conveniently forget to turn in this form so that I would lose my clearance for a senior-year scholarship.

I returned to Cambridge and managed to finish up my few academic responsibilities left over from the fall. But I dropped out of Radcliffe in spring 1968 because I simply could not carry on.

During that semester, I grew closer to Rick. After leaving Radcliffe, I moved into the off-campus apartment he shared with two graduate students in government and their girlfriends. He was finishing his senior year at Harvard, struggling to keep his focus under the shadow of the Vietnam War and the draft. He had applied for a doctoral program at Harvard but deferred his acceptance to get a draft deferment for teaching at a public high school in Washington, DC. I thought he was brave and resilient under pressure.

As I became closer to Rick, I understood that for me, intimacy meant talking about Sherry Zimmerman. With one man early in my freshman year, I had gotten as far as telling him of Charlie's existence, and then, in my recollection, I was pretty much rendered mute. I couldn't bear to say too much to my boyfriend Bob during freshman summer because I didn't want to put my mother in a bad light. I wanted so much for Bob to love my mother.

But after my mother's death, I trusted Rick and he gave me space to mourn. I told him things I had not had time to say to my mother: That I was grateful she lied to me, because I would not have gone away to college if I knew she was sick. That I was angry I had not had time to thank her for that sacrifice. That I was sorry I had not been there to help—I understood it was what she had wanted, but it had added to my grief. I told Rick so much, but I never told him about the trauma of the shower with Milton. My reaction to my mother's death was to idealize her. I rehearsed to myself the good ways I was like her—feminine and intelligent, grateful for new experiences, eager to be seen by the world—and actively forgot, at least for a while, the things I didn't like. Becoming my own person would mean remembering them, little by little, and learning to love and mourn her with full knowledge of them.

Much later, I did the hard work of confronting in myself the qualities of my mother that I'd criticized. Becoming my own person meant that I could be grateful for all she gave me. The upside of all the downside.

. . .

ONCE I DROPPED out of school, I needed to earn money. The sociologist Seymour Martin Lipset had recently moved to Harvard from
Berkeley, and his files were in disarray. He advertised for help and I
got the job. I was given a key to a large, unoccupied office and told I
should start filing immediately.

When I opened the office door, I found a mountain of correspondence about students, colleagues, meetings, and publications. I found
whole filing cabinets about the Congress for Cultural Freedom, a
Cold War organization that turned out to be CIA funded, set up to
support scholars who proclaimed the "end of ideology"—that was
Lipset along with other intellectuals such as Raymond Aron and Daniel Bell. It was my job to put all of this in order.

I billed for a small fragment of the time I spent in the Lipset archive.
I liked immersing myself in someone else's life when I had so little
sense of what I would do with my own. I could imagine myself in an
academic life such as his. Looking at the correspondence, I could see
the web of relationships—how students and colleagues became friends,
how ideas were debated in letters and then on conference floors.

In the Lipset correspondence, I saw how a circle of colleagues who
had once been committed socialists tried to grapple with anticom-
munism during the Cold War. Many of the letters were about wanting to build a new kind of great university at places like Columbia,
Harvard, and Stanford, intellectual communities that could criticize
communism and thrive in the sunlight of enlightened capitalism.

At the time, I was critical of Lipset because of his politics and
hostility to the student movement. But as I worked on his papers, I
identified with many of the values that animated him. He came to
the Vietnam War with a profound distrust of communism, the Soviet

Union, and China. My generation flirted with Mao and the Little Red Book as if they were elements of fashion. Lipset had no patience for that.

I have no idea, really, if I helped the Lipset archives. But they did everything for me. I saw how academic collegiality could create a kind of family, generations of colleagues and students. I would need that. I worried that there were so few women in these files.

I LEFT CAMBRIDGE for Brooklyn and helped move my grandparents to Rockaway. Our old neighborhood had recently been razed to the ground in a promise of urban redevelopment by the John Lindsay administration. But Mildred had found a woman on Beach Sixty-sixth Street who owned a two-family house that had not been torn down. In the summer she moved into the basement and let seasonal renters—that would be my grandparents and Mildred—live on the ground floor.

I spent two weeks there, my bedroom, as it had been for every Rockaway summer, a daybed in the front parlor. My grandparents had lost a daughter. Two of their grandchildren were moving out of reach. Fifteen blocks away from what used to be, we tried to comfort ourselves with the rituals of a lost past. But there was no court. No community of neighbors. Unlike the days on Fifty-first Street, all the neighborhood stores were gone. Now we walked five blocks to a large supermarket.

There were no conversations with the butcher, no flirting with the son of the man who ran the vegetable store. There was no cool alley between the bungalows; we had to sit on the porch for shade. Before, our alley had been private, intimate. My grandmother sat with her feet in an Epsom-salt bath and drank lemonade. On this new porch we stared out onto a street of strangers. Here, feeling exposed, my grandmother wouldn't take off her shoes. We still walked to the board-walk for the late-afternoon breeze.

One of these late afternoons, I sat with my aunt, grandmother, and grandfather on a boardwalk bench. It was the last Sunday of my visit. We ate bagels, hot out of the bag. My grandmother had pre-pared a thermos of coffee, laced with milk and sugar.

An emergency summit: Milton had asked Mildred to marry him. I had warned my aunt this might be coming. Milton's technique had been disastrous, involving an attempt at a hug and kiss. Mildred was white with fury. My grandfather said that he never wanted to see Milton again. I sensed that my aunt had told her parents the story because she wanted her father to have this reaction. She felt he had always favored her sister; she wanted to experience Rob Bonowitz com-ing to her defense. My grandmother didn't know how to react. A break with Milton meant she would never see her two younger grandchildren again. She looked for a compromise.

By the end of the afternoon, the Bonowitzes had a plan. They feared for me if I stayed within Milton's reach. They would send me to Paris at the end of the summer. Why Paris? I told them that when I returned to college—and I would—it would be helpful for my senior thesis. I already imagined it as having something to do with the stu-dent and worker protests that had taken place in France the previous May. My grandfather and aunt gave me the money for a round-trip ticket to Paris, the least expensive one, on Icelandic Air, that took you to Paris through Reykjavík and Brussels. My Lipset work had brought in just enough money to keep me going until I found a job in France.

As for the other two grandchildren: My grandparents would offer to take care of Susan and Bruce on weekends so that Milton could do his waitering jobs or visit with his family or rest or date. But they would not entertain him in their home. That was the cost of his asking me to leave school and proposing to Mildred. I was skeptical. Milton had always wanted to feel accepted by these three; I thought these terms would provoke retaliation. My grandparents and aunt accused me of taking Milton's side, but I was only trying to maintain their relationship with Susan and Bruce. Things fell apart, as I anticipated, but in slow motion. No one wanted a decisive break before Bruce's bar mitzvah, coming up the following year.

I moved to Washington, DC, to spend the summer with Rick. In theory, I was reading books that would help me write my senior thesis, books about troubles in the French university that had predated the May events. But I wasn't reading much. At night, while Rick slept, I sat on the cold tiles of his bathroom floor and ate one of my grandmother's favorite snacks: Lorna Doone cookies dipped in cold milk. I resumed the smoking I had experimented with as a Holmes Hall freshman. I missed my mother, my grandparents, and my aunt. I missed Rockaway, Nancy, Social Studies, and Bertram Hall. I felt guilty that just as I was beginning to assert my identity apart from my mother, I had been called home to attend her death.

I had let Rick take care of me, but that decision had come to define and stress our relationship. He was only a month or so out of college and was struggling to stay out of Vietnam. So, in part to avoid any sign of dependency, which I knew would be unwelcome, I was also telling him that I really needed to flee the country.

I sat on Rick's bathroom floor and summoned the courage to proceed. I remember stifling cigarette smoke and feelings of dread. I took a weekend group-therapy course that asked all participants to compose their own mantras. I settled on one that seemed both realistic and hopeful: "You are not supposed to be happy. You just have to walk toward the light." It was too much to pretend that I felt myself on an adventure. It was enough to do the best I could.

I spent a final weekend in Rockaway before I left for Europe. The morning of my departure, I went back to the rubble of Fifty-first Street where Lafayette Court had been. I sat on my childhood beach and made my way onto its familiar jetties. You needed good balance because the rocks were not placed for easy walking but to break the waves. I had always scrambled on these rocks unsupervised. Now, on this jetty walk, I realized how dangerous it was and how fragmented my childhood—totally controlled yet so often unsupervised, full of treacherous moments of autonomy. Now I felt nothing but autonomy. I felt dizzy, cut loose.

Part Two

1968–1975

8.

Newspapers and Vinegar

I n May 1968, a movement that began as a protest in the French university system ultimately shut down every aspect of French life. The student protestors had taken Marx's ideas about the central role of the working class in revolutionary struggle and broadened them to include a student-worker alliance. They urged everyone to imagine a Marxism that looked beyond class struggle to a critique of the alienations of everyday life. Authority had always spoken loudly in France—the authority of the church, the government, the teacher, the father. But as individuals, people felt isolated and alienated. You could feel that alienation as a student or as a stay-at-home mom. The May '68 movement, almost universally referred to as *les événements* or simply "May," wanted to take on these emotional and cultural discontents as political issues.

French society had always had rigid rules about how to speak and to whom, about what to wear and where to go. At Harvard, I had heard Stanley Hoffmann characterize traditional French mores as built on a desire to avoid unstructured "face-to-face" encounters. May threw people into a politics built on immediacy and spontaneity. It celebrated confrontation and conversation. It politicized daily life—how people dressed, ate, and thought about sexuality. "This is not your father's revolution" was a slogan of the Paris '68 barricades.

I had studied some of the ideas that animated May; now I wanted to understand how abstract ideas, often written in dense, academic language, had been able to motivate practical action.

People hear a slogan and find that it gets them thinking. Ideas become what the anthropologist Claude Lévi-Strauss called "objects to think with." They get picked up, sometimes in bits and pieces, and are used to propel action. And affiliation. I thought about this kind of study as "a sociology of superficial knowledge"—with the caveat that this knowledge is never superficial in the life of the individual.

On my way to Europe only a few months after the student uprising, the atmosphere on my Icelandic flight was electric. I met writers, artists, and activists who wanted to be a part of the historic moment of change that was sweeping across Europe. There was also a group of American students who had dropped out of school to spend time in France. Everyone wanted to know who else was on board. We were all short on money and eager to pool resources. The flight was a party and a hustle.

I met François Weill, a young French artist and furniture restorer, who lived in a small village outside of Paris. François had a practical suggestion. His sister, Catherine, was getting a master's degree in international relations at l'Institut d'études politiques, affectionately known as Sciences Po. It was where I had been planning to take courses that year. It was (and remains) on the rue Saint-Guillaume in the seventh arrondissement. Catherine was renting a room from a French family only a few blocks away. I should check in with her and see if the family had any extra rooms.

Sciences Po was one of the best places in Paris to study history, politics, and sociology. Also, it was not part of the official university system, and so it had been relatively unaffected by the turbulence of the May days. By September 1968, large segments of the traditional university system had not yet announced opening dates. Sciences Po was opening late, but it was definitely going to have a fall semester. I needed to be registered at some university program in order to manage my Paris finances. University registration meant a student card—discounted meals, books, and movies.

But before Sciences Po began, I wanted to visit Germany. My family could see Germans only as villains and followed strict rules about not buying German products. All the years I was growing up, I remembered my grandparents checking labels to make sure that nothing we bought had any bit of it made in Germany. My aunt loved Rosenthal china. To buy it was out of the question. There was some talk that our German boycott was punishment for Nazi misdeeds, but really, we didn't buy German goods because for my family, at that time, to bring such things into our home would contaminate it. I didn't want to live my adult life with that kind of reflexive anger and fear. I wanted to meet German people my age and understand how they were thinking about the war and the future.

Even on my brief trip to Germany in the late summer of 1968, I began to understand something about the fierce confrontation with history that the Germans were attempting. Some Germans my age had left home because their parents and grandparents had been, in their eyes, disgraced. Some had constructed elaborate rituals through which conversations with their elders could begin. Others told me they now believed that during Nazi times their parents had felt too insignificant to confront the horrors of the Third Reich. They had simply tried to wait things out and look after their own families.

I felt a growing connection with the young Germans I met in my travels. Conversations with them reminded me that when people see their society begin to go mad, individuals feel small and disempowered. Political theorist Hannah Arendt called it the kind of loneliness that made it impossible to see yourself as connected enough to the world to act in the world. Totalitarianism thrives on it. During the rise of fascism, many Germans and Jews had believed that things would right themselves. But history had taught that when madness descends, no one can sit on the sidelines.

In a Cologne coffee shop, I had a halting conversation with a German mathematics student who tried to convince me to spend the year studying in Germany rather than France. I tried to explain that this plan would almost surely mean a break with my family. When I told him we avoided German products, he asked if my aunt bought French perfume. When I said yes, he argued that the embargo should be the other way around. It was the Germans, he said, who were facing what had happened during the war. The French were not speaking about their complicity with fascism.

"When your aunt buys French perfume, she supports people who rounded up their Jews to send them to the gas chambers but have never admitted it happened. The French will not say they had a part. What you don't admit you can't heal."

Even from my short previous visit to France in 1967, I knew he had a point. I had seen how little French people knew about what had happened to French Jews during the Second World War, or how commonplace it was for them to deny what they knew.

It was in Cologne, where a lively city had been left a bombed-out shell, that I finally felt a grief about World War II that included Germans. The moment seemed important. I went to a city park and took a photograph of a swan that I carried with me for years. Just from looking at the photograph, it could have been a swan from the Boston Public Garden. But I knew what it was.

ONCE I REACHED PARIS, I called the grandmother of the French exchange student who had stayed with Rick's family during his junior year of high school. Madame Suzanne Mullender invited me to lunch at her apartment on Avenue Niel as a gesture of thanks toward Rick's parents, who had been so generous to her grandson.

At lunch, Madame Mullender made it clear that she expected me to stay with her and Monsieur Mullender, a World War I veteran, until I found my footing in Paris. I would live in her maid's room. Like many older French women with large, elegant apartments, Madame Mullender supplemented her income—and also, I think, amused herself—by renting out her extra rooms to American girls studying in Paris. When I came for that first Sunday lunch, Madame Mullender's boarder for the year was a lively, friendly American college junior named Carol.

In 1968, Madame Mullender had habits and tastes formed before the First World War. We kept to the mealtime rituals she had known as a young girl. At breakfast, coffee and a third of a loaf of bread, sliced and ready for butter and jam. For lunch and dinner, a beautifully set table, with linen napkins that you kept for a week in a ring that was designated as yours. We ate soups and salad, small servings of fish and meat, rounds of French bread, cheese, and fruit. At dinner, a sweet.

Lunch included the two Mullender grandchildren who lived in the suburbs but were at school in Paris. If Madame Mullender's daughter was in Paris, she also came to lunch. After lunch, a helper cleared the table and reset it for dinner.

At lunch and dinner, constant conversation. It was expected that everyone at the table would have gone to an exposition or to the theater or be reading a serious book. It was not enough to have gone to a museum. You had to share an opinion on what you had seen. So this was not only about speaking French. It was not just Madame Mullender's gregarious nature or French politeness. It was about learning how to say something surprising, arresting, perhaps useful.

After about two weeks, I said a reluctant good-bye to Madame Mullender's maid's room. I had found a place to live when I met up with François Weill's sister Catherine.

Elegant and practical, Catherine brought me into her world of couscous restaurants, tea at the Moroccan mosque, and shopping at the local market. She showed me how to cook a full meal—starters, rice salad with anchovies and hard-boiled eggs, wine, coffee, and dessert—all over a camping flame in her room. She was exotic, study-

My dear friend Catherine Weill, with admirers, Morocco, 1968.

ing Chinese politics, language, and culture. She had short red hair and effortless chic. And Catherine introduced me both to Sciences Po and to her landlords, Monsieur and Madame Dumas.

Les Dumas, an elderly couple, lived in a large apartment on the second floor of 70 rue du Bac. Rue du Bac is a glorious street, steps from the place Saint-Germain-des-Prés and a short walk along the boulevard Saint-Germain to Sciences Po. Catherine had rented a large, airy bedroom in the Dumas apartment that she shared with another student—they hung a curtain to divide the room in two. They also shared a bathroom and shower. I didn't have money for anything like that, but the introduction to the Dumases led to something equally precious: a job that came with a room of my own.

Madame Dumas asked if I knew how to clean. "Nous avons besoin d'une femme de ménage, quelques heures par jour." Madame Dumas was clear. Housekeeper. A few hours a day. I said that was perfect and smiled. My grandmother had taught me to clean. "Ma grand-mère m'a bien appris." Another big smile. This was the opposite of the truth. But it was decided: I would live in the Dumas's maid's room, a room on the fifth floor of the rue du Bac apartment building, in exchange for cleaning four times a week.

The question was how soon I would be found out as a fraud.

Madame Dumas usually filled my position with a Portuguese woman, and from the very first, I heard her referring to me in the third person to her husband as the *portugaise*. I said nothing. I existed, for this gig, as an interchangeable nonperson. I was visiting this status. That, too, was part of my French lessons.

UNDER A SLOPING MANSARD ROOF, my room at 70 rue du Bac looked out over the rooftops of Paris. When I first walked in, I found an iron bed piled high with French treasures: a duvet, pillows, linens, towels, everything was white and bleached. All of this reminded me of my grandmother, her love of Clorox, and clotheslines in the Rockaway sun. On one side of the bed was a small set of drawers; on the other, a table and lamp.

Across from the bed was another table with a basin in which I could pour water to wash up. Down the hall were a WC and a large sink, large enough to take a kind of "standing bath," so I never felt totally gritty. But for an American, going without a real daily bath or shower was tough.

Madame Mullender came to the rescue. She was excited about my new position. I would learn so much. Knowing how to clean a French bourgeois home would prepare me to run one. This was the best preparation for a splendid home, a splendid marriage. She sounded like Aunt Alicia in *Gigi*! But Madame Mullender did not want me to go to a public bathhouse. No! I was to come to dinner every Thursday night. Recount my adventures. At school! At the theater! At the expositions! And most certainly cleaning for Madame Dumas. I could also take a bath. And stay the night in the maid's room, where I had started my Paris adventure.

So that became my routine. Cleaning for the Dumases. Sciences Po. Discovering Paris—its streets, its museums, its films, its theater. And endless political meetings. In 1968–69, there were political meetings all the time, debating the Vietnam War, the capitalist system, psychoanalysis and the Left, the end of Gaullism, the next steps after May. And once a week at avenue Niel, I talked about all of these things at dinner. Then a bath and to bed.

On my first day of work, Madame Dumas showed me her cleaning products, all lined up on a shelf in a special kitchen cupboard, and

said that she was going out to *faire les courses*—do some shopping—
and would check up on me later. I began dusting and then went into
Catherine's room and asked if she knew what product should be used
on hardwood parquet floors. Catherine said there was a *produit par-
ticulier* and under no circumstances to use plain water. When I found
nothing in the cupboard that made reference to floors, I decided to
wait for Madame Dumas and ask directly instead of risking disaster.
She showed me a product that needed to be mixed with water and
then applied sparsely to the floor before being hand-buffed dry.

I used too much product, and my circular buffing was leaving
white-gray streaks. I re-rinsed and made the back-and forth-motions,
le frottage, that Madame Dumas had demonstrated. She was patient
but obviously disappointed that my grandmother had not adequately
covered this territory.

It was lunchtime. My job was to set the table and leave. Here, I
was a star. Holmes Hall wait-ons. Gracious living. Two weeks with
Madame Mullender. I did something right.

But I had completed only one room, barely. Madame Dumas said
we would continue tomorrow and on Wednesday, *faire les vitres*.

Faire les vitres. I knew what that was. Wash the windows. How
was that possible? Once a year, my grandmother called a window
washer who dangled outside our apartment building on a harness.
And even if I was expected to wash only the insides of our windows,
I knew of only one window-cleaning product: Windex. Long after
dismissal time, I snuck back into the Dumas apartment and began
rummaging around. There was no Windex. Nothing that made any
reference to cleaning glass. I went to the neighborhood hardware store,
la quincaillerie. There were straw market baskets. Soap dishes. Table
linens. Dishes, cutlery, pots and pans. No Windex.

My next stop was the post office—the only place where I could make a telephone call. You told a clerk the number you wanted to call and were assigned a *cabinet*, a booth where you picked up a handset and could speak with some privacy. My grandmother answered her phone. All at once, I felt ready to end my adventure.

Sherry, are you sick?

No, I am fine.

Are you eating? Are you sick?

Grandma, no. I'm fine. I missed you. I wanted to hear your voice. I love you.

What's the matter?

Well, nothing is the matter. I just have a question.

Here I am sure my poor grandmother was certain I was pregnant or in an emergency room. These long-distance phone calls were expensive. I had to act quickly, or I would terrify her.

Grandma, actually, I have a job doing a bit of cleaning.

Cleaning what?

House, in exchange for a beautiful room in Paris, right next to school.

What are you cleaning?

Oh, regular cleaning, dusting, floors . . .

There was silence. I knew that part of her was proud of me. And part of her was shocked. Her precious grandchild, the Radcliffe student, was cleaning floors. Also, she knew that I did not know how to do this.

I'm calling for your help. Your advice. Only you can help me.

I had her attention.

Grandma, how do you clean windows if you don't have Windex?

No hesitation.

With vinegar and newspaper. You rub the vinegar in
with the newspaper. And then you take clean newspaper
and rub.

Vinegar. Newspaper. Apply vinegar with newspaper. Discard
that newspaper and rub clean with fresh newspaper.

Yes.

Grandma, I love you. Please don't worry about me. I'll be fine.
I'm really fine. I have a great room.

Sherry, don't clean the outside of the windows! Quit your job
and live in a hotel. Mildred will help you figure something out.

I promise. I love you.

I love you.

Just writing this, recalling this, I miss her so. I miss our intimacy—
she sent me Flatbush Avenue–discount–store panty hose to Paris,
three for a dollar. She was proud that she and I knew how to show a
pair of fine leather gloves. And despite her years of trying to protect

me from this moment, I like to think she was happy that she could help me clean a window without Windex.

On Wednesday, I marched into the Dumas kitchen and, as they say in French, *mine de rien* (with the air of its being nothing at all) asked for vinegar and newspaper. Madame Dumas looked relieved. Perhaps the request to do windows had been some kind of test. I had failed elementary dusting and floor cleaning, although I had shown myself willing to learn. But now, only a day later, I had a new self-assuredness in the window-washing department. I picked up vinegar and a stack of newspapers, smiled, and tried for a tone both competent and firm: "Bien sûr, je ne ferai que l'intérieure des vitres." Naturally, I'm going to do only the insides of the windows.

Of course I told the story of "le Windex" at the next Mullender dinner. To great success. In French. I observed myself. I sat around the Mullender table, speaking for hours in French about the adventures of a French-speaking woman who was a part-time student and part-time maid, and who had adopted a swept-back chignon because that kind of hairstyle didn't have to be washed (or put into curlers!) every night. I think of her as my avatar, French Sherry. She was me, or perhaps a braver incarnation than the Sherry I had left at home. The French language, with its cadences and shrugs, seemed to help her along in the development of a certain insouciance. When I had my down moments—English-speaking Sherry was prone to them— French-speaking Sherry seemed able to summon new resources.

This experience of a slight and constructive dissociation from self was something I drew on when, in the early 1990s, I first met people constructing selves in cyberspace. When people built online identities that were braver or more adventurous than who they were in "real life," they did not feel that they had multiple personality disorder. On the contrary, they told me that in "real life" they tried to associate themselves with the strengths of their online creations.

French-speaking Sherry was not unrecognizable, but she was her own person. There was no space in her world for doubts that she could take care of herself. She simply had to get on with it. When English-speaking Sherry felt fear, she threw herself into the persona of the resourceful, French-speaking woman.

WHEN IT RAINED on my sloping attic roof, every drop had its own note and after tone. From my mansard window, I had a view of rooftops, trees, and distant street life. But I was a bit set back from all of these, both in the city and protected from it.

Loneliness in Paris is broken by the warmth of what sociologists call its "third places," places where you can be alone in public, that is, alone but still part of an informal community. During my 1968 stay, there were markets where I was alone yet swept up with familiar people and conversations. There were cafés for perfect coffees and for *citron pressé*, lemon squeezed into a glass with a carafe of water on the side. If I asked for extra water and ice, I could make lemon-refreshed water last for an afternoon of reading among neighbors.

But sometimes, when I wanted comfort food, I bought a liter of milk and a plastic-wrapped loaf of what the grocery store at the end of the block called *pain d'épices*, a kind of autumn quick bread spiced with anise, cloves, honey, and cinnamon, available all year round. If, when visiting Paris today, I smuggle a *pain d'épices* into my hotel room and order a glass of milk, then, no matter how elegant my accommodations and no matter how happy my current circumstances, I can find my way back to my 1968 state of mind, how I felt when I mourned my mother in Paris.

. . .

FOR MY SCIENCES PO DEGREE, I went to lectures, took notes, and wrote response papers, all in French. Once enrolled, I found plenty of students who wanted English lessons. Soon I had more than enough money for laundry, coffees, lemonades, and other indulgences. Most I found at Prisunic, one of the first French discount superstores, with many departments, from makeup to women's clothing, that offered plausible but inexpensive imitations of the "real" thing.

I loved Prisunic. I bought an abstract-patterned "looks like silk" polyester scarf and matched it with a looks-like-cashmere jumper and looks-like-cashmere sweater. I found a shoe bin of inexpensive black patent leather loafers with thick rubber soles. They bore a family re-semblance to the shoes I really wanted, the too-expensive ones from Bally, only a few shops down. They didn't remind me of the desired objects in a bad way, as in "You can't have the real thing, so here are your fake shoes." They reminded me of the Bally shoes in a good way, as in "You can't have the real thing, and someday you will; these will remind you of your future." Back home, Catherine showed me how to tie my scarf with the knot jauntily to the side. She joked that it was a good thing I had a French woman on tap for such matters ("Heureuse-ment que tu as une française pour t'aider à arranger ton foulard"). Her loyal friendship was a cornerstone of my French experience.

I spent hours in the *papeteries* that lined the boulevards Saint-Michel and Saint-Germain. I bought all the objects that Sciences Po students carried around: Quadrille-lined Rhodia pads with easy-to-tear-off top-perforated sheets. Short wooden rulers with metal inserts to make sure those Rhodia tears were clean. Loose papers that got organized in color-coded files and then were swept together in card-board document folders with large buckled clasps. I came to believe that the right paper, the right binder, the right fountain pen could confer special powers. Catherine wrote only with cobalt-blue ink. I, too, adopted this as my signature color.

All of these *papeterie* objects had wonderful names, *les classeurs, les feuilles, les trousses, les cahiers, les dossiers*—to me, they were like Madame Toquet's special words in *The Glass Slipper*. And there was ritual in how we were asked to write papers for Sciences Po. I was in a special section for foreign students working toward the Certificat d'Etudes Politiques, and we were given instructions for how to approach composition in the French style, a style I was told had something to do with the first words of Julius Caesar's *Gallic Wars*: "Gaul is divided into three parts."

As we understood it, the essay had to be in three parts, with each of the three parts having three parts. We had one week to write the outline and two more weeks to write the essay, which had to match the outline. The French style posed particular challenges to me. I don't compose with an outline. From as far back as I can remember, I have built up my ideas by writing paragraphs. I think of them as provisional building blocks. Then I move them around, try them in different combinations, and rewrite. I develop new ideas, and older ideas are cast away. A structure emerges as I decide how to frame my argument. Then I refine that structure. There are many drafts. It sounds exhausting, but I work happily through many iterations.

Each Sciences Po assignment challenged me to work backward. First I wrote my essay by writing and rewriting on my Rhodia pads. I cut out useful sections and pasted them onto a large sheet of oak-tag paper on my bed and moved the sections around. Sometimes changing the order of things gave me a whole new idea and I started from scratch. By the end of a week, I had a three-part paper, with each of its parts divided into three parts. I then extracted the outline and rushed to turn that in. Then I came home and wrote out a neat copy of my full paper, editing for style. I carefully put the completed paper in my dresser so that it would be ready two weeks later when the assignment was due. The constraint of a structured paper encouraged clarity of thought. I was pro-outline. But I could get there only by working as a tinkerer.

This experience came back to me later when I studied children learning to program. It was a common assumption in the 1980s that "good programming" was done in an "engineer's style," that is, in a top-down, divide-and-conquer way. But when I studied expert programmers as well as children learning to program, I found a range of styles. To learn or make something new, people have to work in their own style. It's as true of engineers as it is of poets. And it was particularly relevant to women who were trying to find a way into programming in the early years of a computer culture that was unwelcoming to them.

My grandfather and I took apart old clocks and watches when I visited him on weekends, but I remember my irritated mother telling me, "Don't touch it. You'll get a shock," when I sent away for a kit to make a crystal radio in sixth grade. Twenty-five years later, computer science teachers told girls that if they wanted to program, there was one "right" way, that top-down style. But many girls (and a fair number of boys) preferred to program in the style I used for writing, the tinkering style that I called bricolage or "soft mastery," paying my respects to Lévi-Strauss. You try one thing and then another; you make false steps and then revise. Equity would be served by epistemological pluralism, a message that engineers were not eager to hear. This notion, which would become so foundational for my future work, was one of my French lessons, born as I struggled in my attic room with Rhodia pads, cobalt-blue ink, scissors, paste, and oak tag.

. . .

ONE THURSDAY EVENING, as usual, I was on my way to dinner
and a bath at avenue Niel. As usual, I stopped at a local florist and got
Madame Mullender a small bouquet. What was not usual was that
she was waiting excitedly for my arrival. She had torn out a small announcement that had only just appeared in *Le Figaro*. Something called
L'Académie was opening a program where French intellectuals would
be periodically lecturing, seemingly to an international group of college students. Madame Mullender said my credentials for this kind of
thing were obviously *impeccable*. The first meeting was the following
Tuesday at 3:00 P.M. at 3 rue Royale. Madame Mullender said that
this didn't sound right because that was the address of a "well-known
restaurant." But I should go anyway and present myself with my letters of reference. On Tuesday, I showed up at 3 rue Royale. I was, in
fact, in front of a "well-known restaurant." I wasn't prepared for it to
be *Gigi*'s Maxim's!

Madame Vaudable, the wife of the owner of Maxim's, was the
head of a junior-year-abroad program organized primarily for American women. She was speaking. Every week, she said, enrolled students would have access to lectures and discussions with well-known
French intellectuals. The lectures would be at Reid Hall, in Mont-
parnasse, a historic home to American junior-year-abroad programs.
The program would begin with Jean-Louis Ferrier, the art critic of
L'Express.

There was no discussion of financial arrangements. It seemed that
the other girls in the room already knew one another and had signed
on. The announcement in *Le Figaro* was meant not to invite new participants but to make the world aware that l'Académie was in session.
At the end of the meeting, I walked up to Madame Vaudable and told

her that I was a Radcliffe student on a leave of absence, studying at Sciences Po, and was interested in the lectures at l'Académie. She said nothing. She looked at my letters of reference and seemed most interested in the one from Laurence Wylie, who had just returned to Harvard from his post in Paris as American cultural attaché.

Perhaps Madame Vaudable hoped that having a Wylie student in l'Académie would lead to some endorsement and a new level of accreditation for her endeavor. I only know that she looked up from the Wylie letter, smiled, and said that I was invited to the Reid Hall lectures and also welcome to participate in all aspects of l'Académie. As her guest. There would be theater visits, studio visits, and intriguingly, outings at Maxim's where we would be taught about food, wine, and guest placement at significant social occasions, things it would be hard to learn at any other junior-year-abroad program.

I asked a friend at Radcliffe to please send along the gown I had worn to the South House ball during the spring of my sophomore year. I had stored it in the Bertram Hall attic. It was strapless, made from frothy tiers of white lace. I had long white gloves packed in with it, these a gift from my grandmother. If I could pretend to be a cleaning lady, I could pretend to be a debutante.

Sometimes I could see the Dumases watch from their landing when I descended from my attic aerie for a Maxim's event. Did they think I was kept by a very particular man, someone who wanted me only on rare occasions? We never spoke of it.

And we never really spoke of whether the Dumas floors were getting the *frottage* they deserved.

After giving me a long time to prove my worth, Monsieur and Madame Dumas told me they had found someone else to clean their apartment, someone who, they politely said, was not also tied up with student life. Thus, they needed their fifth-floor room for the new cleaner. I was sad to lose my view of the Saint-Germain rooftops, but I was also relieved. The money I had earned from tutoring English was sufficient to rent a tiny studio in the seventeenth arrondissement. It had a bed that pulled down from the wall, a sink, a hot plate, and a bathroom with a shower. I savored my first real apartment. I bought it fresh flowers and a set of stoneware mixing bowls. Madame Mullender told me that I was still welcome for Thursday dinner, even though I didn't need to stay for a bath.

CATHERINE WAS GENEROUS in sharing the other members of her family—her three siblings, her parents—I think she, like Madame Mullender, understood that what I needed most was a sense of family. Catherine's father, Robert Weill, a biologist, had a presence that loomed large. In 1939, he was named a professor at the University of Bordeaux. But he was fired in 1940 because of anti-Jewish laws. The family at first tried to live in a part of France that during the Vichy years was administered by the Italians, less hard on the Jews than the Germans were, but when the German authorities took over, the family obtained false papers and went into hiding—five children, two parents, a grandmother, and a great-grandmother. After the war, which Catherine's father spent in the French Resistance, the family returned to Talence, a Bordeaux suburb.

Catherine's family had been torn out of their lives because they were Jews. But after the war, they did not have the options for a life as Jews that I had as an American. In postwar America, I grew up with the message that I could choose how to be Jewish. Minimal participation in organized Judaism would not make me less Jewish. My grandfather's religious practice consisted of eating the traditional foods that went with each holiday season. And on the eve of Yom

Kippur, he listened to a recording of Jan Peerce, a great American operatic tenor of the 1940s, singing Kol Nidre, the prayer in which Jews ask for forgiveness for sins committed in the year that has just passed.

In France, the only synagogues were Orthodox. If you weren't Orthodox, there seemed to be no traditions of participation in Jewish life. Compared with me, Catherine operated in an atmosphere of all or nothing. Non-Orthodox Jews didn't do Seders or have Purim parties or compete with Christmas by making Hanukkah a big deal. They participated in Christmas as a *French* holiday and sometimes went to church as a social event.

When I told French people I had visited Drancy, where French Jews had been detained before being sent to Auschwitz, some told me that no such thing had happened. Or that they had never heard of such a thing. Some said I was perhaps making up this story to excuse my own country for its moral crimes in Vietnam.

But in the months after May 1968, at least in Paris, things were changing. A film by Marcel Ophuls, *The Sorrow and the Pity*, about collaboration and the Vichy years, would not be released for another year, but already it was much discussed. One of its central themes was that collaboration with the Nazis was made easier because France was riven by a deep strain of anti-Semitism. I went to meetings where students asked the most difficult questions about French complicity with the Nazis: Why was it still taboo to talk about what France had done to its Jews? Why were the French still telling inflated stories about the Resistance during the war?

In my presence, an American Reform Jew at ease about being Jewish, I found that some French people would shyly tell me that they were Jewish "by ancestry." Usually what came next was a terrible explanation of how their family had managed during the war, what they had lost, and what had never been given back to them. Houses. Jobs. Apartments. Jewelry. Art. I heard how neighbors had taken these things and how, after the war, it was sometimes easiest to leave the neighborhood. You didn't want to visit people who were living with your furniture and walking on your rugs.

I made one visit home to Brooklyn that year. To Bruce's bar mitzvah in April. My grandfather sent me round-trip tickets to New York and Rick drove up from Washington to be my date. Mildred took me shopping for a party dress fancy enough for the occasion. I was expecting the worst, but it was much worse than anticipated. Milton managed to fit in a speech in which he said that only the presence of Bruce, his son, his heir, had given him the strength to endure Harriet's loss. Susan ran out of the hall. Bruce and Milton followed her. I followed them. Rick and my grandfather followed me.

AFTER THE BAR MITZVAH, preparation for final examinations at Sciences Po were upon me. They were oral exams that emphasized a special kind of academic "sweet talk," the ability to speak eloquently on a narrow subject, even if you were not well informed. Each exam had the same format: All the students in the course gathered in a room that had a large glass bowl on a center table. When your name was called, you went up to the bowl and drew out a folded slip of white paper on which was written a question. You then had ten minutes to prepare your answer. And then perhaps ten minutes to give your answer. Ideally, your answer should be in three parts, with each of the three parts having three parts. Then you could leave the room. From exam preparation sessions, I got the impression that you got almost as many points for presentation as for mastery of the content related to the question on the white slip.

I took four courses that year, so I made four ten-minute speeches. My efforts to "think French" were adequate but not spectacular; I got a respectable *mention bien* across the board. But my French-style exams prepared me for the most hostile Q&A sessions of academic life. You breathe and make sure to sound super organized.

And I had good news from home. My time in Paris would be counted as a semester of course work in social studies. It would make up for the time I had "dropped out." And a scholarship was cleared for me to come back for senior year. Radcliffe found a way to bend the rules.

I HAD ARRIVED in Paris with two pieces of luggage—a backpack that I had bought before my hitchhiking tour to Brittany in 1967 and the red leatherette suitcase that I had brought to Radcliffe at the beginning of freshman year. I was determined that the red bag would not come back with me. I became obsessed with luggage. I had few possessions. I didn't need anything big.

I picked up the pace of my tutoring. I earned enough money to afford a capacious duffel at my beloved Prisunic. But really, I wanted something beautiful as well as practical, something I would keep for a long time. Something that would symbolize what I had achieved here. English-speaking Sherry would perhaps never be as brave as her French-speaking counterpart. But increasingly, she could hold her own.

In the window of a luggage store on the rue de Rennes was a traveling bag of taupe and brown jacquard fabric. I went in to inquire about it. I was told it was officially called "the Boston Bag." That seemed like a sign. But this bag had another name because of its shape. The salesperson kept referring to it as "the Speedy."

Over fifty years later, it is hard to say what the Speedy meant to me. I was searching for what a woman of substance would carry as she traveled the world. Something that would hold her notebooks, her manuscripts. Who were my idols? Susan Sontag. Joan Didion. Lillian Hellman. They would have a bag that would never need to be replaced. It would have an unusual, elegant shape. They would take it on the airplane when they flew off to give a lecture so they would never have to check luggage. From time to time, as I studied for my Sciences Po finals, I visited the Speedy. I would pick it up and imagine myself having places to go, papers to deliver, books to write. I had no way of buying it.

Mildred visited me in late May, just before it was time to return home. We had breakfast together in my studio. I made her an omelet. She was worried about me. When I had come home to attend Bruce's bar mitzvah, I had seemed depressed. I had gained weight. Young girls are supposed to go to Paris and slim down. And I had worn a wig. Why was that? Was I losing my hair? She was proud that I had made it through the year, but she could tell it had been a struggle. Had Paris been a mistake? Had she abandoned me to what seemed like the right thing, sending me off to a strange country where I knew no one, just because it seemed as far as one could get from Milton?

I tried to reassure her. I was on some kind of journey. I was not always happy. I confessed that I sometimes ate *pain d'épices* instead of real food. I had seen a French doctor who said that I had a kind of hair loss that comes with stress. The body takes a shock. Happily, my hair seemed to be growing back. I answered the question she did not ask. I was not in danger. I never thought of suicide. I could tell that I was going to be some kind of writer. I even had an idea for my senior thesis and thought I might try to be a professor, but I worried that I didn't know any women academics. Mildred shrugged. "I think you should take it as far as you can take it. Until you are stopped and you don't see a way around." I stared at her, moved. Mildred had served her bosses and didn't know how to break out of that cycle. She had no confidence in herself. She only had confidence in me.

Over breakfast in my tiny kitchen, Mildred asked if I needed anything, wanted anything. I said no. Having her with me in Paris was my unexpected treat. She said that she wanted to buy me a birthday present. I was going to be twenty-one, a special birthday. Since my mother died, we had not taken time for any real celebrations. And so I told her about a piece of luggage so fancy that it had a name.

Mildred laughed. She wanted to see it immediately. Together, Mildred and I put our faces against the glass on the rue de Rennes and she came up with a plan: During her Paris visit, we would eat pâté sandwiches and sidewalk croque monsieurs. She would check out of her hotel and sleep next to me in my Murphy bed. If we did all this, we could buy the Speedy. Mildred consoled me about the price by assuring me it was timeless. It was made by Dior. It would last forever.

I was carrying it, twenty-five years later, when I went to pick her up at an Arizona airport where she was to fly to meet me for a holiday vacation. She never made it to the plane. She had died, in her apartment, as she prepared to take this vacation with me. I had long before bought her a Speedy of her own, a blue one she carried whenever we got together.

9.

Things for Thinking

The crowd on the Icelandic Air flight back to New York in June 1969 was subdued. Race riots and Vietnam protests raged in America. A year ago, moving toward the European protests seemed exciting. Now I felt pessimistic and frightened for my country. I returned to my grandparents, already in Rockaway. They were withdrawn. Since Bruce's bar mitzvah in April, they had seen Susan and Bruce only occasionally.

It had been a year since my mother died, but I woke up every morning to a lump in my stomach. Now my anxiety focused on Susan and Bruce. My thoughts played on a loop: *They are children. Have I abandoned them? Milton used my leaving for Paris as an additional reason to keep them away from the Bonowitzes.* (His argument: I refused to come home to help him, but I had time to go to Paris!) And then I heard the voices of my grandparents and aunt: *Sherry, you, too, are a child. You must allow yourself to be a child. A child goes to Paris. She has a boyfriend. She returns to college. All of these are things that your mother would want her child to claim.*

After a few weeks in Rockaway, Rick and I had a romantic plan. He had a new car, a white Volvo. We were going to drive it cross-country on a camping trip. Rick asked me to buy a few things at a camping store. There was one in Queens not far from our Rockaway bungalow. Mildred offered to drive me. My grandmother said she wanted to come along. On our shopping list were a Coleman camp stove, collapsible pots and pans, cutlery on a ring, and special soap packets for washing dishes at a campsite. Here, in the camping store, my grandmother was Isak Dinesen in *Out of Africa*. The store stocked not one Coleman stove but many. She examined them with the expertise of someone who has cooked in every exotic circumstance. My grandmother was proud of my Radcliffe education and my time in Paris, but these things were abstract to her. Now, however, she was studying waterproof matches, powdered eggs, and tiny eating utensils. She had a new sense of participation in my adventures.

On the camping trip, we drove across what I only remember as the "middle of the country" and experienced the exhausted satisfaction of pitching a canvas tent in 1969. I have since participated in the revolution in camping technology, with lightweight tents that open when you throw them in the air, and I have new respect for our efforts. I laughed just because rain sounded wonderful on canvas.

Rick and I made tentative plans to live together when I returned to college in the fall, but then he changed his mind. "Cold feet," he said. I had considered him my family, and now I faced this new reality. I found a three-bedroom apartment on Fayette Street in Cambridge to share with Amy Gutmann, then a junior at Radcliffe, and Deborah Fiedler, who had just graduated and was now at Harvard Law School. We ate delicious meals that Amy's mother precooked and left frozen in our freezer, as many as it would hold. Debbie introduced me to the pleasures of Lanz flannel nightgowns, which became my official writing outfit, usually over tights and a sweater, since I was always cold—then and now, fifty years later. Radcliffe was modernizing a dormitory and had a tag sale of old furniture. I bought an ample wooden desk on which women had carved their initials since before I was born.

My senior thesis grew directly out of my time in France. In 1968, every kind of intellectual told a story of what had just happened—political analysts, sociologists, and historians on the left, right, and center. For my thesis, I would take a group of prominent French thinkers and analyze what they had written about May. My hypothesis: When intellectuals looked at the May events, they could see only what their previous theories suggested would occur.

And indeed, I found that if you read someone's work *before* May, you could predict what they would say *about* May. Bureaucratic dysfunction. A sclerotic educational system. The expression of a new working class. The May events were a Rashomon story. How we prepare ourselves to see the world determines the world we see. When, later, I found engineers approaching human problems with engineering solutions, their narrowness of vision did not surprise me. They were acting in the same tradition as the sociologists and political scientists who projected their pet theories onto May.

I asked the social historian Barrington Moore to be my thesis adviser. He agreed, and at our first meeting he gave me advice that I remember this way: "When you start a big project, you should have done enough research to know what your story will look like if you find the data you need, if everyone you want to interview is able to talk to you, if everything goes perfectly." In other words, at the beginning, you face a lot of work ahead. It's possible you will come up with nothing. But be sure that in the best case, you will end up with something you will love.

I applied the Moore test to my thesis plan and to all of my later projects. And I ask a version of his question to my students: Do you have a great story to tell, if everything in your research falls your way? Can you see where you hope to go, and will it delight you if you get there? As a woman, the advice had special meaning to me. If I was going to succeed, I would have to do something special. If I was not going to have a successful career, all the more reason to have one in which I explored my passions.

Writing my senior thesis confirmed my decision to pursue an academic career. But I was paralyzed about where to apply for graduate study. I couldn't even decide what department I belonged in. My teachers suggested I was interdisciplinary. But what I felt was not so much that I needed to carve out a space between disciplines as that I needed to learn more disciplines.

Thinking about May 1968 brought me to questions about how people take up ideas—political ideas but also ideas about the self—and bring them into everyday life. I hadn't been able to get to this question in my thesis, but it was what I wanted to look at next. My interests were moving from ideas in the abstract to the impact of ideas on personal identity. How did new political ideas change how people saw themselves? And what made some ideas more appealing than others? After all, many students had taken up radical ideas that had only recently seemed foreign to them. I wanted to explore this not theoretically but in one-on-one conversations. The more I worked on my thesis, the more interested I became in the inner history of ideas: the psychology of how people change their minds.

I wasn't sure what these interests suggested about graduate school.

Perhaps this was a sociological style of intellectual history? I applied to Harvard's graduate program in history.

I thought I needed to learn more about psychology, and in the most comprehensive way. I thought of how I had once put my kelly-green "Courrèges" dress and white boots in a Massachusetts Avenue trash can when I felt that this outside skin couldn't represent me anymore. I wanted to study the kind of psychology that could understand that.

Up to then, I had read only a few of Freud's classic works. By the mid-1960s, he was out of intellectual vogue. Experimental psychologists saw him as a historical footnote within an increasingly scientific psychology. Anthropologists examined kinship but left out the messy dynamics of the life of families. They studied cognition but excluded the emotional lives of thinking individuals. My classmates who specialized in social theory were trying to boil down Freud to bullet points. But I was drawn to his fine-grained analysis of language and motive. What if you examined people's beliefs about themselves, including their political ideas, with the kind of detail that Freud brought to the study of their dreams and fantasies? What about if you brought that kind of detail to their ways of thinking about their minds?

My senior thesis had focused on the analysis of political texts, but I wanted to go back to France and have the conversations that would fill in the beating heart of how people had experienced May: How had new political experiences changed their relationships with parents and friends? With themselves?

I thought back to reading Erik Erikson in my freshman year. And I remembered my impressions of him—tall, distinguished, with white hair framing a beautiful head. When I first saw Professor Erikson walking across campus, it was like watching my childhood representation of God in a blue blazer and knit tie, carrying a briefcase. In a series of clinical, then historical writings, Erikson described identity developing over the life cycle. He made it clear that no gear shifts to graduate you from one stage of development to another. So, for example, the issue of basic trust comes up in infancy and identity is most pertinent in adolescence, but you work on both of these all your life, always bringing different skills to bear, always using new resources to work on familiar problems.

Erikson's thinking had been helpful to me during my year in Paris, particularly the idea that identity is constructed and reconstructed over the long haul. By winter 1969, I saw young people rethinking what they had dreamed for themselves in 1968 as they reconciled with their families and made plans to resume their educations. I took comfort in the idea that we each have many chances to rework our identity. I never gave myself space for any kind of identity crisis in high school. In college, I took some first steps away from my mother, but this was cut short by her death. When she died, I felt guilty for those first steps and idealized her to keep her close. I couldn't bear to think of her as she really had been. I tried to reclaim only what I admired, beginning with her relentless optimism, which I so needed.

Erikson helped me come to peace with this. I could think, *You are here to mourn your mother, yes, but you'll be doing that for a long time. What you are doing now is your best possible first step. Or rather, it's the only step possible for you now.*

So, in my senior year, I returned to Freud and Erikson and broadened my psychoanalytic readings to the British writers known as "object relations theorists"—Ronald Fairbairn, David Balint, and Donald Winnicott. For these writers, object relations meant people relations. Objects and people have this in common: When we lose them, we bring them inside us, with the objects carrying bits of the people associated with them. That's what happens in mourning: What we lose comes within and takes on new life.

So all of those objects in the memory closet, they were inside of me. I used them to think things through just as I found ways to keep alive the people I had lost. My mother. And Charlie, those shards of what I had gathered about Charlie. This made sense to me. Whatever came next, wherever I moved intellectually, I had found some grounding within the psychoanalytic tradition.

Erikson and the British theorists provided some of my first tools for thinking about identity and a basic idea for how people resolve identity confusions. You talk yourself out of them. In this way, they planted the early seed that psychoanalysis was the treatment designed for the kind of life troubles I had been presented with. Through them, I first considered becoming a psychoanalyst myself, especially once I learned that to become an analyst, you began with a personal analysis. You start with self-knowledge and then you generalize what you have learned to help others.

But in 1970, psychoanalysts in America were, for the most part, medical doctors who had also received psychiatric training. Getting psychoanalytic training with a doctorate rather than a medical degree would pose its own challenges.

Before I even thought about crossing that very big bridge, I had a smaller one in my own backyard. During the events of May 1968, people tried to invent a politics that would bring together how people thought about family, career, and sexual life. When I wrote about May, I needed to bring together psychological and sociological perspectives. That effort had me essentially trying to reunite departments at Harvard that had just split from each other.

The Social Relations Department at Harvard had been founded after World War II so that clinical psychology, social psychology, sociology, and physical and cultural anthropology could be studied together. But by my senior year, Social Relations was splintering into its component parts. There was general pressure to adopt formal and mathematical models, but different disciplines had competing visions of what these models should be.

Intellectual and administrative fragmentation was embodied in space. At Harvard, the people who studied the psychology of thinking were on different floors from those who studied the psychology of feeling. I wanted to do academic work that put thinking and feeling on the same floor.

A more holistic path made the most sense to me in part because I could see my own reactions to people and events unfolding on multiple sliding screens. Home-hungry in Paris, I was comforted by the ritual of Madame Mullender's lunches and Catherine's lessons in how to tie my faux-silk scarf like a bourgeois wannabe. Now, back at home, I was increasingly caught up in the antiwar movement and training to be a draft counselor. My mother had just died. When I spoke to friends about her, I talked about her bravery. In my secret life, I wondered if Charlie was alive, but I was ashamed to be even thinking of him.

For a brief time, in May 1968, old institutions did not seem important, but there was nothing new to take their place. I began to read social scientists who studied communities in transition and to correspond with Victor Turner, an anthropologist at the University of Chicago, who studied them. In *The Ritual Process,* Turner called transitional moments "liminal," literally, threshold states. He argued that on a personal level, liminality encouraged change and creativity. On a social level, it fostered new symbols, rituals, art, and language.

The idea of liminality gave me a way to think about the May events but also about how much had changed during my own college years. In fall 1969, I returned to a politically charged Harvard/Radcliffe, one that was beginning its first experiments with having Radcliffe and Harvard students live in the same dorms. The sisterly retreat of the Radcliffe quadrangle was now nostalgia. My private expectations, too, were derailed: I was raised in a family where virginity before marriage was an assumption. Now I lived in a culture where it would be a near embarrassment. In my family, it was understood that a woman with a serious career made a statement that most men would find hard to deal with. In my current circle, a career was an expectation. There was no scholar more relevant to my life than a theorist of life on the threshold. I asked Victor Turner if I could study with him at the University of Chicago.

Victor Turner wrote back to say that he was coming to Cambridge and invited me to join him for coffee. He was fifty years old, dressed in tweeds, a large, solid man with a sparkling conversational presence. We drank coffee from a machine in the sitting room of his suite in a Harvard Square motel. We cut its bitter taste with packets of powdered milk substitute that he found next to the coffee machine. I remember thinking that either this nonchalance meant that I was a very unimportant guest, or it was a sign of warmth and simplicity. I decided on the latter.

When I met Victor Turner in the spring of 1970, he managed to give me the feeling that we had been talking for days, had been interrupted, but now were happily carrying on with our important work. We talked about how I might fit into the program he had recently joined at the University of Chicago, the Committee on Social Thought. He hoped I would take his seminar and explore my growing interest in ethnography—the documentation of individuals and cultures by living and working with as well as interviewing those you study. He liked that I was interested in Freud. *The Interpretation of Dreams* was a book that he had his best students read in detail. I loved how Turner sailed bravely against the prevailing winds of academia, where psychoanalytic thinking was on the way out. We talked about my Paris experience. I tried to say why it had been so important to me. I told him that a generation had grown up thinking that if a political action didn't lead to a general strike, it hadn't been important. But something else had happened during May: a revolution in how people thought about themselves.

I decided to begin graduate work in Chicago. Turner encouraged me to study the May events from the perspective of liminality and what he called *communitas*. When habitual structures dissolve, so do boundaries between people. They experience new intimacies and become open to change.

I carried this idea forward to my later work: When individuals meet transformative technology, that technology can change their inner life and relationships.

Rick and I had continued dating my senior year. Dutifully, he had applied to law school at the same universities where I had applied to graduate school. But as he put it in a much later conversation, "When you decided to go to Chicago, I withdrew my application from Chicago and decided to go to Harvard." We had each waited for the other to grow in ways that would finally allow us to separate.

10.

Great Books

I left for Chicago with my first car, a used red Saab model 96—elegant, rounded in shape, timeless. To me, it was Nancy Drew's red roadster, which had kept her safe on so many of her adventures. This car would give me freedom in my new life in Chicago.

I found a Chicago graduate student who had a bedroom to spare. The room came with a mattress and a desk. I put a cardboard dresser in the closet and, with loving ceremony, settled my grandmother's taupe electric portable typewriter on the desk. On my first night, to celebrate, my new housemate took me to the local favorite Chinese restaurant. It was Cantonese and had all of my grandmother's favorite things. When I drank the sweet tea "for the table," I was pleasantly reminded of home, from the happy remove of my new life.

My Chicago classes included an anthropology seminar with Victor Turner, a course on the novel with Saul Bellow, and a seminar on Thucydides with David Greene. The goal of all Committee on Social Thought classes was to help you choose an adviser and develop a

In my red "Nancy Drew roadster" at Radcliffe
graduation, June 1970.

reading list of about twenty-five books that would make up your
"Fundamentals Exam." During this exam, ideally taken at the beginning of your third year, you were asked to consider these books indi-
vidually and to weave their themes together. After the Fundamentals
Exam, each student wrote a dissertation.

Some students, it was said, had been on the committee (on and
off) for close to a decade and had never made it to the Fundamentals.
There was a second kind of student, equally storied, who had passed
the Fundamentals Exam but never completed their dissertation. At
Chicago, it was easy to set the bar so high that no achievement seemed
like enough. The books that you were encouraged to put on your Fundamentals list were intimidating. A typical list might include *Ulysses*,
the Bible, or *Capital*. Perhaps all three.

The "great books" curriculum seduced me. In high school I had
studied from review books, and I still had persistent feelings of inadequacy despite my successes at Harvard. I always felt I was trying
to catch up with students who had gone to private schools. They had
read the "real" books. I had read too many review-book summaries of

history and philosophy. The Chicago program seemed an alluring diploma in authenticity.

At Chicago, I read for many hours a day, and only great books. I learned that (for me) there is never a list that sets you free. You never finish a great book. You keep reading it, doing your best to make it your own. Chicago calmed me down for a life of reading. I no longer felt I needed remedial work before I could pursue my academic career.

Victor Turner agreed to be my official adviser. I was fortunate because his emphasis was on how the Fundamentals Exam could help me develop my own intellectual identity. I encourage every graduate student to use this big question to think about their generals exam. It can seem daunting or pretentious when you are just starting out, but it's the right question. With Turner encouraging me to be ambitious, I could see elements of the scholar I wanted to become, a psychologically astute ethnographer, with a special interest in how people think about thinking. My fundamentals list began with classics of psychological literature: Marcel Proust, *Remembrance of Things Past*; James Joyce, *Ulysses*; Gustave Flaubert, *Madame Bovary*; Aeschylus, *The Oresteia*; and William Shakespeare, *Hamlet*. Since I was interested in tinkering as a form of cognition, there was Immanuel Kant, *Critique of Pure Reason*; Ludwig Wittgenstein, *The Tractatus*; and Martin Heidegger, *Being and Time*. Then there was the core of the list: Sigmund Freud, *The Interpretation of Dreams* and *The Psychopathology of Everyday Life*; Émile Durkheim, *Suicide*; Max Weber, *The Protestant Ethic and the Spirit of Capitalism*; Karl Marx, *The Eighteenth Brumaire of Louis Napoleon*; Marcel Mauss, *The Gift*; and Claude Lévi-Strauss, *Structural Anthropology*. The list was a work in progress. At the time, I was reading all of Turner's work and that of the anthropologist Mary Douglas, so I put *The Ritual Process* and *Purity and Danger* on the list. I remember Turner adopting a "wait-and-see attitude" about how they would hold up to Durkheim. He would often remind me that the list didn't matter; what mattered was the product: me, developing a more secure sense of what made me unique.

Every week, about twenty-five graduate students and anthropology faculty met for a seminar at Turner's home in Hyde Park, walking distance from the university. It began with food and drink. I remember hearty cheeses, and often something exotic and sweet. And then there was a presentation by a student or faculty member that used Turner's ideas about liminality to illuminate their work. On personal and social change. Or the creation of new myths and symbols. Victor Turner talked about the Ndembu of Zambia. Terence Turner about the Brazilian Kayapo. Arjun Appadurai about Indian temples. Barbara Babcock about trickster myths. I talked about May 1968.

I noted how none of the sociologists—across the political and methodological spectrum—I looked at in my senior thesis had found a way to explain the festival-like aspects of May. The May protests often took the form of street celebrations, with food and music. Most academic onlookers thought that if students and workers were on strike, things should be somber in tone. But through the prism of Turner's work, the celebratory side of May made sense. In liminal periods, personal boundaries blur and people are available for the intimate social connection of *communitas*. And they look to moments of *communitas* in the past, which is why the references to the Commune of 1871 were so prominent in May slogans, art, and symbols.

Turner made the point that traditional social science has looked at festival-like moments such as May as pathological, a symptom that social order has broken down, revealing an underlying disease state. Turner argued that the opposite was true. Disorder could be generative and healthy. And social science had a role here: We needed to pursue ethnographies of antistructure, those chaotic moments when new social forms emerge. In Turner's seminar, it occurred to me that the delicate tools of clinical listening would be well suited to such ethnographies.

Turner encouraged us to read critically but be open to good ideas from writers we didn't like. Sometimes in class, when students would criticize a reading, he reminded us that some researchers have terrible "global theories," but they might have a few wonderful ideas scattered through—use them! Turner called these the "nourishing raisins in a cellular mass of inedible dough." So to what Sam Beer had called my intellectual tool kit I added the idea that some "nourishing raisins" could glisten in bad theories.

In Chicago, I made a close friend, Merilyn Salomon, who shared her enthusiasm for psychoanalysis with me. She also shared her love of fashion and style and gave me my first designer dress, a black Fortuny formal that, over fifty years later, I still wear on special occasions. Merilyn was married to an artist and lived in a downtown townhouse they were renovating. I decided that this was how I wanted to live when I "grew up." In my conversations with Merilyn, we kept going back to a set of ideas about the importance of early attachments. How our lives are shaped by the things and people who have mattered most to us, even (and especially) when we have lost them. How what we remember and forget is motivated. Forgetting is not just a way to avoid the unpleasant; for some people, it's their main way of defending themselves against what they can't face. I was learning to think of these as the foundations of a psychoanalytic culture—the way ideas originally inspired by Freud had made their way into everyday understanding.

Once there, they influenced people who had never read a psychoanalytic paper or visited an analyst.

Merilyn recommended a book, David Shapiro's *Neurotic Styles*. In *Neurotic Styles*, Shapiro translates what Freud called neuroses (and thought of as illnesses) into a series of styles through which people cope with life's troubles. Where illness was, let defensive style be.

When I was about eight, my mother gave me a white cap. We had just moved to Murdock Court and it was after the holiday season. It was unwrapped and she held it behind her back. "I made you something," she announced. She drew me close with the arm that was not holding the present. My mother did not really make things—she did not sew and for dinner might broil a steak or make some spaghetti—so I was curious. She produced a white knitted cap. It was what in those days we called a "tam," a sort of beret. It had a pom-pom on top. "I knitted this for you." I didn't believe her. I thought I recognized the cap from Lamston, the five-and-dime store near my grandparents' apartment. I was ashamed of doubting her. But I did doubt her. I held the cap in both my hands and didn't know if I should say "thank you."

Of course, by then I knew that my mother did not take the truth too seriously. But I understood that the lies we participated in together, the lies about my name and about Milton's being my father, served a big purpose. But I didn't know what to make of this lie that seemed to serve no purpose, except perhaps to turn my mother into a knitter of caps.

I kept the cap for years but forgot the story. When I read David Shapiro, it came back to me. The hands behind her back. Her conspiratorial smile. Now I think that when my mother presented me with the cap, she felt as though she *had* knitted it. When she saw the cap in the store, what was on her mind was her attachment to me and the overwhelming truth of her love. My mother wanted to be a perfect mother. So she forgot the things that stood in the way of living up to her ideal of what that might mean. Being a mother who knitted this cap perhaps made other things easier to bear.

I WAS TWENTY-TWO when David Shapiro provided me with tools for thinking about my mother's vulnerability. Later, Shapiro would help me consider the thinking styles of MIT engineers. For my mother, what looked like a lie was the fear of remembering something about herself she didn't want to face. For the engineers, what looked like a lack of empathy was a fear of becoming flooded by emotion. Shapiro explains that some people would rather remain engaged in the details of an experiment than look at the human being before them. Other human beings almost always have mixed feelings toward us; we are ambivalent toward them. If you are afraid of that, it's comforting to look at certainties, even if they take you away from what is most relevant to a relationship, the complexity of human emotions.

In my practice as a clinical psychologist, I have often had the opportunity to work with young scientists and engineers. What so many of them had in common was that they lived their lives on computer screens and could most easily experience their feelings if they turned them into thoughts or, better yet, into lines of computer text. Sometimes what suited them best was to express feelings by playing characters in computer games or avatars in virtual reality. All of these could be ways to deal with feelings in manageable bits.

AT CHICAGO, I continued to develop the idea not only that psychoanalysis would help me personally but that its core ideas could deepen ethnographic practice.

Real life is lived with thought and feeling joined. I thought that people steeped in psychoanalysis respected this. I thought it was their comparative advantage in academic life.

And there were concrete ways that a psychoanalytic sensibility could contribute to ethnographic work. Understanding the feelings that patients and analysts have for each other becomes a key element of analytic treatment. They reveal a special kind of projection, transference and counter-transference, where the shadows of past experiences fall on this new relationship. Projection shows up in field research as well. In any interview, researchers should ask: To whom is this subject speaking? For whom is this subject potentially performing? If this subject is belligerent, whom or what might they be frightened of? And further questions for researchers: Whom does this subject remind you of? What feelings does this interview arouse in you? If ethnographers better understood their own pasts, they could see the objects of present study with greater clarity.

Psychoanalysis encourages patience. A research interview isn't a therapy session. But it should allow space for people to discover something about themselves. Psychoanalysis teaches that people tell small, unconscious lies. In this spirit, ethnographers should continually reflect on the truth of what they are hearing and respect its emotional reality even if it is not the literal truth. For example, some participants in the May events told me they were in analysis, but subsequent conversations revealed these declarations to be aspirational. The literal truth was often that they had gone to a few preliminary sessions with therapists they might like to see *someday*. But their aspirations told their own compelling stories.

Finally, it seemed to me that ethnographic empathy can have some of the effects of a psychoanalytic interpretation. The things that come out during the practice of ethnography can transform the relationship between ethnographer and subject. And change their lives. A naive ethnographer could stir a lot up without knowing what was going on.

BY LATE SPRING, I had greater clarity about what I wanted in my graduate education. And I saw a more direct path to my doctorate. I would leave the Chicago program and return to Harvard for a joint degree in sociology and psychology. The sociology degree would prepare me for research and teaching about self in society. And to give my ethnographic work clinical depth, a PhD in psychology was my first step to becoming a clinician and psychoanalyst. Also, since I would be in Cambridge for a while, I could begin serious psychotherapy, a personal treatment. I didn't have the money for a four-times-a-week classical psychoanalysis. But I could start face-to-face therapy once or twice a week with a psychoanalyst.

Harvard no longer had a formal clinical psychology graduate program, but it still offered most of the courses that were required for clinical accreditation. Additionally, I would have to set up predoctoral clinical supervision hours and a full-time predoctoral internship. After graduation, I would need more supervised clinical hours before I took the state licensing exam. My program was ambitious, but I was determined. I had a name for the kind of work I wanted to pursue: the intimate ethnography of contemporary life.

11.

The Lacanian Village

Early in my graduate work at Harvard, I took a reading course with the anthropologist Laurence Wylie on contemporary French authors, among them Jacques Derrida, Michel Foucault, and Jacques Lacan, all of whom he introduced as "vexing." He wanted a small group of students to read along with him, "to keep him company." I recall the conspiratorial atmosphere of our meetings, as though we were in a secret society where even the books were hard to obtain. Wylie had brought some copies home with him from a summer visit to Paris.

I found the texts hard going but personally relevant. For Derrida, everything seemed to be about how to create distance from the familiar. To fully understand the "normal," you have to look at what it suppresses.

That was a new way to look at my family secret. My mother's desperate quest for her Brooklyn Jewish normal kept a lot of Bonowitz and Bearman "otherness" hidden from our family. After her death

I learned of a lesbian, two Catholic converts, and an evangelical. With each new revelation, I felt ashamed for what I hadn't seen and who I hadn't recognized. Derrida taught that my blindness was part of the game.

Foucault, too, made the familiar strange. When we fill out bureaucratic forms, we are being shaped into the kind of subjects the modern state needs us to be. Prisoners and patients play their restricted roles because a guard or psychiatrist might always be watching, even if no one is watching at that very moment. Foucault was with me when I turned my attention to life on the screen. Online, we perform a self because we always imagine ourselves seen.

As for Lacan, the texts were harder to read, but I was pierced by a sense of personal affinity. He wrote about the importance of the father's name in the development of a child—or, more subtly, the mother's relationship to the father's name. I seemed to have a past that required Lacanian explication. I was lucky to come of age with Wylie's vexing theorists.

And in the three years since I had returned from Paris, I had been hearing about Lacan not only in academic circles but from students I had met during my time there. Most intriguing, several friends who had been politically active during the May days were now pursuing or planning to start psychoanalytic treatment with analysts who declared themselves Lacanian. They said that involvement with Lacanian ideas felt like a continuation of their political lives. This was strikingly different from the role that psychoanalysis was playing on the American political scene. Students on the American left saw psychoanalysis, if they thought of it at all, as an extension of psychiatry's tendency to reduce political protest to the expression of personal distress.

American psychoanalysis in the 1970s was dominated by psychiatrists who talked about their work using a medical model: They

diagnosed and treated patients. This model made it easy to patholo-
gize protest and protesters. In contrast, Lacanians saw psychoanalytic
theory as something that could support political action. Lacan argued
that society constructs the individual through language and therefore
we can understand ourselves only in the context of our social sur-
round. In this way of thinking, psychoanalysis doesn't treat a patient
for "cure" in an isolated consulting room. An analysis was a search for
the truth of a speaking, social subject.

In fact, American and French psychoanalysis had been on different paths from the start. In America, Freud had inspired early enthusiasm (provoking Freud's famous remark to Jung: "Don't they know I
am bringing them the plague?") as psychoanalysis was made into a
medical specialty and reshaped for American taste by associating it
with ego psychology. Here, a sensible observing ego (your "I") could
master a wayward id and a too-punitive superego. This "I" was so
stable it could even form a "therapeutic alliance" with the ego of the
analyst, an alliance that was an engine of the cure. Freud's ideas about
childhood sexuality were conveniently dropped.

Meanwhile, from the earliest days, French commentators were critical of Freud. They didn't like that he was Jewish and Austrian. They
found his theory of childhood sexuality distasteful. French psychology
already had a theorist of the unconscious in their own Pierre Janet,
who was Catholic and conveniently didn't talk about childhood sexuality at all. But by the late 1960s, a philosophy of finding your own
truth made more sense in France. And Jacques Lacan was Catholic,
with deep connections to the art world and the Surrealist movement.
He said he wanted to return to the early Freud and focus on language.
He compared psychoanalysis to doing crossword puzzles. This struck
even casual observers as Cartesian. Finally, a French Freud.

In the early 1960s, there wasn't even a standard edition of Freud in

French, but by the early 1970s, just as American psychoanalysis was beginning to wane, in France, analysis was in high demand, as both an intellectual movement and a therapeutic modality. Psychoanalysis was finding its way not only into the education of psychologists and psychiatrists but into the training of social workers, schoolteachers, and massage therapists. It was the subject of articles in popular women's magazines and the French equivalent of *Reader's Digest* on how to raise children and save marriages. This was the background against which I decided to write my dissertation as a kind of intellectual-history mystery with three big questions: What was behind this infatuation with Freud? What was Lacan's role in the story? Why had things taken off after May?

My work on the May events had gotten me interested in studying how people "changed their minds" about how to think about themselves—their past, their present, their possibilities for change. Exploring the new French interest in psychoanalysis seemed a logical next step. People were changing their minds about the nature of mind.

I WAS INTERESTED in social change and the inner life—the inner history of ideas—just as the field of academic sociology was becoming more quantitative, focused on measurable outward behavior. In order to have guidance for my somewhat unorthodox academic agenda, I turned to two mentors in the sociology department—George Homans and David Riesman—who envisaged the social sciences as a broad humanistic enterprise.

George Homans was the chairman of the Sociology Department when I returned from Chicago in fall 1971. He helped me organize my joint degree program and became my primary thesis adviser. We were an odd couple: He was a Boston Brahmin, a descendant of John Adams, who studied rational exchange. I was a descendant of Wolozin Jews, increasingly taken up with theories of the unconscious.

But we had a firm point of intellectual connection. Homans's first work—a close study of an English village—had this premise: Sociology should begin its analysis from the observed behavior of individuals and not from definitions of roles, structures, institutions, or other abstractions. Homans saw the sprawling French psychoanalytic culture as analogous to his English village. It was the Lacanian village. My planned fieldwork in that village included time with Lacan and his circle but also with members of all French analytic groups—at one time, they had all been colleagues of Lacan. I would interview analytic patients. I would go to psychoanalytic seminars (certainly Lacan's, but not just Lacan's). I would also analyze television shows and women's magazines. I would visit the university departments and centers of professional education where psychoanalysis was now part of the curriculum—this would put me in front of what seemed like an army of newly minted psychologists, many of whom were in some kind of analytic treatment.

And of course, the village included students who had only recently thought of themselves as political activists and who now saw some kind of Lacanian affiliation as a continuation of rather than a break with politics. In conversation with Homans, I worked out a key element of my methodology: It didn't matter if my informants had read more Lacan than I had or understood him better. They were villagers, so they naturally were going to be immersed in the byways of Lacanian lore. If I had a good relationship with them, they would explain things to me. But equally important, if I discovered that the villagers had not read Lacan or were unclear on key points, that was also important, just as important as what they understood.

Homans prepared me for the complexity of these encounters, and for talking to Lacan himself. Lacan had repeatedly split the French psychoanalytic world apart, and by 1973, there were four psychoanalytic schools, all formed with him as the flash point. With each schism, he had lost some of the students he loved most. Analysts who had left Lacan might want to talk to me to get a message back to him. Of anger, loss, and, yes, regret. And Lacan might want to talk to me to get a message back to some of them. As in any love affair, no matter who leaves whom, all parties feel abandoned.

During these years of graduate school, preparing to do my fieldwork in France, I kept in touch with Marty Peretz, my sophomore Social Studies tutor. One day at lunch, he said abruptly, as though announcing a new stage of my life: "It's time for you to meet David Riesman." Riesman was a professor in the Harvard Sociology Department who focused on undergraduates. I hadn't met him as an undergraduate because I had so quickly turned to studying European history and theory, but I knew that his course Social Sciences 136, "Character and Social Structure in America," was legendary. With Marty's recommendation, I was quickly called to an interview with Riesman, who hired me as a teaching fellow for this course. He became a mentor and friend.

Riesman's classic work, *The Lonely Crowd*, was an attempt to understand what lay beneath a particular American loneliness. Riesman encouraged my interest in psychoanalysis. He himself had been analyzed by Erich Fromm, a sociologist who had received analytic training in Vienna. Riesman reworked the postwar warnings of Fromm, who believed that, in America, people see themselves as commodities and find their identities by looking to the opinions of other people. In Riesman's formulation, Americans were once inner-directed.

Now they had become other-directed, seeking identity in external validation.

I had this idea of other-direction in mind when, later in my career, I turned to studying the new culture growing up around social media. On social media, people talked about authenticity but curated a carefully constructed public self, a self for Facebook or Instagram. I framed it as a new psychology of "I share, therefore I am" and called it "other-direction brought to a higher power." I wrote my book *Alone Together* at the dawn of the age of texting. I wrote *Reclaiming Conversation* when people were fleeing face-to-face encounters for the safety of social media. In these works, I wanted to revisit the ideas of *The Lonely Crowd* in the era of digital culture. Where my research was hopeful, it pointed in directions that were low-tech. If we had lost ourselves to the alienation of our screens, there was evidence that the immediacy of face-to-face conversation could be a talking cure.

Riesman was more than a mentor; he was a champion. When anyone suggested that my choice of dissertation topic might be obscure, Riesman had a ready response: I had framed my question around a classical sociological proposition—namely, that every society shapes the therapies it can use. The Americans made an American Freud. The French would have a French Freud. He was proud that I had chosen something ambitious. Once, when reviewing my Paris field notes, he paid me a compliment that kept me going for decades. As an ethnographer, he said, I had taste and tact. When I worried aloud to David Riesman about how few women there were in academics, he acknowledged that there was reason for my anxiety, but he said that in his opinion, things were about to change and that I would be part of that change. Riesman also said that if I was going to make a difference, I should write for as large an audience as possible.

Riesman gave a weekly lecture in a large hall, and then his class broke up into smaller groups to discuss the week's reading. Our list was eclectic. It included Alexis de Tocqueville, Willie Morris, Nathan Glazer and Daniel Patrick Moynihan, Mark Twain, J. D. Salinger, and, of course, *The Lonely Crowd*. The teaching fellows met to discuss the readings at a weekly dinner at Riesman's stately home on Linnaean Street near Radcliffe. During the years I taught with Riesman, other teaching fellows included the historian Nina Tumarkin, Frank Fisher (who ran Harvard's Office of Career Services), the photographer Bobbie Norfleet, the psychologist Eric Olson, and the sociologist of media Michael Schudson. The Riesman dinners had their own ritual. As I recall, we were served sherry in the living room at six thirty, joined by Riesman's wife, Evie. Our working group was seated in the dining room at seven and served dinner by two women in white. I remember a soup, a salad, a meat course, a dessert, and coffee. With the coffee there were always Pepperidge Farm chocolate Milano cookies. I sometimes imagine many generations of social scientists, Riesman teaching fellows all, who find themselves stocking up on these addictive cookies when they are about to write something challenging, unaware of all the other Riesman alumni with Milano cookies on hand for writing emergencies.

Conversation at dinner was about the past week's sections, how they had gone, and how they could be taught better the next time around. Then at eight, back to the living room and one of the fellows would talk about how to present the following week's readings. From time to time, there were visits by former teaching fellows—I remember after-dinner talks by Doris Kearns Goodwin and Rosabeth Moss Kanter. Both of them spoke about work in progress that was relevant to the themes of the Riesman course. At nine we adjourned. These

Riesman dinners had a different emphasis from Victor Turner's living-room seminars in Chicago. With Turner we tried to illuminate field-work with theoretical ideas. Riesman wanted to train master teachers. In his home, we focused on how to deliver a great undergraduate course. But for me, the Turner and Riesman evenings had something in common. They confirmed my choice of an academic career. In these places, I felt: *This is where I belong.*

Ideally, David Riesman wanted his students to write final papers that engaged them with the world. To prepare for that, the first section meeting class members asked to interview one another about their lives—their experiences on high school sports teams, their first jobs, how it felt to go away to camp. In my section, I offered advice about how to conduct these conversations. I told them that my most vivid memories of growing up centered around standing on a chair and try-ing to pull things out of a musty cupboard over my grandmother's kitchen table. The best way to get *me* talking about my life would be to ask me about the objects I found. I suggested that students begin their life-history interviews by asking their classmates about the ob-jects of their early lives. The class looked puzzled. I clarified that, yes, I meant *concrete* objects. *Things.* Surprised, they started throwing out ideas: Toys? Clothing? A first camera? A Spalding pink rubber ball? Yes, I assured them, that's exactly what I had in mind.

By coincidence, Mildred had come to visit me in Cambridge dur-ing the week when I taught my first section of Riesman's course. It was early February, deep winter, her favorite season. I was wearing a gray Persian lamb coat that she had given me as a hand-me-down. Of course, I carried all of my books and papers to class in my Speedy. I felt her pride as she watched me teach in a Harvard classroom. I knew how happy it made her that I led off the conversation by talking about an object of my childhood, my grandmother's "best dishes," the ones she had been given as a wedding gift by her own mother, bought from a pushcart on Manhattan's Lower East Side. These were Czechoslovakian white porcelain, with a border of pink roses on black trellises. My grandmother protected them by wrapping them in faded purple flannel and then putting them away in special cardboard boxes on the highest shelf in our hall closet.

The dishes only came out three times a year: Thanksgiving, Rosh Hashanah, and Passover. They were the only

My grandmother's special occasion dishes, her most precious possession, my most evocative object.

possession that my grandmother could imagine living beyond her. She believed that my children would eat on those dishes. My daughter does. On Passover, we tell the story of the flight from Egypt. The dishes have their own journey.

I've since found this idea of focusing on objects in so many places—including in books about how to teach writing or start a memoir—that I claim no originality for it. But because of my own experiences with my memory closet, whenever I meet an idea about the power of objects to think with, I stop to explore it.

As I worked on my joint degree, I became more comfortable seeing the number of things I wanted to accomplish (clinical training, psychoanalytic training, training as an ethnographer) not as signs of personal indecision but as necessary steps. I was always tempted to reduce my problems with choice, even the most mundane choices about decorating decisions, to my experience in the courtroom, where I was presented with a question ("Do you love your father?") that had only wrong answers. But during those graduate school years at Harvard, my refusal to narrow things down worked for me. I didn't make choices; I chose a starting point.

12.

Chère-cheur

I left for France in September 1973 to immerse myself in a story of how a psychoanalytic movement, something that concerned analysts and their patients, had become a psychoanalytic culture. My first ethnography of a science of mind. I was nervous because reading Lacan was daunting. But I was confident that once I was living in his social and intellectual world, the words on the page would take on new meaning. Perhaps more daunting was that in his world, key participants were at war with one another. That might be hard to navigate.

From early in his career, Lacan saw patients in short, sometimes five- or seven-minute sessions. He justified it theoretically, but the International Psychoanalytical Association (the IPA) would have none of it. In 1953, the IPA told Lacan and his students, all members of the Paris Psychoanalytic Society, that they could not train analysts, largely because of these unorthodox practices. Lacan left the Paris society and founded another school, which immediately began courting the IPA. In 1962, Lacan and his students were once again rejected. He called it an excommunication. By the time I arrived in Paris, there had been two more dramatic splits.

French analysts compared the story of their schisms to those in Freud's circle. Freud argued for the existence of a new science of mind, but he rewarded fidelity and handed out rings to loyal disciples. Similarly, some analysts who left Lacan said that what drew them to him was his idea of psychoanalysis as a subversive science. It should explore any path, unafraid. But when Lacan demanded that they accept his unorthodox practices, wasn't he saying "agree with me" rather than allowing an open conversation about psychoanalysis? What happens to people when they are caught between the pursuit of science and loyalty to a *maître*? When Lacan demanded fidelity, he got schisms. I was deep in a story that had elements of a passion play.

CATHERINE NOW LIVED in Hong Kong—this was a blow! I found a place to live close to our old neighborhood, a small, furnished studio on rue Saint-Victor in the fifth arrondissement, a short walk to the famous market on the rue Monge. Most of my floor space was taken up by a double-bed mattress pushed against a wall. Piled high with pillows, draped in madras cotton, by day it was both couch and work space. An adjacent room had a small kitchen, with a little table next to a window that looked down to an interior courtyard. Without a refrigerator, milk had to be put on a ledge outside the kitchen window. In France, I happily learned, cheese was not refrigerated but simply put under glass.

I began to send handwritten letters of introduction to members of the four French schools of psychoanalysis and followed up with calls. I wanted to get my bearings, and I remember beginning with the more traditional analysts (the ones who had left Lacan), whose writings were easiest for me to understand. But I was soon going to seminars at Lacan's Freudian School and interviewing Lacanian analysts, and my fears fell away. By the end of the year, I had spoken to over a hundred French psychoanalysts: Lacanian disciples and critics and a group of analysts who disagreed with Lacan on questions of technique but were influenced by his theories.

I had a great advantage: I was talking to people who were invested in my topic. Everyone situated themselves in some relation to Lacan. Almost everyone had an opinion about May 1968 and its impact on psychoanalysis. And the fact that I was American was an odd asset: Even members of the "traditional" groups had their own critique of American ego psychology. So most analysts assumed we could begin there, with the assumption that any French analyst would take a different approach from anything my colleagues would consider. I was easy to talk to because I was the ultimate outsider. That also meant that people were gracious in answering my most basic questions.

I went to Lacan's seminars, now being held at the law school on the second and third Tuesdays of the month at 12:15 p.m. These were lectures in a large, traditional hall. Anyone could attend; I remember being surprised that I just had to show up and walk in. Lacan wore a long jacket, longer than a standard suit jacket. He wore a bow tie. He was gray haired, elegant in carriage, beautiful in his way. Sometimes his jacket was velvet, embroidered with a kind of soutache. Once I thought his jacket was navy blue, but I was sitting too far back to be sure. The first two rows were taken up by young men who were dressed more or less in his style—in 1973–74 this meant, at the very least, a bow tie. A hand-tied bow tie. I remember them as thin and black. *Les noeuds papillons.*

The seminars were hard for me to follow. Lacan would read,

speaking very softly. Then there would be a louder declamation. Loud or soft, the content was not always clear to me. But even as I struggled with how little I understood, there were things about that seminar that stayed with me, that still are with me—beginning with the title of the seminar during the year I attended: "Les non-dupes errent." This was a play on Lacan's classic discussion of the importance of the name (*nom*) and the no (*non*) of the father, which sound the same in French. *Les noms du père*. Also, those who are not duped are in error.

The "no and name" wordplay refers to Lacan's retelling of the Oedipus story, in which he puts the emphasis not on the father's forbidding a physical sexual act with the mother but rather on what is at stake symbolically when the son (or daughter) takes the father's name. With this interdiction and naming, children accept their father's authority and find a place in their family, and more broadly in the social order. What the child needs above all else is *le nom du père*, the father's name, which goes along with what it sounds like in French: *le non du père*, the father's "no."

This is one of the many ways that Lacan describes society shaping the individual psyche. The linguistic action, heavy with meaning, is something in which mothers must participate. In the winter of 1968, I attended a lecture by Jean Clavreul, one of Lacan's close colleagues, in which Clavreul presented case studies of widowed, pregnant women. And women whose husbands had been off at war when their children had been born. The dynamics of the "name of the father" operate even if there is an absent father. The mother holds the meaning of the father's name for the child in how she talks to the child about the father.

I came upon Clavreul's presentation at the Clinique de la Borde, a psychiatric hospital at which several Lacanian analysts worked. The

Clavreul lecture was the "grand rounds" for the day, a teaching lecture for the hospital staff. I listened to Clavreul, both making and not fully making the connection with how my mother had denied me my father's name and, when it was spoken, had tried to hide and denigrate it. I stared ahead in a psychiatric hospital in the château country outside of Blois and listened to a lecture that stunned me. Of course. The name of the father is communicated with or without the father's presence. It's all in how the mother presents him. Or erases him. Later I would come across the thought that an absent father makes everything seem possible and nothing seem safe. You have no name. You can be anyone. But there is no guardrail, no backup, the reality that is implied in an interdiction. I sat in Clavreul's lecture, crying.

Clavreul lived in Paris, and a few weeks later I interviewed him at his apartment in the Marais district. After the interview, he took me to lunch at a restaurant on the place des Vosges and I told him how much I had liked his lecture at the Clinique de la Borde. We talked about the cases he had presented; I wasn't ready to tell him what they meant to me personally. For dessert he said that this restaurant specialized in a dessert called a tarte tatin. I had never tried it. It remains my go-to favorite dessert, one of the many small signs I have that my French research marked me more than intellectually. How could it not?

Waiting every week for Lacan's law school seminar to begin, I found myself in conversations about what Lacan might mean by the play on words in his title: Those who are not *duped* make mistakes? Who were the nonduped? What mistakes were they making? One of the things he might be saying was that one of the greatest dangers of psychoanalysis is to assume that it allows one to achieve a position above all the other dupes. I became superstitious that I had come to

Paris in just the right year. My destined year. The *nom du père* year. The year Lacan was talking about those who are duped or not by their father's name. As soon as I began talking to other members of Lacan's seminar audience, I found that I was not alone. There were so many people who also thought that this year, this seminar, was their special year.

It took me a long time to get up the courage to write to Lacan and ask for an interview. I tried not to be, but I was intimidated by the seminar. What I feared most was a direct question such as "So what have you found most interesting in what I had to say this year?" I would simply have to answer honestly and describe my struggle. I wrote that I was a Harvard graduate student writing a dissertation on the French psychoanalytic movement and he, of course, was central to my story. He responded by return post. He asked me to call. Within an hour I had an appointment.

He addressed his note with a play on my name: He addressed me as "*Chère-cheur*," "dear researcher." But the play on words also meant "dear Sherry." And "dear dearest"—*chère cherie*.

My professor Bruno Bettelheim flashed through my mind, sitting in a chair on the stage at the University of Chicago. He made the point that relationships are often determined by the way they begin, by dynamics that are set up from the start. His native language was German, and so the thought came out in a sentence whose syntax was foreign: "In the end is the begin. In the end is the begin." Or as my friend Merilyn Salomon, who sat next to me in Bettelheim's classes, would always rephrase it as a joke between us, "Een zee end, zee begeen."

My relationship with Lacan continued as it began. He was responsive. Respectful. Playful. I think he wanted something from me: to tell a story that would present him to an American audience in a good light. And he wanted those who had left him to hear this positive story as well. So he told me the story he wanted me to tell. But he answered my questions directly. He was not evasive.

For that first meeting, I was at his office on a day when the other people waiting to see him were all men, almost all young, and, as at the seminar, almost all dressed in black trousers and white shirts and thin black bow ties. I came to that meeting wearing an outfit that my grandmother had gotten for me at Macy's before I left, "something beautiful to wear at your interviews," she said. It was a tan cotton dress in a safari style. It had brown plastic buttons up the front and tabbed short sleeves. When I got to Lacan's office, suddenly I felt like an American teenager imitating a British colonial waitress. But the safari outfit reminded me of my grandmother, and that was good.

I told Lacan the essence of my project. He listened quietly and said we would meet again. After this first daytime meeting in his office, future meetings would be at restaurants, always at the end of his workday, usually on the late side, always after 8:00 P.M. At the time, the format seemed exotic. Now it strikes me as practical. Lacan was not befriending or enlisting me. He was helpful and gave us plenty of time. He was charming and wanted me to tell his story, but he did not want to complicate things. There was no attempt to turn me into a comrade, a friend, or a warrior in his cause. I was invited to no social occasions. He did not

Leaving for Paris in the safari dress my grandmother bought me for interviewing French psychoanalysts, Cambridge, September 1973.

approach me romantically. Once, but only once, he called me Mademoiselle Tur-kelll. Usually he called me *chère-cheur.* We always met at his office, 5 rue de Lille. I was always asked to arrive early, when he still had several patients to see.

I can attest that he did see patients for five minutes or seven, but it seemed more usually for ten. I never waited more than twenty minutes for him. I assumed I was asked to come early to avoid the possibility that he would ever have to wait for me.

After the last patient, I was asked into his office. We exchanged pleasantries. He put away some papers. And then we took a short walk to a local restaurant, where we would be quickly escorted to a back table. There was little fussing with the menu. He always asked if he might make a suggestion. I always said yes. And then the menu was fixed: caviar on toast points. Champagne. Sparkling water.

I had never eaten caviar on toast points before. They came with little pots of many other side delicacies: sliced lemons and capers, chopped egg yolk and whites, chopped onions. Perhaps crème fraîche? The actual "toast points" referred to a very thin white bread (my grandmother would have called it "Arnold's thin white," but I am sure in France it was called something else). This bread was grilled hot, with grill marks, so that the caviar did not make it soggy. Then the square bread, without its crust, was cut on the diagonal twice, so that you ended up with four triangles.

I have since developed migraine headaches, and all alcohol makes me violently ill. As does raw onion. One of the questions for me and my many therapists, neurologists, and, yes, psychoanalysts over the years has been when exactly I developed these violent allergies. In 1973–74, I drank champagne and ate toast points with raw onion, and Jacques Lacan lectured me on the history of French psychoanalysis, on what was wrong with American psychoanalysis, and on how he had inspired the students at Vincennes. All without migraines.

In the years since I had these conversations with Lacan, the question I am most often asked is "Were you nervous?" I suppose a little. But actually, not so much. I put on no airs. I explained to Lacan that I was reading his work and struggling with his ideas but that my study was not only about his ideas as they were written but also about his ideas as they were read. And misread. And even about how he was understood by people who had not read him at all. But I also said that it would be helpful to me if, on a few points, he could explain his intentions. And indeed, on several occasions, when Lacan explained some idea to me, I found myself almost laughing with pleasure.

I remember that when we talked about his notion of the mirror stage, Lacan warned me not to think of it, as others had, as a stage of development. It's an image that captures our inescapable alienation from any stable "self." Our restaurant banquette faced a mirrored wall, smoked over by a kind of brown gilding. And there was a similar mirror behind our table. Lacan pointed to our reflection in the mirror we faced, reflected back in the mirror behind. Our figures could hardly be made out. As he stared at us together, he paraphrased something I remembered from the mirror paper—you are always lost when the first recognition is a misrecognition. And I thought, *This is a beautiful idea. I (almost) understand this idea.*

Once, I was bold or perhaps naive enough to ask him why he didn't explain things this simply in his writing, and he said that he wanted people to struggle with *themselves* as they unpacked his work. Reading psychoanalytic texts should be self-analytic. *Ecrits* should be read in little bits and puzzled over. It's like reading poetry. You don't try to speed-read. The idea is to have an experience that changes you.

As I recall, Lacan took me to toast points three times. I was always his guest. At the end of each dinner, we walked back to the rue de Lille. I said, "Thank you." And he said, "My pleasure."

MY EXPERIENCE with French psychoanalysis left me with three stories to tell. First, there was a story about the sociology of how we think about the mind: New ideas about the self take root when old pieties have lost their hold. During May, schools and businesses closed. In Paris, people poured onto the street. Singing. Sharing food and life stories. A postwar generation had never seen anything remotely like this. They had been raised to respect traditional forms in dress, respect for family, church, and social hierarchy. Now they were open to new ways of thinking about themselves. In the festival-like atmosphere of May, people felt a sense of community where markers of class and status fell away. In Victor Turner's language, May participants experienced *communitas*: New ideas were formed in the crucible of broken hierarchies.

In the end, it took only a short radio address by General de Gaulle to end the May events. He did little more than declare that the time for fun was over and that he had the army behind him. People were not ready to fight a real war. But they wanted to continue something, even if it was not clear what.

This brought me to my second story—why certain ideas became "good to think with" for thinking about May. The uprising was over, but its questions remained: What makes people both ready for and resistant to revolution? How does bourgeois society make radical change hard if not impossible? The Lacanian take on Freud that was circulating during May spoke to these questions: The self does not develop independently from its social surroundings. The individual is fixed within a *symbolic* order that has to be taken out of the Oedipal context of mother/father/me and understood within the larger social world, including the realities of class.

After May, people were interested in how social forces had limited individual action. The question was not new. After World War I, when bourgeois Europe survived moments of what should have been revolutionary crisis, Marxists acknowledged that "objective" conditions alone could not "force" revolution. Bourgeois society shapes individuals in ways that inhibit them politically. Theodor Adorno asked for a social psychology that could "reveal in the innermost mechanisms of the individual the decisive social forces."

Lacan's idea of the symbolic order can be read as one response to what Adorno was asking for. This, for Lacan, is when human beings are constructed by language and law. "Man" comes into being and becomes social with the acquisition of language. This myth of passage served as a framework for thinking about the relationship between the individual and society.

Before language, the infant is alienated in an "imaginary" realm in which everything is illusion, the smoke and mirrors of the bistro where Lacan took me for caviar and toast points. In the symbolic order, we speak and find ourselves, but within limits. Because the imaginary realm always remains within us.

In Lacan's version of the banishment from Eden, there is no natural man and therefore no way of thinking about society as coming after to thwart man's nature.

Or at least, this is how Lacan was *read* by the students during May. So when, after May, the music stopped, pursuing an analysis at the École freudienne became a way to feel that you had not given up on your dreams, *that by doing a Lacanian analysis, you were pursuing politics in another form.* Psychoanalysis was seen as a way to learn about the inevitable connection between self and society. It was a way to rid yourself of the illusion that there was an Eden where you had once been free or could once again be free of social constraint. It is in this belief that I am most a Lacanian. I had begun my political education at Harvard during the years of opposition to the war in Vietnam. I hadn't thought of this protest as tied to my interest in psychoanalysis. In France, I came to see my personal and political interests as one. Social wounds show up in symptoms.

"Thinking through" the passage to the symbolic order was a way to think through or work through the May experience. That is one of the things that was being expressed when people said that a Lacanian psychoanalysis could deepen a Marxist political education. From a more strategic perspective, a Lacanian analysis could enhance one's political contacts on the left. And there was simply this: Going to seminars by École freudienne analysts meant that you would see the same people who only a few years before you had been with at political rallies. The students I talked to wanted to continue life in a community that felt political even as it was psychoanalytic.

The third story was how the Lacanian schisms brought up essential contradictions or "knots" that had plagued psychoanalysis from the start. To take one example, analyzing the transference, the feelings that analysands develop for their analysts is central to analysis. We learn who we are through examining them. But if transference is replaced with the requirement to be devoted to a *maître*—or, for that matter, devoted to opposing one—there is a problem.

People fell in love with Lacan and his ideas, among these, his insistence that psychoanalysis was about their owning their own truth.

But acting on that might put them at odds with Lacan. If they were in Lacan's group, disagreeing with him usually caused trouble. If they had left Lacan's group, this would interfere with the imagined reconciliation they hoped one day to have with him. One in which they were understood or forgiven. Or forgave.

13.

The Perfect Shortcake

I began writing my dissertation during the summer of 1974, back
from Paris, about to start a clinical psychology internship at
Harvard University Health Services. I wrote it sitting on a couch
in my apartment on Lee Street in Cambridge, with my grandmother's
taupe electric typewriter perched on a coffee table in front of me.
From time to time, George Homans and I would meet in his office in
William James Hall, and we would talk about Lacan.

The thread of my dissertation that Homans liked best was the
story of the outsize European intellectual who had created a theory
that required him to tear down the standard hierarchies of a psychoanalytic school, although he seemed to want to be king of his own
school all the same. Homans said that Lacan reminded him of all the
would-be-king academics who talked about having a democratically
run university department or university but also wanted to be in charge
with no votes or discussions. To him, the Lacan story was universal
and, in its way, *funny*.

As a clinician in training, I was drawn by the complexity of people's life stories and my need to confront my own. I was in psychotherapy, but increasingly, I wanted to be in analysis, the first step to becoming an analyst. At the time, there was only one institute in Boston that was affiliated with the International Psychoanalytical Association: the Boston Psychoanalytic Society and Institute (BPSI). I investigated what was involved. It turned out that training at BPSI posed a problem: The institute accepted only medical doctors, psychiatrists, or psychiatric residents, for full analytic training. For those with doctorates, there was a research track where you had to sign a waiver stating that after your analysis, your course work, and being supervised on analytic cases, you would do analysis only for "research purposes."

All these years later, when PhD psychologists are routinely admitted to full training as analysts, it is hard to put oneself back in that moment, but that was my moment. Years of interviewing French analysts who put affiliation with the IPA at the center of their concerns meant that I did too. Being trained in a psychoanalytic society affiliated with the IPA meant that I could practice in any country. At that time, I was considering the idea of living in France, so that was important to me.

I felt strongly that signing this waiver would put me in a position of bad faith. I would be seeing analysands, who would be coming to me because they were in some kind of pain (no one goes to an analyst four days a week for fifty minutes a day who is not in some kind of pain), but I would have signed a document promising that my work with them was not "therapeutic."

But what could an analysis be if not a response to whatever the analysand brought to you? To promise a "research analysis" seemed to undermine the open nature of the analytic contract. Wasn't this just another impossible "knot," another contradiction in psychoanalysis?

I had lunch with Harvard Business School professor Abraham Zaleznik, who had been a research candidate at BPSI, and pressed him on this question. He shrugged. What I understood from our conversation was that signing this waiver was in the spirit of a white lie. If you weren't a physician and you wanted to be an analyst, you signed the waiver and put it out of your mind.

One positive effect of being steeped in Lacanian thought was that I worried about the effects of this white lie on my own analysis. And on the analyses of those who would technically sign on as my "research subjects." Lacan might not have lived up to everything he inspired, but he inspired the right questions.

So while I was in graduate school, I decided to go to medical school in order to become an analyst free to state her true intentions. I took premedical courses during summer vacations and began medical school as I worked on my dissertation. Almost immediately, I realized that medicine was not right for me; my priority was to be an academic and clinical psychologist whose work was informed by psychoanalysis. I never made peace with the waiver. I decided in the end to have a personal analysis and do course work at BPSI, but I never took analytic patients. By the time the waiver would have come up, there was a lawsuit in progress (of clinical psychologists against the American Psychoanalytic Association) to dismantle the waiver system. The knots of psychoanalytic politics were becoming undone in my own backyard.

MILDRED WAS LIVING IN CALIFORNIA. For more than a decade, she had worked at Twentieth Century Fox Television in New York, happy to be assigned challenging work in their legal department, but in 1973 the company decided to close that office and transfer its operations to Los Angeles. Mildred would lose her job if she did not move to the West Coast. She hesitated. Her mother would soon be seventy-five. Mildred wanted to spend more time with her but feared that if she did not move with Fox, her lack of a formal title meant that she would not find comparable work in New York. Mildred decided to try California.

I love this photograph of Mildred, mid-conversation, having coffee with her best friends, Brooklyn, mid-1960s.

A few women of Mildred's generation had made successful careers. But my aunt did not have the emotional capital that this would take. She was shy and easily hurt. She had been told all her life—by both her parents—that she was the less attractive, the less charismatic sister. She had tried to stand up to her authoritarian father but really only wanted his affection.

I visited Mildred in Los Angeles during my spring vacation in 1975. As always, she met me at her door, having already changed into cotton pajamas and a robe. She offered me a similar outfit. Later I would think that visiting Mildred was like going to a Japanese *ryokan* where all the guests wear the same *yukata*, except Mildred gave out pajamas and a robe from Macy's.

We slept together on her foldout sofa. I carried my Speedy and taupe portable typewriter. I wore my best dress to California, a Marimekko embossed with large brown flowers from the Design Research store on Brattle Street. My aunt had helped me so much. I wanted her to see I was doing well and had not let her down. But when she talked about her job, I heard disappointment and resignation. As usual, she was seeking approval by doing the work of the men she worked for and getting no credit for it.

She asked me about my next professional steps. I was relieved to tell her that I had a job offer. David Riesman had called to say that I would be hearing from MIT—they were recruiting for a new program they were starting in the social studies of science and technology. I fit because of my interest in "sciences of mind." They were counting psychoanalysis as a science of mind, a bit of a stretch for MIT.

Shortly after Riesman's call, I had met with an MIT dean, Harry Hanham. He asked me to come on board as a guest of the School of Humanities and Social Sciences, finish my dissertation, and then decide if I would like to stay as an assistant professor. I told Mildred what I liked about his pitch: He said that the group he was assembling was not being chosen to fill "slots." He was looking for people whose minds he admired. He said, "If you come to MIT, it's to define a new field." The thing I had always seen as my vulnerability, that I didn't quite fit, Harry Hanham saw as my strength.

That June, Mildred visited Brooklyn for a quick visit. My grandmother had been postponing an annual checkup and she wanted Mildred to go with her. Mildred had left her car in Los Angeles, so I drove the three of us to Dr. Collini's office. He was the Turkle-Bonowitz family physician, who had cared for my mother throughout her illness. The trip took us down Ocean Parkway to Avenue Z, steps from Murdock Court. We were tense at being so close to where my mother had lived out the last chapter of her life. Tenser still that we might run into Milton or Susan or Bruce. By this point, their estrangement from my grandparents and Mildred was complete.

I brought my aunt and grandmother to the doctor's door and drove around the block a few times to find a parking space. By the time I walked into the waiting room, the examination was over. Dr. Collini said he would call when my grandmother's blood work came back.

A few days passed. The tests needed to be redone. Something had not come out right. Three days later, my aunt and I were alone with Dr. Collini in his office. This was the conversation between my aunt and the doctor.

She has pancreatic cancer.

What can you do for her?

Very little. For this, there is very little. She should be made comfortable.

Can we keep her at home?

I interrupted them and, with too much Harvard in my question, asked if we should perhaps have a fuller diagnostic workup, a consultation with a senior oncologist. Dr. Collini offered no resistance and reassured my aunt. "Of course she can stay at home. Let's just begin with this second round of tests that Sherry wants."

I answered the phone when Dr. Collini called with the results from the new tests. Nothing had changed. He was so sorry. He would do everything he could to make Edith comfortable. Mildred was standing by my side. She asked softly, as she had at his office, "Can we keep her at home?" I asked the doctor this precise question, and Dr. Collini said, "Of course." I nodded to Mildred. And then my grandfather shouted out something unexpected: "No nurses. No home nurses. I need that money for me." It broke the silence like an obscenity.

He said that he knew his insurance policy. It would cover hospital stays but not home care. He said it again. I ran to him: "Grandpa? I love you. I love you. It's okay. Don't be upset. Don't say these things. And shah, Grandma could hear you." He ignored me. "I don't have enough money for home nurses. There can be no home nurses."

Suddenly, he wouldn't talk to me. He didn't want me to touch him. I sensed that he wanted to find a way to be shut down and didn't know how. He moved toward the bathroom, right next to the bedroom where my grandmother lay. Now he was in the bathroom and had locked the door behind him.

I ran to my grandmother's bedroom to close her door. I couldn't bear to look in. Then I turned and found my aunt, still in the kitchen, close to the phone, where I had last seen her. She had not moved. She had said good-bye to Dr. Collini and hung up the phone. I tried to comfort her, but she pushed me away. "That son of a bitch."

I stayed at a distance. She was waiting for my grandfather to leave the bathroom. I thought she was going to attack him.

Mildred took her pocketbook and walked out of the apartment.

In about fifteen minutes, my grandfather came out of the bathroom. I was waiting for him. "Grandpa, don't worry about the nurses. You won't pay anything for nurses. Just don't say anything to Grandma about money or nurses. You must promise me. You will not pay for the nurses." And I put my finger to my lips and pointed to the bedroom where my grandmother slept. My grandfather's face had no expression. I wondered if he was ashamed, but he did not apologize. He had his daughter and granddaughter near him in a moment of crisis, and he had only known how to go into battle against them and his dying wife. My grandfather, silent, went to his bedroom, taking the bed next to my grandmother. Her eyes were closed.

At some point, I knocked on their door and asked if I could bring in a tray. My grandmother asked for tea and saltine crackers. My grandfather said nothing. They were each in their own bed, their backs to each other. I noticed that my grandmother had a puppet made of fabric rounds on her bedpost. I didn't remember how long it had been there, but all of a sudden, it seemed important to know what it was. I asked her: "Grandma, this looks handmade. It's really nice." She said, "Oh no. It's nothing." She looked as though it was her secret.

Mildred was back by ten thirty. She made a large pot of coffee. We each had three cups and ate a whole plastic sleeve of Lorna Doones. We agreed that we would keep Grandma at home. Mildred would quit her job and get out of the lease of her Los Angeles apartment. She would move back to Brooklyn. I would come to Brooklyn whenever I could. I thought I could make most weekends. We didn't even discuss home nursing. We didn't want strangers in the house. We wanted to take care of my grandmother.

Visiting my grandmother for the Jewish holidays during graduate school, Brooklyn, fall 1972.

In the months that followed, my grandparents had moments of familiarity. They played cards at the kitchen table. Sometimes my grandfather cooked scram-

With Mildred on that same High Holiday visit.

bled eggs for them both. But alone with her husband, Edith turned her head away.

On her birthday in August 1975, my aunt and I made my grandmother a strawberry layer cake—my mother, my aunt, and I had made this as her birthday gift since I was a young child. My aunt always took me to the supermarket so I could pick out its ingredients: flat rounds of sponge cake, strawberries, and heavy whipping cream. Then the three of us assembled the confection: a round of sponge cake on a pretty plate, whipped cream spread on top and dotted with strawberries, a second layer of sponge on top of the first. Then we covered the whole thing in whipped cream and strawberries. We called it a strawberry shortcake.

My special job in this annual production was to make the whipped cream, accomplished by taking an eggbeater to heavy cream until it formed peaks. This job is delicate because if you whip for even a few extra turns, the cream turns into butter. I always worked in terror, waiting for the moment when the cream turned into perfect peaks. Nevertheless, more than once, I ended up with butter in the bowl. My grandmother was sentimental. She wanted her granddaughter to help with her cake. When my cream turned into butter, she never lost her temper but just encouraged me to finish making the butter and start again. She wrapped the "mistake" butter in a cool wet cloth, put it in the refrigerator (it was perfect butter, after all!), and started me on another round of making whipped cream for her cake.

This time, for the first time, my grandmother did not supervise my work. It was odd and joyless when I got perfect whipped cream the first time around.

When fall came, my grandmother grew listless and would eat only shortbread cookies and saltine crackers with smooth peanut butter, taken with tea. But Mildred wanted to fortify her mother by cooking my grandmother's holiday recipe for chicken soup. This formula had been closely guarded, not shared with her daughters, and certainly not with me. Now my grandmother handed over a small pile of used envelopes on whose backs she had scrawled her recipes. This was a terrible moment for Mildred. She wanted the recipes, but the fact that her mother had relinquished them felt like an admission of being close to death. I hugged Mildred and told her that we would cook the chicken soup together.

In Edith Bonowitz's small cursive hand, the recipe said: *Take a good kosher chicken. Clean. Salt and pepper. Add water and celery and onions and carrots. Soup greens and string. Cook. Get rid of fat. Drain. Reheat with noodles. Make new vegetables to put in.* My aunt and I put pillows around my grandmother so she could sit more comfortably in a kitchen chair as we tried to re-create her secret sauce.

In mid-October 1975, a movie about Jews at the turn of the century on the Lower East Side of New York opened at an art theater in Greenwich Village. We worked out our strategy: I would put a chair in the elevator. My grandmother would sit in that chair while she and I took the elevator to the lobby of her building. I would leave the chair in the lobby. Mildred would have her car parked in front of my grandmother's apartment building. I'd walk my grandmother from the car into the theater while Mildred parked the car. After the movie, we'd work the system backward. I think my grandmother liked *Hester Street*, but I fear my memory plays tricks. All I know for sure is that for Mildred and me, that we got my grandmother to *Hester Street* was our only triumph over the ravages of her disease.

By December, my grandmother rarely left her bed, on whose bedpost was that curious clown made of circles of felt and fabric. I slept next to her. I tried to remember how calming was her scent.

While I was attending a meeting in Boston, Mildred called an ambulance to take my grandmother to Brooklyn Hospital. She explained that she did not want to remember her mother's bedroom filled with tubes and machines. And then Mildred said, softly, "After all, Grandpa has to live in that room . . . after."

The next time I saw my grandmother, she was in a blue-and-white hospital gown and bathrobe. Her hair was combed back, flat, not ruffled by the little curls she had set for herself every night with bobby pins. She said little. I thought she recognized me. She gave me a kiss. She did not smell bad, but not like herself. My aunt said again and again that my grandmother was in a chair. "Sitting in a chair. She is sitting in a chair." Mildred was comforted by my grandmother's dignity restored.

The next day, I drove my grandfather to the hospital to visit his wife. He stroked her head. "Eda, Eda." I forgave him. My aunt could not, not yet. I wondered if she took comfort that my grandmother did not seem to recognize my grandfather. I drove him home, made sure he had some dinner in the refrigerator, and returned to the hospital. Now my grandmother was sleeping. My aunt told me that my grandmother opened her eyes and saw her. I knew a moment of not wanting anything more for myself. My aunt had been recognized. I felt included. We sat at my grandmother's bedside and she took a shallow breath that became tinny. There was not another.

"Do you see it?" My aunt asked. I did. My grandmother was glowing. I wanted to disbelieve my eyes. Unspoken between us was that my mother did not glow when she died. But here, before us, my grandmother was bathed in light.

Mildred asked me to help with the funeral arrangements. Together we chose the dress that my grandmother would be buried in. Together we took it to the funeral home. Together we found a casket made of my grandmother's favorite wood—a golden-toned cherry. Then I took my aunt home so that she could nap, and I arranged for my grandmother's shiva. I knew what to buy. I knew whom to call.

Mildred said to me, "Sherry, thank you. You have come through for me." When she said this, something in me took shape that was not there before. Later I told her how much her "thank you" meant to me. Mildred gave me the gift of seeing me as separate from her.

I realized that in my family, I had usually been asked to do things as the family representative, but rarely thanked. I was treated as an extension of the membership. But all at once, as Mildred thanked me, I remembered that in a phone conversation with my mother about helping with her paper about *Les parapluies de Cherbourg*, she did thank me. I'm not sure I registered this at the time. And now I realized how important that was, how different. I silently sent my mother a message of acknowledgment. I started to cry, and I know my aunt assumed that I was missing my grandmother. She comforted me: "She is worthy of your tears." But right then, I was thinking of my mother and the friendship we never got to have. I was beginning to see the shape of what that could have been. She had decided that I would be a Turkle, not a Zimmerman. I tried to fulfill her desire. But, like her, I was also a Bonowitz, before all that struggle began.

14.

Knots

J ust before my grandmother died, I had to make some quick progress furnishing my apartment in Boston—I settled on a plush couch in merlot velvet—because Jacques Lacan was about to arrive in America. He had written to me to say that he would be visiting colleagues in New York and New Haven in November and he wanted to visit Cambridge as a guest of MIT as well. Considering who he was and who I was (still a graduate student at Harvard, on a fellowship at MIT to finish my dissertation), I was surprised and terrified when he thanked me in advance for making the necessary arrangements.

I went to my dean, Harry Hanham, who seemed intrigued by the possibilities of MIT hosting Jacques Lacan, international psychoanalytic superstar. Hanham said that the School of Humanities and Social Sciences would fund the Lacan visit and certain of his special requests—a higher-than-usual honorarium, a stay and a dinner in his honor at the Boston Ritz, and even a room for his traveling companion, Thérèse Parisot, an analyst at the Freudian School.

After spending time in New York and New Haven, Lacan was finally in Boston. At his request, I had arranged a dinner meeting with Boston psychoanalysts and one-on-one encounters with the MIT linguists Roman Jakobson and Noam Chomsky and the Harvard philosopher Willard Quine. I found the meeting with the Boston analysts compelling. Lacan spoke about his skepticism of what psychoanalysis becomes in psychoanalytic institutions. At a certain point, he said, institutional psychoanalysis had tried to silence him. After that, he became afraid of getting caught up in psychoanalysis as a profession. He preferred to think of it as a calling. Whether or not you agreed with his ideas, he said, these were the deep motivations for his defection from institutional psychoanalysis. Lacan asked the group to talk about their personal decisions to become analysts and wondered if they could bring this question into the training of analytic candidates. I recognized the relaxed Lacan who had tried to explain things to me over toast points.

In contrast, the meetings with the academics proceeded like a series of small train wrecks. Jakobson was rushed and Lacan was annoyed. Quine tried to recruit Lacan to a group of intellectuals working with the Reverend Sun Myung Moon. I was translating this conversation and, at first, Lacan thought I had heard wrong, so Quine had to repeat several times that, indeed, he had just been to a Reverend Moon event and wanted Lacan to come to the next one. Lacan was icy, French polite. At the MIT Chomsky meeting, Lacan shared his hopes for a psychoanalytic science and asked if linguistics could help him develop a mathematical theory of punning that broke it down to equations. Chomsky said no, that what he was trying to do was closer to looking for the "language organ, like the ear." In response, Lacan commented that compared with Chomsky's project, he was a poet. Later I learned that Chomsky summed up the meeting by characterizing Lacan as a "genial charlatan." I remember hoping that Lacan had not heard the comment.

With Jacques Lacan during his visit to America, November 1975.

To relax before his afternoon seminar at MIT, I took Lacan and Thérèse Parisot to lunch at the Ritz dining room, a beautiful space overlooking the Boston Public Garden. Seymour Papert, an MIT mathematician and developer of computer languages for children, who had been the translator at the Chomsky meeting, came with us. As soon as he learned that Papert was a mathematician, Lacan wanted to talk about knots, which Lacan thought were key to future research on the unconscious. Seymour was a specialist in topology, a branch of mathematics that studies geometric properties and spatial relations, so I felt very relaxed.

We entered the large, sunlit room. Lacan was dressed in slacks and a jacket, with a white shirt that had a high banded collar. We were seated, and then a server brought a silver tray with several ties to our table. He politely informed Lacan that all gentlemen in this formal dining room needed to wear ties. Lacan took the tray in silence and placed it next to his plate. The server did not object. Seymour and I said nothing. This was the moment when we should have insisted that Monsieur Lacan was dressed impeccably, as he truly was. The waiter, in silence, took our orders, assuming, I suppose, that compliance was minutes away. Wine was ordered and brought to the table, and all four of us ordered an elaborate array of starters. The ties remained discreetly folded on the silver tray. I thought the moment of confrontation had miraculously passed. However, when the waiter returned with the first course, he raised the question of the tie again. Now Lacan stood up abruptly. A glass fell over. Wine, water, and silverware fell to the ground. Lacan left the dining room and the three of us followed, rearranging ourselves in the lobby. In what seemed like an instant, Seymour had us in a taxi to Anthony's Pier 4, a fish restaurant in South Boston. I can report nothing of what took place there. I no longer cared if I was participating in intellectual history.

Lacan wanted to get to his seminar room early. For an hour before he was scheduled to begin at four, he painstakingly sketched in colored chalk a series of knots. In his audience were analysts, linguists, literary theorists, and mathematicians.

He began the seminar by explaining that these knots were called "Borromean," made of interlocking circles. When one knot is cut, the whole chain of circles becomes undone. He drew the knots in four colors and explained that each color represented an order of analytic understanding—the imaginary, the real, and the symbolic. The fourth was the "symptom" (*le symptôme*). "The symptom is the special mark of the human dimension. Perhaps God has symptoms, but his understanding is most probably paranoid." The diagrams were more than illustrations. They were integral to a challenge Lacan offered the scientists. Were they receptive to the idea that science should be more connected to the body? If so, he had a practical way to shatter inhibition and get started: *play with knots.*

The scientists at MIT were having none of this. Lacan was saying that doing mathematical theory, topology, had a role in self-reflection. And more than this, he was suggesting that working on knots, practicing the manipulations, could be critical in the emergence of insight about the self, in the same sense that psychoanalytic insight grows out of the lived relationship with an analyst. Lacan was trying to engage his audience in a style of discourse to which they seemed allergic. The discussion period made things worse. Lacan answered a question about exterior and interior in reference to the topological metaphor by stating that, as an analyst, he was not sure that man had an interior. The audience was expecting a rational discourse about topology and got this instead:

> The only thing that seems to me to testify to it is that which we produce as excrement. The characteristic of a human being is that—and this is very much in contrast with the other animals—he doesn't know what to do with his shit. He is encumbered by his shit. Why is he so encumbered while these things are so discreet in nature? Of course, it is true that we are always coming across cat shit, but a cat counts as a civilized animal. But if you take elephants, it is striking how little space their leavings take up in nature, whereas when you think of it, elephant turds could be enormous. The

discretion of the elephant is a curious thing. Civilization means shit, *cloaca maxima.*

Lacan's audience might have accepted a talk about elephant shit as an example of Dadaist poetry. But Lacan was not speaking *about* mathematics or poetry or psychoanalysis. He was trying to *do* them— together. When Lacan was asked why he came to the United States, he said, "To speak." Really he was saying that he would not speak *about* psychoanalysis but that, whenever possible, his speech itself would be a psychoanalytic discourse. He hoped that people would enter the circle of his language and let it work on them. That they would ask themselves the questions he posed. At MIT, grumblings about his lack of preparation gave way to questions about whether he was altogether in his right mind.

Somehow the seminar ended. Everyone had been invited to dinner at the Ritz. During cocktails, Octavio Paz walked up to me with a champagne glass in hand and said, "Vous avez les seins très beaux"— you have beautiful breasts—and walked away with a happy smile on his face, a moment that somehow fit entirely with the spirit of the day. A tweedy MIT chemist came up to mumble that this trip would do nothing for my tenure case. I mumbled back that reading my work would explain the very difficulties of this trip. It was such an excellent answer that he smiled, but I was not smiling inside. If there was a market for these French ideas in the United States, I would have to be part of creating it. I wondered if this was really my vocation.

Lacan left town. I never heard from him again.

JUST BEFORE CHRISTMAS IN 1975, I had the taupe typewriter with me in Brooklyn to write my grandmother's eulogy. The tombstone wouldn't go up for another year, but already my aunt had told me she knew exactly what she wanted on it: *A truly gentle woman*. I told Mildred it was perfect.

Now, in late December, with holiday lights everywhere, I was back in Boston, back with my typewriter and my dissertation, as the snow fell outside my apartment on Marlborough Street.

Soon after, Mildred came to stay with me. She looked pale. I knew she had ulcers. I'd seen her seized by pain and nausea. Everything, she said, had flared up since Grandma's death, and she'd reconnected with her New York doctors. She was on new medication. I was glad that she had turned to me for support. She told me she had come for the comfort of one of our sleepovers, but this time "at my house."

After I went to college, I was painfully aware of how many advantages I'd had that Mildred could have used, and I always tried to be upbeat in her presence. To be anything but happy with all I had been given seemed an affront. But on this visit, I let my guard down. Mildred had shared her vulnerability and I wanted her to know me. I told her I had decided that I needed psychoanalytic treatment.

Mildred was shocked. She knew about psychoanalysis. "The five-times-a-week kind?" she asked. "Four," I answered, trying to smile. She said she couldn't understand why someone like me, with my talent and education, could need that kind of therapy. I told her:

I've been in psychotherapy for a while; now I'm starting this more intensive work because I feel I need it. I often feel paralyzed. Any decision brings me to the panic of being in a courtroom and being asked if I love Charlie.

I'd done it. I'd said his name. This was something we never discussed. Mildred objected: I'd accomplished so much. I admitted that this was true but told her I was struggling. I'd allowed myself to use accomplishment as the metric by which I judged myself. But there were other things. I decided to tell her about my recurring nightmares, so intrusive that I was often afraid to sleep.

> I think I am in a park with Charlie. We are drinking milkshakes. We have rowed in the lake. We come out of the boat onto the shore. We sit for a moment on a bench. I glimpse a man behind a tree. We begin to walk, then run, but everywhere we go, men in suits, with fedora hats, lurk behind trees. Everywhere we go, a man emerges from behind a tree. I look to my father. He stares ahead; he cannot help. I am terrified.

I lowered my eyes as I spoke. Now I looked up to Mildred. Her eyes were clouded. There was a flicker of surprise or something else, an emotion I didn't recognize. "But there *was* a man," she says. "We hired detectives to follow you."

MARLBOROUGH STREET BLOSSOMED in May. I delivered my dissertation on French Freud to George Homans. And, now committed to an academic path at MIT, I became fascinated by the MIT environment. In France, I had an opportunity to watch ideas that usually are only debated in seminar rooms—psychoanalytic ideas—catch on in the wider culture. At MIT, I observed another sea change in how we think about our thinking. Computer scientists and artificial intelligence researchers were developing models that imagined the mind as a computational machine. They saw behavior as programs, as software as yet undetermined.

At MIT, I could hear this new science of mind trickle down in how people spoke in the halls, the student lunchrooms, and the faculty club. I remember a conversation with an excited colleague who wanted to finish a complete thought. He said: "Don't interrupt me; I want to clear my buffer," referring to his mind as a mental terrain that needed to be cleared and crossed before he could have access to full processing capacity. If interrupted, he would not be able to function, as he put it, "at full revs." A student told me he had girlfriend trouble; their relationship needed to be "debugged." I came to MIT interested in how we think about our minds. And like a tourist in a new country, when I met computer science professors and students, I put myself in their place and found a new place for me. In recent years I've often been asked if I planned my career because young people want to plan and certainly I did, never wanting to make a false step. But in truth, I found my life's work by navigating as a bricoleur, trying one thing and stepping back, making new connections, and most of all, by listening.

At MIT, I had a front-row seat on a movement from a psychoanalytic to a computer culture. A shift from meaning to mechanism. And since I would be spending time both in a personal psychoanalysis and studying at a psychoanalytic institute, I would also, in those mid-1970s-to-mid-1980s years, be able to see the two cultures as they existed in full flower, in relative isolation from each other. At the Boston Psychoanalytic Society and Institute, analysts talked about language, the body, attachment, relationships, connection, the meaning of a glance, a tone, a gesture. At MIT, the Psychology Department had recently changed its name to the Department of Brain and Cognitive Sciences. In the new discipline of cognitive science, people's feelings were analyzed in terms of their thinking. Or rather, the states of mind that we code as feeling are a result of the same neuron firing that results in thinking. As one of the great founders of cognitive psychology, George Miller, put it, for this new discipline, if it was legitimate to study memory, it was only because computers had them. I was going to have the luxury of a full life in two parallel worlds.

In France, I had studied psychoanalytic ideas carried by politics. Now new ideas about the mind as a program were being carried by an object: the personal computer. In 1975, there was the Altair 8800, a real computer that you could build from a kit, much as you could build a radio or stereo. In 1976, the young Apple Corporation released the Apple I, another personal computer you could build from parts. But by 1977, the time of tinkering was past. Radio Shack sold a fully operational, out-of-the box personal computer in its retail stores and Apple released its Apple II—no longer something you had to build, this computer came with a screen and keyboard and expansion slots for a printer and floppy disks, a place to store your work. Some would say that was the official beginning of our new computer culture.

By the spring of 1976, I was swept into an ethnography of a new science of mind, crystallizing around computation. Ideas about things on the threshold—the power of the liminal—that I had used to think about the May days now seemed to describe the computer as an object betwixt and between many worlds. It was almost-mind; it stood between the animate and the inanimate. Indeed, once programmed, computer systems seemed to take on a life of their own. When I began to conduct interviews about computers, I expected to hear people wondering whether machines thought like humans. Instead, I found computer users considering another, age-old dilemma: Had humans always thought like machines?

Part Three

1976–1985

15.

The Xerox Room

ll the buildings at MIT have numbers rather than street addresses. My office was on the second floor of building 20. Built during the Second World War as a temporary structure, building 20 was the place where radar was born. Hastily constructed, with no basement, wood-shingled outer walls, and a flat tar roof, building 20 was loved by researchers because you could easily reconfigure its space. Because it always seemed like "throwaway space," building 20 became a place where intellectual experiments could easily grow. That's how it came to be home to Linguistics and Philosophy and Cognitive Sciences, and to the program I had joined: Technology Studies, which would later evolve into Science, Technology, and Society, or STS. I also joined another quintessentially "building 20" enterprise, the Division for Study and Research in Education, which translated into the acronym "DSRE."

At the DSRE, Benson Snyder, a psychiatrist who had studied the educational culture of MIT, was working with Seymour Papert and the urban planner Donald Schön to promote self-reflection as an educational strategy, a consulting strategy, and a first step for thinking about how to program digital computers. Management consultants and school administrators brushed shoulders with psychoanalysts and the founders of artificial intelligence, which was then defined in my MIT world as the science of getting computers to do things that would be considered intelligent if done by people.

Papert, who had been so helpful during the Lacan visit, had run a series of workshops on what he called "loud thinking." There, people solved problems while talking them through in front of others, already a valued method in building artificial intelligence. Papert was trying to broaden this reflective thinking strategy. He wanted to make learning itself an object of thought for a large community of researchers. Papert's famous slogan "You can't think about thinking without thinking about something" was a mantra to this research community.

The power of thinking about thinking by "thinking about something"—all of this was familiar to me from my research on how psychoanalysis had caught on in France. I had seen how Lacan's "symbolic order" was an idea-object that allowed people to think about the self in relation to the social world. Now it seemed a near miracle that I had fallen in with this smart group of people who were considering concrete thinking and self-reflection just one floor down from where I had landed in building 20.

By early spring, I had thrown myself into writing a short proposal to the National Science Foundation to study the "social and psychological impact of computers." I brought my work to Harry Hanham, who helped put it into better "proposal" form, and by a Sunday in late April 1976 I was ready to make copies so that the dean's office could distribute it for administrative signatures on Monday—and then send it off to Washington. When I got to building 20, the Xerox machine in the dean's office had run out of toner, but Hanham had given me his code for the DSRE Xerox room, and I made my way down there. I found Seymour Papert in that Xerox room, photocopying last-minute proposals of his own.

As I waited for him to finish his copying, we spoke about the connection between free association in psychoanalysis and loud thinking. He said that he was trying to make more transparent our resistance to learning, inspired by how psychoanalysis makes more transparent our resistance to certain memories and feelings. And he was trying to borrow the nonjudgmental tone of the analytic relationship. In a "loud thinking" group, a speaker should be respected, never judged. He wanted a supportive, open space. We chatted about how Lacan fit into all of this.

I said that Lacan talked about psychoanalysis as a space of complete intellectual freedom, but my dissertation depicted the Lacanian world as quite judgmental. You were in or out. Seymour nodded. We talked about an additional contradiction: Although the official Lacanian message was that any "master" discourse is incompatible with psychoanalysis, in his own analytic societies, it was hard not to see Lacan as a *maître*.

We laughed about the Lacan visit. About the silver tray with the ties at the Ritz. I thought we were finding reasons to say each others names, "Sherry" and "Seymour." I noticed his strong features. Soft gray hair framing a beautiful head, an almost Talmudic face, sparkling gray eyes.

"What is this proposal?" Seymour finally asked, looking at my papers. For the first time, he seemed to register that I was there for any other purpose than to talk to him as he used the copy machine.

I told him that I had been struck by his work with children and computers—the idea that the computer is an object to think with for thinking about mathematics. Papert was teaching children, even very young children, to program in a language he had helped to design. He was on a mission to convince educators that while, in 1976, children could only meet the principles of computer science in his laboratory, very soon, inexpensive, small computers would bring programming to children everywhere.

As a clinical psychologist, I told him, I wanted to know about children's emotional attachments to these machines. Computers crossed standard cognitive and emotional categories. They were in some ways like Freud's uncanny—something that seems both familiar and deeply unfamiliar. One minute you think the computer is like a calculator, but then it does something that makes you consider it as almost alive. One minute people were referring to computers by saying things like "garbage in, garbage out," and the next they were wondering if someday a computer might be their best friend. For me, that made the computer a perfect example of an evocative object, an object that opened up your thinking to other things. This idea was keeping me at MIT.

Seymour helped me collate my proposals. Our decades-long conversation had begun. We decided that sometime soon we would meet again to talk about all this. I didn't know if this man, twenty years my senior, was married. Or romantically available. But I was in love with him. Just like that.

A FEW DAYS after our Xerox-room encounter, Ben Snyder threw an end-of-term party for the whole DSRE. I had planned to skip that party—but I went, hostage to my curiosity. I went to see who Seymour Papert showed up with. Naturally, Seymour was there with a beautiful woman. But wait! He seemed to be there with several beautiful women. One worked at MIT. One was a visiting European. Two visiting Europeans? Seymour was taking photographs with several elegant blond women. I was ready to go home. I turned to say good-bye to Ben and his wife, Judith Wechsler, a professor of art history at MIT. Seymour seemed to be flirting with her as well. Now I was jealous of my married hostess. In less than an hour, I had seen something true. All of Seymour's relationships were seductive. It was how he related to friends, coworkers, colleagues on every level. He felt most comfortable when everyone, man or woman, was in love with him. When I first saw it, I did not want to heed it or take the full measure of what it might mean.

I said good-bye to Ben and Judith. As I walked toward the stairs, Seymour was at my side with a spinach tart that he had cooked for the occasion. He reminded me that we had to get together to continue the conversation we had started in the Xerox room. He said that he had been thinking about my analogy between psychoanalysis and artificial intelligence as subversive sciences that de-center the human subject, one with the idea of the unconscious, the other with the idea of the program. He thought I was onto something. I should give a seminar about this at the DSRE. I nodded absently. I had recalibrated. Old enough to be my father. Many women. This was not boyfriend material.

Then I looked at his eyes, already familiar to me, and felt a sudden clarity. This man was going to be my first and best colleague at MIT. He understood exactly what I was trying to do. And he had yet to consider the emotional implications of the computer revolution he was suggesting for children's education. I had a lot to offer him.

But if he wanted something more, all of these women would have to go. The ones in this room and the ones, I sensed, who were not in the room. I felt lighter, unburdened. I knew what I couldn't do. What I didn't take into account was what he might want to do, truly want to do, but would not be able to do.

Two days later, Seymour called to ask me to dinner, and we made a date for Thursday at Casa Romero, a Mexican restaurant in the Back Bay. Seymour showed up in a beige linen jacket. I wore a white silk dress with pink roses. After dinner, Seymour asked the waiter to give us our coffees to go. We walked to the Boston Public Garden and sat under a willow next to the swan pond. Seymour put down his jacket for me to sit on. My dress was beautiful, he said, and he wanted to protect it from grass stains. I decided I would count this as the *beegeen*.

THERE WERE ONLY a few weeks between the Thursday of Casa Romero and my formal graduation from Harvard University. My PhD. I invited my grandfather and aunt and two close friends who I knew would help me take care of them. My aunt, my grandfather, and I needed a genuine celebration. My aunt and I were learning to see my grandfather's outburst in a more generous light. My grandmother had taken care of him for over sixty years. He had no confidence that he could manage without her. The three of us were family. We would give one another what we could, whenever we could.

Walking with my grandfather during my Harvard doctoral graduation, Cambridge, June 1976.

Once, after a disagreement, my grandfather had written me his only letter of apology, in which he said, "I have to say what you always say. I am sorry. Please forgive me. Let us be sweethearts again." I took a special trip home just to make it right, to kiss him, reassure him. I'd forgotten about this letter until I was going through some papers while researching this book. When I read it again, something entirely new occurred to me: From my grandfather's point of view, I had taught him empathy.

After graduation, George Homans shook my grandfather's hand and said with a big smile: "You must be Sherry's grandfather, Mr. Bonowitz. Sherry is one of our best students. She is going to write a wonderful book." My grandfather talked about the smiling professor for the rest of his life.

With my dissertation advisor, George Homans, on Harvard graduation day.

SEYMOUR ANNOUNCED THAT he would celebrate my graduation by cooking me a festive meal.

He lived in Chinatown, in a loft on the sixth floor of a large, square industrial building. The first floor was occupied by a cavernous dim sum restaurant. The fifth floor was a martial arts academy. Our first dinner at the loft established a pattern. I drove to Chinatown and parked in front of the dim sum restaurant. Seymour told me that there would always be an empty spot, and there always was. I rang a buzzer that only sometimes alerted Seymour to my presence. More often, I had to go into the dim sum restaurant and call Seymour's telephone. Then Seymour would take a freight elevator down to street level. He would roll up a heavy door that worked on a pulley. The elevator would ascend to six.

In the loft, worn oak bookshelves and steel baker's racks lined the walls. In the center of the space, electronic equipment covered large wooden tables. There was a pile up of cables, modems, printers, keyboards, and the first computer terminals that were attached to the ARPANET, the precursor to the internet. Telephone cables linked them to central servers at MIT and from there to the world. The floors were stacked with books opened and put aside, manuscripts started and abandoned. The manuscripts were all computer printouts, which I had never seen before. Writing on a computer was altogether new to me.

On my first visit to the loft, Seymour gave me a demonstration of what a computer at home could do. He typed: I LOVE YOU. It came up on a rectangular screen in small green fluorescent letters. And then, with two or three strokes on a keyboard, the screen was filled with I LOVE YOU. I LOVE YOU. I LOVE YOU. From edge to edge. Top to bottom. I touched the screen and felt deep relief. I was going to follow my heart.

Seymour had arranged the kitchen area so that it had a large work table surrounded by industrial shelving. French ceramic pots. Woks of many shapes. Families of pots in stainless steel, cast iron, and copper.

Grinders, graters, blenders, food processors, deep-fryers, fish poachers. And bookshelves of cookbooks. The collection was international.
Wherever Seymour traveled, he brought back things to cook with.
My grandmother had not wanted to teach me to cook, for fear that I
would fall into the routine of her life, responsible every day for putting several meals on the table. Here was a solution that my grandmother had never considered. A man who showed his love by cooking.
When Seymour first invited me to his loft so that he could cook dinner, he asked me my favorite food. I thought back to Maxim's in Paris
and replied, "Steak au poivre."

And that is what he made. With four cookbooks open, Seymour
had spent the hours before my arrival experimenting with glazes and
reductions. We ate dinner on the roof. I told him the steak was "wonderful." He wanted more. Texture? Intensity of the sauce? The granu-
larity and flavor of the pepper? He had many choices of pepper. And
what about the wine he had used in the preparation? I didn't know
the answers to his questions. I didn't know how to talk about food.
He made it clear that he would fix that. I would know food talk in no
time. And he said that now that he knew my favorite food, he was
going to cook it over and over, until it was perfect for me. At first, I
heard the sexual overtones in this culinary metaphor as so close to the
surface that I started to smile—it seemed more heavy-handed than I
would have expected from him—but when I raised my about-to-smile
face to his, Seymour was not smiling. He was announcing a learning
plan. He was going to perfect my favorite food for me through repetition. I didn't know what Seymour Papert understood about love or
commitment or being there in sickness and health. But he was a master of intimacy on his terms. And perhaps not only on his terms. I
recalled how happy I was to try out Charlie's exotic malteds, my delight when Lacan arranged the caviar and toast points.

In part, my love for Seymour grew because I was so happy with who I became when I was with him. Through Seymour's eyes, my desire to be more and learn more was not gluttony. I was cultivating a unique style. I was developing needed resources. My college and graduate school mentors told me that I was a gifted student and should press on. The kind of understanding that Seymour brought me was granular, intimate. He understood that psychoanalysis and AI were two ambitious sciences of mind. He understood that I was developing strategies for interviewing through which I could see people actively using one or another to think about themselves. I could sometimes see them shifting from one style of thinking to another, trying to juggle both. Mind as meaning or mind as mechanism. Seymour encouraged me to think of my ability to get people talking this way as a gift. But also as a professional skill that needed to be cultivated.

At the start of my career, my closest colleagues encouraged me to stay in my lane. If I was a sociologist, why was I also seeing patients and getting certified as a clinical psychologist? And why analytic training? Wouldn't that make tenure more complicated? Psychoanalysis was unscientific. MIT would hold it against me. And certainly, there were strong signals that the MIT culture did not want to be studied. At best, my work would turn out to be some kind of critique of computer science at MIT. This couldn't possibly be a good career move. Was I doing the rebellious thing and expecting to be rewarded for it?

When I talked to Seymour about all this, he shrugged. I was doing something important. I should be patient. I had no right to expect the people I was studying to welcome my inquiries. The French psychoanalysts certainly hadn't. I needed to respect my style of creativity.

And now my intuition was guiding me toward the interplay between a new kind of theory of mind and the rise of a new object in the culture. People, I excitedly told him, would use computers to think about mind (and relationships and decision making). An evocative object. Seymour was supportive. I had come up with a fine idea, he said. Several. He liked evocative objects. He liked computer as Rorschach, the notion that people project themselves onto this new betwixt-and-between object. All I was missing, and only sometimes, was courage. Like the lion in *The Wizard of Oz*. He bought me tiny plastic ruby slippers to put on my key ring.

We made plans for me to spend more time at Seymour's laboratory so that I could observe, in greater depth, how children engaged with the computers of the future. In the meantime, about two months after we began dating, he said he had a surprise for me.

"I have a daughter. Diane. She is coming tomorrow. She lives in Switzerland."

"Switzerland?"

"With her mother."

"Mother. Why didn't you tell me?"

"I was afraid you would be angry at me."

Here was the thing that Seymour was not eager to share. His wife, one of Piaget's collaborators, and young daughter had lived with him in Cambridge for a while when Diane was a baby, but then, after about a year, had returned to Geneva. For a long while, he had been in only sporadic contact with them. He had visited Geneva from time to time, usually to attend some professional event, but had missed most of Diane's childhood. When Diane was about eleven, he said, their routine had changed. She told him she wanted to see him more, and on a more consistent schedule. She began to visit him in Cambridge over school vacations. She came with him to work, befriended his colleagues, became known to everyone in his lab. Now she was fourteen, and these Diane visits were a regular thing. Tomorrow, on the Fourth of July, she would come to visit until the end of the month. He told me how grateful he was to Diane. He had let their relationship slide. She had made it happen.

I did not focus on how he had let things slide. Instead, I heard the story of the young girl who had successfully brought her father back into her life. Diane, fierce, daughter of Jupiter, had hunted her father down. She had done the necessary. She did what I had not been able to do. I admired her.

Later I heard Diane's account of this change in their relationship. Diane said that her mother had initiated it. I believe Seymour sensed that presenting their reconnection as Diane's idea would be a way for me to bond with his daughter. It would make her my hero.

Seymour had not wanted to tell me that, in his view at least, he had abandoned his child. He needed to hide that from a woman who had been let down by her father. I was shaken, but love is not deterred when it wants to love. I identified with Diane and couldn't wait to meet her.

He said that he had not yet told Diane about me. He would introduce us at a proper dinner, cooked by him, at his loft. As soon as I saw her, I felt the physical shock of how much I wanted a daughter, how much I wanted a child. I was twenty-seven, and, until that moment, I had not allowed myself these feelings, except in the most abstract way.

Diane was small and compact, marked by Seymour's beautiful, strong features. Seeing her standing next to her father collapsed space and time for me. I turned her into me at fourteen, but this time a me who had Charlie's attention. By the time I was fourteen, I had lost all claim on Charlie. Milton had legally adopted me. My name was Sherry Turkle for real. But here Diane was, with Seymour sharing his life with her. And her pursuit of him made him happy.

It was during Diane's visit that Seymour and I officially had what we laughingly called our *début de couple*. Diane, Seymour, and I went to dinner at Marvin Minsky's home. Seymour had a brother and sister-in-law in Boston, and I would meet them at a later occasion, but this dinner with Marvin Minsky and his wife, the Boston pediatrician Gloria Rudisch, was my official introduction to Seymour's social world.

Marvin Minsky was one of Seymour's closest colleagues and friends. Together they wrote *Perceptrons*, a book that changed the direction of artificial intelligence, at least for a while. In its day, *Perceptrons* closed down the idea that neural nets, as they were understood at the time, could become general learning machines. In the end, artificial intelligence programs found a way to learn through example, but *Perceptrons* demonstrated that the learning algorithms of the time did not have this promise.

It was a wonderful thing to hang out with Marvin Minsky. He was interested in everything. Curious about everything. He expressed an opinion on everything. Science fiction. How to explore space by building a ladder instead of shooting rockets. In our first conversation, he probably wanted to goad me, so he began with a litany of reasons "why Freud was wrong." Then, like an elegant British hostess who turns to her opposite side midway through the meal so that her guests, too, can have new conversational partners, he abruptly began to argue "why Freud was right."

Even at that first dinner, the questions came up that would come up again and again: Why would we want to build machines of such profound intelligence that they might want to take over from us? Would we want to upload our brains to a giant computer when we die and achieve immortality as a machine? The people Minsky liked best fought back against whatever side of an argument he took, secure in his love. I was insecure, easily silenced. But I appreciated him. And sitting with Seymour on my left and Diane on my right, I felt like a member of the family being introduced to the in-laws.

Too soon, Diane was gone, and Seymour and Marvin were about to leave for Brazil, on a long-planned writing retreat. They were working on a new book about the mind being made up of decentralized programs. They called this idea "the Society of Mind." Seymour, at home and in his office, worked on an international, networked computer system. One of the important innovations of the network project was its decentralization. Messages from one center to another did not travel directly but were broken up into data packets that were then reassembled at the destination. The packets could take many routes before reassembly. Radical decentralization became an idea, resonant with the work I had been doing in psychoanalytic theory, that turned out to be crucial to the early internet.

WHEN I LEARNED in late June that Seymour would be spending August in Brazil, I decided that I, too, should get away. My project was to turn my dissertation on French psychoanalysis into a book. I rented a small cottage in Annisquam, near Gloucester, on the North Shore of Massachusetts. It was nestled high in the craggy rocks above the harbor. One woke up there to birdsong. Everyone called it the tree house.

My plan was to leave for Annisquam right after Seymour and Marvin left for Brazil. The night before their departure, we drove to Newton to visit my friend Nancy, now married to Richard Rosenblum, a sculptor. Nancy, my best friend since Social Studies 10, was as close as I had to Boston family. This was my chance to present Seymour to my family, just as he had presented me to the Minskys. My new man. I thought the evening went well, although Richard seemed overly protective of me. At the time I thought that, as an artist, he might have sniffed out that Seymour was a bit too, well, artistic. I had an answering machine and checked it before we drove home to my apartment on Marlborough Street. I wanted a serene end of the evening. Seymour's loft was an exciting environment for work and cooking. But it was chaotic. Tonight, just before Seymour's departure, I wanted the serenity of my Back Bay apartment and Seymour's undivided attention.

There were vulgar messages from one of Seymour's ex-girlfriends on my answering machine. She said that she would get rid of me as she had gotten rid of the others. I was no different. I was not special. She would stalk me. Seymour said he would postpone his trip. I said that I would not tolerate calls like this, threats like this. Others might have given him a pass; I would not. Seymour promised to take action.

He said that the next day, he would be in touch with his exgirlfriend. I made it clear that one more call and I would alert the police. But for all my tough talk, I was rattled and after I took Seymour to the airport, I did not want to go back to my apartment. I left immediately for Annisquam.

There, I walked on the wild trails around the old abandoned settlement known as Dogtown, and up and down the beach. Seymour wrote to me every day, long letters about his love for me and the new life he wanted to start with me. I began to calm down.

I will give Seymour this: When he fell in love with me, he did not fall in love with a woman who saw him realistically and loved him for who he was, as he was. He was a magician who conjured up many selves, and I let him. I adored him in bits and pieces that I fit into compelling narratives I already had in place. This was true when it came to how I filled in the story of his relationship with Diane, and it was true as I navigated the minefield of Seymour's other women.

What helped the most during that period was that I lost myself in work. The feeling was familiar. As a child, I withdrew from what I could not fix about my name, my mother, and Milton by devoting myself to academic achievement. I mourned my mother and grandmother by using ideas as well as people to keep me company. Now I calmed myself by writing all day. What mattered most to me now were the things that Lacan's psychoanalytic culture had in common with the computer culture I was getting to know. Most of all, this was the notion of a de-centered self.

Artificial intelligence and psychoanalysis shared common challenges in thinking about the decentralized mind. For ego psychology, the ego was a kind of mini-me living within each person. It was as though the ego were your eyes, ears, and brains too, smart enough to keep your impulses in check. Object-oriented psychoanalysis and Lacanian theory turned away from that. Seymour and Marvin's "Society of Mind" model did the same thing. A person had to be constructed without a "homunculus" core. The grounding premise of AI was that the human mind, like a machine mind, was built up from a multitude of simple, decentralized programs.

If the mind is built up from many different learning programs, millions, perhaps billions of them, how are they organized? How do they communicate? In the Minsky/Papert solution of 1976, it's probably best to think of them as members of a society. If so, what kind of mathematical ideas would best explain their social relationships?

That summer, I realized how close were the key problems in artificial intelligence and psychoanalysis. Debates about consciousness in the twenty-first century would be fought on this new terrain of how consciousness emerges from "de-centered" mind. People ask me if my interests shifted from psychoanalysis to "computers" when I arrived at

MIT. I suppose it might look that way, but that's not how it felt. It felt like the same debates moved from one venue to another.

But something did change. As my career developed, I watched people cycle through different versions of how they thought about their minds: Freudian-style memory catcher, information processor, and a biological system, ready for chemical manipulation. People now use all of these models, depending on the circumstance. We take medication and interpret our dreams. We do behavioral therapy and have a personal mantra for meditation. If there's a movement, it's toward psychological and therapeutic pluralism.

ONE OF SEYMOUR'S LETTERS said that after his time with Marvin, we should have a proper vacation. Since he was in remote Brazil, why didn't I call a travel agent and arrange it? He would get himself to Miami on the appointed day. We would proceed from there.

He was up for anything but thought that the Bahamas might be romantic. His only request was that we *learn* something together. How about spending a week learning to scuba dive? We should take the full course. I was coming to understand Seymour's ways: Every love opportunity was a learning opportunity. Every learning opportunity, a love opportunity. During our scuba diving adventure on Eleuthera, Seymour proposed. I had two questions. I asked him if he could be faithful. He smiled. "I will be utterly, completely faithful to you." And what about Judaism? Seymour came from a Jewish family. At thirteen, he had been a bar mitzvah. But we had not spoken about Jewish holidays, a Jewish home. I wanted children. Jewish children. Seymour took me in his arms. "We will have seders. We will go to temple this Rosh Hashanah in Brooklyn when you introduce me to your grandfather." After the words "Rosh Hashanah" and "grandfather," I said I would marry him.

When we got back to Boston, we celebrated our engagement by making a special chicken dinner. We froze the leftovers and labeled them "love chicken." Our relationship, from the start, was stressed. Seymour was in debt and didn't tell me. Seymour had fraught relationships with students and ex-lovers that were never quite resolved. The love chicken, over time, became inedible, but its presence reminded us, whenever we opened our freezer, of what had brought us together. We loved each other and were unembarrassed in the joy we found in each other. One day, shortly before our wedding, a cleaning person threw out the frozen love chicken, knowing that it had been in the freezer too long to defrost and consume. Seymour and I became frantic. Together we searched the garbage to find the love chicken. We rooted through dumpsters in South End alleyways. It was gone.

16.

Building 20

O ver that first summer, while Seymour was still in Brazil, I
told my aunt and grandfather that I was in love. I tempered
the disappointing news that Seymour was forty-eight with
the good news that he was Jewish. Of course, they wanted to meet
him as soon as possible. A date was set for us to have an early-fall
dinner in Brooklyn.

While in Brazil, Seymour's bohemian side had flourished. He
came back with long hair, a scraggly beard, and a decidedly more
absentminded-professor look.

Worried about the first impression he might make on my wary
relatives, I told Seymour that even though we were going to be having
dinner at my aunt's home, my grandfather would be wearing a suit.
He would greet us at the door in his jacket and then remove it for
dinner. From my grandfather's point of view, meeting a prospective
son-in-law was a formal occasion. Seymour understood immediately.

"We should go to Louis," he said. That was Boston's most elegant men's store. "I will get a 'Grandpa outfit.'"

"Grandpa outfit" became our code phrase. When we arrived at Louis the next day, I was shocked when several salespeople approached, clearly acquainted with Seymour. They called him "Professor." What had I missed? I had never seen Seymour dressed in anything that could have possibly begun its life at Louis. But Seymour was being treated as a regular customer.

We were given espressos as the Louis staff fussed over Seymour, asking him the occasion for which he needed to be dressed. Seymour said: "The first dinner with the family of Sherry-Love." The salesmen swooned. Grandpa outfits were assembled. Gray flannel slacks and elegant khakis. A white shirt with light blue stripes and a blue shirt, both of soft cotton. A silk tie with a delicate pattern of light and dark blue. A second tie, gray—at Seymour's insistence, as he said that he always got soup on his tie, and there was sure to be soup. And best of all: a tweed sports jacket and a blue blazer, both of these beautifully cut, tailored to perfection. And then, without my asking, Seymour took me in a cab to Gino's in Harvard Square, where he got a haircut. I looked at Gino and wondered if he could be the same man I remembered only as "G" who had cut my hair in Harvard Square during freshman week so long ago. I could not be sure; I had been in such a daze on that first visit. But here at Gino's, as at Louis, everyone seemed to know "the professor." His gray hair now shone close to his beautiful head.

Despite the grand spiffing up of Seymour, I was still nervous. I assumed my grandfather would be naturally disapproving of any of my friends—to say nothing of a boyfriend—who was over forty, with a beard. But Seymour was a hit. Seymour had our taxi from the airport stop at the iconic Zabar's delicatessen on the Upper West Side before we made our way to Brooklyn. After offering my grandfather pickled herring in sour cream, Seymour quite unexpectedly took out small red balls that he had in his travel bag and began to teach my grandfather to juggle. My grandfather, as expected, was dressed to meet Seymour in a white shirt, blue suit, and tie. No one had ever seen him as the kind of man who might want to juggle. But now we were in his living room on East Seventeenth Street, and he had taken off his jacket and was passing a red rubber ball from hand to hand. The first step in juggling.

Seymour Papert on the charm offensive with my grandfather, Brooklyn, September 1976.

The two men stayed focused on the juggling lesson for an hour, with snack breaks for Zabar's delicacies and moments of frustration. But my grandfather learned to juggle—enough. And more extraordinary, at some point, Seymour began to ask him how he felt about it. Loud thinking. What was working? Not working? How could they fix it? What was coming to mind?

My grandfather told Seymour that, as a young man, he had been a bookbinder. The juggling brought back distinct, happy memories of being young and working with his hands. Of being good at the discipline of work with unforgiving, demanding materials. He talked about the repetitive motions involved in making book seams. He was describing the pleasures of procedural thinking.

So it was all there in the juggling lesson, all of the things that made Seymour such a skilled teacher—he got my grandfather to learn through objects and learn through his body. And that wonderful extra thing: Seymour had used these red balls to directly engage the emotional life of his learner.

My grandfather had dropped out of school when he was twelve in order to earn money for his family. In juggling he saw, probably for the first time in a long time, that he could still learn something new. He became a bit smitten with juggling and a bit smitten with Seymour. But in the conversation, and in the reminiscence after, something else kicked in. My grandfather became a bit smitten with himself—as a learner. And as someone who could think of his learning life in a positive light.

After the juggling, Mildred made us dinner, and I had an afternoon in which I felt my life repaired. That is the word that came to mind, both then and now. I had brought a new family member to my beloved aunt and grandfather. One who was worthy of being Bonowitz. He knew to teach my grandfather to juggle. He engaged my aunt in a discussion of apartheid in South Africa. I was loved by someone who understood what all of this all meant to me.

I HAD THE SAME FEELINGS of contentment as I started my new job. At MIT I was put into the Technology Studies Program with the understanding that something new was under way. The former president and the provost of MIT, Jerome Wiesner and Walter Rosenblith, had an idea to start a new college within MIT that would look at science, technology, and society. I would be part of that. Over a few years, a group of senior faculty were hired to be the core of the enterprise. Carl Kaysen, an economist and political scientist; Leo Marx, a literary critic; Kenneth Keniston, a psychologist; Merritt Roe Smith, a historian of technology; Loren Graham, a historian of science. I was a junior hire. Members of the Technology Studies Program at MIT—people like Larry Bucciarelli, David Noble, Kenneth Manning, Elting Morison, Nathan Sivin, Langdon Winner—they, too, would become part of the new unit. After my first day as a professor in fall 1976, Seymour picked me up after work with a bottle of champagne to toast the milestone. He had a particular way of celebrating a significant event. He would stand before me with his hands above his head and jump up and down. So, after my first day teaching, Seymour was standing in front of building 20, jumping up and down, holding a little sign: S-L LOVES S-L ON HER FIRST DAY OF SCHOOL! In our special language, we were both "S-L," Sherry-Love and Seymour-Love.

I felt the excitement of inventing a field. Many of my students worked all day and through the night on mainframe, time-shared computers. They were excited to think with me about how to consider computers as part of the larger culture. In my classes, we read Norbert Wiener's *God & Golem Inc.* and *The Human Use of Human Beings* and considered the ethics of mechanical life. We read Alan Turing's "Computing Machinery and Intelligence" and talked about whether behaving intelligently meant a machine was intelligent. With prescience, we asked, would behaving empathically mean a machine was empathic? We read Freud's "The Uncanny" and talked about computing machines as sitting on the boundary between things alive and not alive. We read the psychoanalyst Donald Winnicott on transitional objects. These are the objects of the playroom (the teddy bear, the bits of silk from a blanket) that children treat as though they were part of their own bodies and also separate from them. They are in a space betwixt and between self and not-self. Later in life we have experiences—sexual, artistic, creative, and spiritual—that bring us back to the feelings associated with those early objects. The compelling nature of programming, that feeling of getting lost in code, seemed to have something of the power of transitional objects. In programming, people get involved, body and mind.

I asked students to analyze the digital world using these lenses and had them write a paper about an early object in their life that had great meaning to them, perhaps one that had brought them into science. This was close to the paper topic that I had assigned when I taught for David Riesman. And at MIT, my early experiences with "object papers" evolved into courses on "things and thinking" where the writings of Proust, Freud, Marx, Lévi-Strauss, and Piaget got matched up with essays I commissioned from friends and colleagues about objects that had served as touchstones in their intellectual and emotional development. A master architect described a boyhood fascination with terraces and steps; the president of MIT wrote about how microscopes led her to science; for a molecular biologist, Venus Paradise paint-by-number coloring pencils made three-dimensionality and the idea of shapes fitting into other shapes come to life. Students wrote about mud pies, Legos, key chains, and Easy-Bake Ovens. In the end, I edited three books about objects in loss and love, in mourning and learning. I repaid my debt to the memory closet.

At MIT, I was not only fascinated by what I was teaching but felt deeply connected to my students. When I assigned a paper asking them to consider how their work with computers influenced how they thought about other things, they often wrote about thinking of their minds as programs. In one class, a computer science student reinterpreted a Freudian slip as an information-processing error. In Freud's thinking, an error is always meaningful, indicative of inner conflict. Not so for my student. When the word "open" is substituted for "closed," she said, one of Freud's famous examples, there is no need to look to explanations that depend on meaning. The person who makes that slip is not showing complex emotion. "The mind is a computer. In a computer, closed = (-) open. There has been a power surge. A bit has been dropped. No problem." She repeated that final flourish, "No problem."

For me, my MIT class on computers and people was a turning point. In computer culture, you didn't need ideas such as ambivalence when you modeled the mind as a digital machine. You didn't need shades of gray. Thinking of mind as program trained you to think in absolutes.

IN MY FIRST YEAR of teaching, Seymour encouraged me to apply for a small research grant from the Laboratory for Computer Science at MIT. It would be good to have the funds, but more important, I should introduce my technical colleagues to the idea of studying the computer as culture. I told the lab director, Michael Dertouzos, that I wanted to observe the life of the laboratory and to ask its members— among them MIT's most distinguished computer scientists—how their ideas about computing had affected their ways of seeing other things. Dertouzos liked the idea. He gave me an office in 545 Technology Square, the center of computer and AI research at the time, money to furnish it for interviewing, a professional-grade tape recorder, and a computer terminal. I was on the Net! In 1976–77, I was living in the future.

I worked my way through Technology Square—interviewing computer science and artificial intelligence pioneers and computer hackers. Among many others, I talked to Hal Abelson, Fernando José Corbató, Robert Fano, Daniel Hillis, J. C. R. Licklider, Chris Stacy, Gerald Sussman, and Patrick Winston. The hacker interviews were my favorites. The term "hacker," at that time, did not connote crime. It referred to a culture of deep mastery of the computer. Hackers talked about elegance, still defined as writing the smallest and most compact program possible. Computers in the late 1970s were on time-sharing systems. During the day, when many people were using them, they worked more slowly. At night, the hackers had them almost to themselves. That was prime time. The computers were located on the ninth floor of Technology Square. I would sit on the floor and watch the hackers at work. The computers were objects of devotion. One hacker told me: "Marvin Minsky wants to create a computer beautiful enough that a soul would want to live in it."

I was also studying the children who were learning to program in Seymour's laboratory. In 1976, they worked on stand-alone Logo machines, typing commands to move a screen cursor, called a "turtle," or to control a robot on the floor that had a pen attached to it, a "floor turtle." If you typed the command PEN DOWN, the floor turtle would be ready to draw. PEN UP would retract the pen and you could move the robot without leaving a trace. On the screen or on the floor, you told the turtle what to draw and it followed your instructions.

When you walked into the Logo lab, there were children programming at low tables, working with the screen turtles. Sometimes children (and child-friendly grown-ups) were curled up on the floor or crouched next to a floor turtle or running from a computer to a floor turtle. In all cases, every time a new child came into Seymour's laboratory, that child was meeting something no child had ever seen before: a computer. And it wasn't like the image of the computer in the culture, something imposing and whirring and taking up all the floor space of a big room. This was an intimate machine. Personal and compact. Waiting for you to express your ideas. As one thirteen-year-old described her experience programming in the Logo language, "When you program a computer, you put a little piece of your mind into the computer's mind and you come to see it differently." That's what I was trying to capture. The computer as a second self. An extension of mind. And also an extension of body.

Consider what it took for children to make a Logo computer draw a circle. First they had to figure out how to draw a circle with their bodies. Take a step forward, turn one degree, and then repeat. Again and again until you closed a circle. The next step was to tell the computer to do what they had just done. After 360 of these step-and-turns, the turtle, too, would have completed a circle. And if you had begun with the command PEN DOWN, the turtle would have left a trace. In this way, those computers made a *physical* connection with their users, because you could move your body a certain way, then program a Logo turtle to do the same thing.

If you liked your program, you saved it on a plastic disk that was waiting for you the next time you came into the lab. I remember having this thought: "I don't like my work being on the same disk as all these other people. It feels like sharing a notebook. As though I am allowed to write on every third line and other people are writing on the other lines. Can't I have my own private disk?" An MIT senior working in the lab patiently explained to me that my work was electronically segmented from everyone else's. The old kind of privacy didn't matter here. Given what has come since, I think often of my first response to digital storage and the first time I thought it wasn't private enough.

It was not surprising that Logo was evocative. It was designed to transparently carry powerful ideas in computer science—for example, the power of breaking things down into what one young programmer called "mind-size bites," the idea of debugging, the power of recursion. Before I met Seymour, I had never encountered these ideas. And this was not surprising, since people who were not exposed to computer programming would have little reason to run into them. Seymour believed that these ideas could be accessible to everyone, even children, if they were taught to program in a language that led with such notions.

No one is surprised, said Seymour, that French children learn French in France. It's because they are immersed in a culture that brings French to them every day. So, according to this analogy, French children learn French in France, a Frenchland. For Seymour, the computer should be a Mathland, what he called a "microworld" for teaching mathematics. But this will happen only if children have access to a computer language that puts them in contact with powerful ideas in mathematics and programming. That is what he tried to accomplish with Logo. The worst thing, to Seymour, was to give children a computer that presented them only with games or opaque applications. The machine might be useful or entertaining. But a learning opportunity would be missed, because you would have masked the intellectual power of the machine. Sadly, this is what has happened. Seymour's dream of every child with a computer no longer seems utopian. But few children who have laptops, tablets, or phones live in Mathland. A child immersed in opaque apps is not learning powerful computational ideas.

Beginning in 1976, I talked with children learning to program in Logo. The experience got them thinking about the idea of machine as mind and, more than this, about other things on their minds. The thirteen-year-old who said she "put a piece of her mind into the computer's mind and thought about it differently"—a pretty philosophical notion—also used programming to work through more emotional concerns. Even in fifth grade, she had trouble with smoking and overeating. But in the world of the Logo computer, all her elaborate designs were built from rotations of thirty degrees. Her control over a Logo "microworld" gave her confidence that she could master things beyond programming.

After a while, I was not so surprised to find children using programming to think about personal matters. Like blocks or modeling clay, programming was a plastic, expressive medium. More surprising to me, an outsider to the mathematics culture, was how certain computational ideas were themselves emotionally charged. Take recursion. It means, most simply, that you define a thing in terms of itself. But again and again, I watched people sit down at a computer, create a program that could go on forever, and quite simply freak out. Meeting recursion was like looking at objects of infinite regress, contemplating horizons, trying to find the end of the stars, all of these experiences that frighten and fascinate children—and adults.

At the same time that computer models were representing human emotions as cool algorithms, the actual response of people upon meeting algorithms was heated.

I had studied psychology at Harvard's William James Hall, where the researchers who studied thinking were on one floor and those who studied feelings were on another. I had committed myself to a career that explored thinking and feeling together, "on the same floor." Studying people learning to program was a way to do just that.

In my many grant applications to explore how computers might change how people think, I began to use a kind of mission statement:

"I want to study how computers change not only what we do but who we are."

SEYMOUR TAUGHT ME to assume that computers would become commonplace objects, in every classroom, in every home, and very shortly, something that every person carried around. Alan Kay, one of Seymour's colleagues who worked at Xerox's Palo Alto Research Center (PARC), was working on something he called the Dynabook, a precursor to the laptop computer. In January 1977, I went with Seymour to visit PARC. There I saw the same thing that Steve Jobs and Bill Gates both said changed their lives: a demonstration of the Alto personal computer.

On the Alto, a computer screen evoked for the first time a physical desktop. Projects in progress showed up in windows on the screen. You made them come alive with a pointing device, a mouse that you operated with your hand. Once you were working on a project, say, a document, that pointing device served as your way of working on it. Change a font. Move a paragraph. No more moving text around by typing screen commands—that's what Seymour and I were doing on our computer editing program at MIT—working the old-fashioned way.

On the Alto in 1977, I had something close to the writing experience I am having now, working on a MacBook Air more than forty years later. I walked away from the Alto knowing that the world was going to change. It was an odd feeling—to know that this future was coming. It wasn't a secret, but very few people seemed to know.

MICHAEL DERTOUZOS ASKED ME to host a dinner for Jobs at my Marlborough Street apartment when he visited MIT in spring 1977.

He had only just launched the Apple II computer. With the Apple II, Jobs went from a device that needed to be hooked up to a TV screen to having the machine that defined personal computing. Those in the know treated him as future royalty.

Jobs had spent the afternoon before my dinner in meetings at MIT. I was told that Jobs had asked that dinner be something intimate, relaxing, and off the record. Close to campus would be best because he would be tired. And of course the meal had to be vegetarian. Michael Dertouzos called me. I lived in the Back Bay. Could I throw this relaxing and vegetarian event? I was delighted. I made arrangements with a local Japanese restaurant to deliver large platters of rice and vegetable sushi. Seymour arranged for spectacular French pastries. When I saw them, I had a moment of doubt. French pastries are made with butter. Butter comes from cows. Dertouzos had said vegetarian. But perhaps Steve meant vegan. I made sure my fruit bowl was overflowing.

Dertouzos estimated about forty people. They would just fit in my apartment. It would be, in my mind, one of those memorable, casual but elegant evenings where everyone drinks champagne, eats delicious food, and falls in love with their hostess.

I spent the day getting ready for Steve's feast. Everyone would taxi over from MIT. My place was less than ten minutes away. Drinks were scheduled for six o'clock. I decided that to simplify drinks, it would be an all-champagne-and-sparkling-water evening. With vegetarian appetizers. Crudités. Guacamole and hummus with pita chips, tofu on skewers, these dishes prepared by me. And then the sushi.

Amazingly, by 6:10, the most famous names in computer science were in my living room, eating vegetarian appetizers before they were trendy. By seven o'clock, Steve had not yet arrived, but people were hungry, so I passed the sushi. When Steve arrived, he said he had another appointment, so he could stay only a little while. I said that I would be happy to introduce him to his guests, they were all eager to chat, and of course, if he was hungry, we had food that I hoped he would enjoy. He looked at the food and said, "This is the wrong kind of vegetarian." He left soon after, and all of the other famous people were left to amuse one another.

I was getting an MIT reputation as a hostess who could not keep a guest of honor happy at his own party.

When summer approached, Seymour said we had to escape in order to get work done.

One April morning, he got up at 6:00 A.M., got into my car, and took off. He was going to find us summer lodgings. He came back that night, triumphant. For June, he had found us a studio apartment on the beach at Plum Island. For July, we would move to a rental in Gloucester. And then, in August, we could return to the tree house in Annisquam. This was a defining moment for Seymour, and perhaps a dangerous one. He wanted to show himself (and me) that we could have no plans, but then he could start a day at 6:00 A.M. with a pad of paper and a pen and return at midnight with everything in order.

These particular plans required a new car. At that time, our family car was my graduate school yellow 1970 Opel Kadett. When I met Seymour during the academic year 1975–76, he had a 1960s-era Cadillac convertible. But I had never seen it running, only in the MIT parking lot, with a plan to have it repaired someday.

Now Seymour wanted us to have a "love car," something that suited us as a couple. An Alfa Romeo. I knew nothing about cars, but when we drove to the Alfa dealership, Seymour immediately bonded with the handsome salesman, who had been a race car driver. Espresso appeared. He and Seymour were talking car talk, and suddenly Seymour knew how to speak Italian. "What do you desire in a car?" the tanned race car driver asked, politely switching back to English but looking only at Seymour. He repeated the question, this time appreciatively staring at me. *Bella!* Now they were pouring grappa. The two men had shifted gears and were talking about what a beautiful *woman* desired in a car.

The handsome Italian took us to a vintage blue Alfa GTV coupe. It had wood paneling and leather seats. By the end of the week, it could be ready to take us to Plum Island. For Seymour, there was no question. This was our love car.

As the happy owner of the Alfa Romeo "love car," summer 1977.

Seymour related to this car, a precision object, the way he related to planes. I had known for a while that Seymour was a pilot, and he explained to me that, in part, it was for therapeutic reasons. Another highly disorganized AI researcher, someone Seymour claimed was even more disorganized than he, had recommended it to him years ago. In flying, you have a checklist. You have to satisfy that checklist. Once flying, you know that any deviation is fatal. So you don't deviate. Seymour enjoyed instrument flying in particular. There, the constraints on him were even greater, the checklists even longer. So Seymour was an untidy housemate; he was disorganized about money and possessions. He was, however, a fastidious pilot. And a fastidious owner of an Alfa Romeo GTV, a car that would run only if everything about it was maintained to perfection.

In the terms that Seymour invented, flying, like Alfa owning, was a microworld in which he could feel free precisely because he was constrained. On our first flight together, we drove out to Hanscom Field, where his teacher, Pat, had a small Cessna plane ready for Seymour. And sure enough, just as Seymour had described it to me, I waited as Seymour and Pat went down a checklist. There was no side talk. Just the checklist. Auxiliary fuel pump—off. Flight controls—free and correct. It went on for a long time.

I had never seen Seymour as serene as when he went down the checklist. His flight plan had us flying to Plum Island to visit the summer house he had chosen for us. There was a small airfield. Once there, we rented a car and drove around the island. At the time, it was wild, almost deserted. After he showed me our summer place, we flew out again. Our lodgings were perfect: a second-floor studio overlooking the water.

On Plum Island, I worked on *Psychoanalytic Politics*, my book on Lacan, and Seymour and Marvin continued to collaborate on the "Society of Mind" project. That there was only one room was no problem because Seymour worked on an outdoor porch, and when we were alone, I wrote, as I always did, on the couch, with my legs up on a coffee table, with Grandma's taupe electric portable in front of me. When Marvin visited, he drove up in a vintage trailer that he parked on our front lawn. He and Seymour worked on the porch, and I sometimes moved to the table by the window, so as to overhear their conversations better.

With Seymour during a brief experiment sans
beard, summer 1977.

They were debating the fine points of emergence, how to think about mind as a machine that didn't require the invention of any brilliant organizing agent, only the collaboration of many simpleminded ones.

WHEN I MET SEYMOUR, he was in psychotherapy with Grete Bibring, a Cambridge psychoanalyst, then seventy-seven, a member of Freud's Vienna circle who had moved first to London and then to

Boston to escape the Nazis. During our time on Plum Island, Seymour went into Cambridge several days a week for his hour with Dr. Bibring. On one of Seymour's days in Cambridge, Marvin was on Plum Island with me, waiting for Seymour's return. Seymour had called ahead and told us to meet him at a restaurant in Newburyport for dinner. He was running errands in Cambridge after his appointment. We agreed on six o'clock. By seven thirty, there was no word, and Seymour had not called the restaurant. Seymour was often late, and Marvin seemed content to quietly wait on the restaurant porch, looking at the sunset and the summer sky. I was not so happy.

I tried, foolishly, perhaps, to ask Marvin's advice. Seymour, I now realized, was habitually late. Today was more the rule than the exception. This way of life, in which I was so often waiting for Seymour to show up, made me anxious. And I was upset that Marvin, too, had now been waiting several hours for Seymour. Marvin's calm expression did not change. He said, "Having the opportunity to talk with Seymour is a great privilege. You have a great privilege." He did not try to comfort me. Or offer me tips on how to cope. At 8:15, we decided to order. Marvin and I ate our seafood in silence. Marvin's attitude was that there was no fixing this or coping with this. Could I do this? If I could, I knew the terms. If I could not, that was understandable, but I would lose a great privilege.

Marvin and Seymour made a world where intellect was valued more highly than empathy, a good conversation more highly than common courtesy. Seymour was being as rude to Marvin as he was to me. Marvin was sharing his code: To be interesting, Seymour did not have to be kind. He had to be brilliant. I knew that the two men saw each other as lifelong friends. But that evening, as we ate in silence, this friendship seemed oddly transactional. And since the transaction was about computational ideas, it made sense that I seemed to have nothing to offer Marvin. I had a moment during that dinner when I felt competitive and thought, *Well, I could try to say something brilliant about Freud or Proust or someone else on my Chicago Great Books list*, but then I fell back. I wonder if I really believed that I could come up with something brilliant enough, something Marvin level. Also, I was angry (but at who?) because I was there not just for the privilege of conversation but for love and consideration. And I wanted to be Marvin's friend, not just a brainy purveyor of conversation. I rejected the game.

In the years since his death, Marvin has been associated with the scandal that surrounded the MIT Media Lab, an organization Seymour and Marvin had helped found. When the news erupted, Marvin was dead and we had not spent time together for decades. But my mind went back to this Newburyport dinner when he was willing to tolerate anything from Seymour and didn't see my intellectual usefulness. I understood why I had made the connection. Marvin spent his career in a value system where brilliant ideas laundered bad behavior.

Seymour was home at midnight. He apologized. Things had gotten hectic at MIT. The two friends were up at dawn, working on the porch.

Marvin Minsky and Seymour, summer 1977.

. . .

THAT SUMMER, just before our move to Gloucester, Dertouzos held a meeting to which I was invited, a retreat at which the leaders of the MIT computer science world were asked to come up with ideas about what the new personal computers might be used for. How might we keep them busy? Of course, "we" academics used computers for writing, but why would "regular" people have so much to write?

Seymour suggested that we would all become programmers. There were shrugs. Seymour's colleagues found this idea improbable. Computers for calendars? Tax returns? Address books? Somebody held up a tiny black book given out for free by the MIT/Harvard Cooperative Society, the campus bookstore. It had, he said, plenty of room for all of his appointments and contacts. And he had an international reputation and many international engagements. No one needed a computer calendar. No one really had a comeback. I thought of the Alto—the computer that would inspire the Macintosh. At that machine, I hadn't given a thought to what I could accomplish. It simply felt compelling.

It helps to remember that not that long ago, I was surrounded by cutting-edge researchers at MIT who were not sure how we would keep computers busy. Now it is clear that they keep us busy. We are their killer app.

17.

The Marriage of True Minds

I n fall 1977, Seymour and I went apartment hunting. We found a duplex apartment on Saint Botolph Street in the South End. Our furniture would be familiar to any graduate student in the 1970s. A round table on a cork pedestal. Director's chairs. Butterfly chairs. I brought the deep wine-colored velour couch from Marlborough Street that I had acquired just in time for the Lacan visit. It was our first real home together. I prefer a no-clutter atmosphere. Now that Seymour had vacated his loft, this would no longer be an option. Electronic and computer equipment trailed from room to room, cables from floor to floor. There were families of woks and fish poachers everywhere. Scraps of manuscripts everywhere. I struggled to live in greater harmony with what Seymour charmingly called his "bits and pieces." We planned our wedding for December.

When I met Seymour, I was committed to training as a psychoanalyst. That plan begins with course work and a personal analysis. I began my analysis during the fall that Seymour and I moved to Saint

Botolph Street. Dr. Philip Holzman's office was at Harvard in William James Hall, home to the Sociology and Psychology departments where I had recently received my joint doctorate, a detail that I didn't think much about when I met him.

I had for so long anticipated this analysis that it had a feeling of unreality when it actually began, as though I were in the movie of my analysis. I laid down on a couch four times a week. And said whatever came into my mind.

By early November, I had started to worry, because all I seemed to have on my mind were doubts about my life with Seymour. For a week, everything would be idyllic. And then Seymour would disappear—he would forget to tell me he had scheduled a trip to Europe. Or a conference in New York. I lost my bearings as to whether these were big things or little things. I didn't know whether to shrug and say, "Absentminded professor, harmless." Or were these signs of significant trouble? When I let my "psychologist self" think about it, I found myself trying to not think.

Then, as we planned the details of our marriage, I found out that I wasn't going to be Seymour's wife number two but wife number three. It wasn't the fact of it that bothered me. It was how I found out. Seymour hadn't told me. It emerged. In September, I told Seymour I wanted to start talking to rabbis, and of course, to get a marriage license, we would need his divorce papers from Diane's mother. Seymour nodded. Then he frowned.

What was the problem? Before he had married Diane's mother, he had been married, as a young man, to another woman. I remember having that same sick feeling as when Seymour had not told me about Diane. Why not tell me about this first marriage?

Seymour felt shy about this marriage because it had been traditional; he had been in a tux, married by a rabbi to a beautiful Jewish woman in South Africa. And he had been unfaithful. I tried to follow his reasoning. He hadn't told me because this first marriage would have reminded me of us. He had been unfaithful in a Jewish, white-wedding marriage. He thought *that* would wound me.

He hadn't been in touch with his first wife in a long time. And getting divorce papers from this marriage might be tricky. It was not so much that the wedding had taken place in South Africa as that it had been performed by a rabbi. For us to be married in a traditional Jewish ceremony, Seymour and his first wife needed to obtain a Jewish divorce. Seymour and I went to a Boston council of rabbis. We sat at a long table of men in robes. We asked to be excused from the requirement to bring a *get* (a Jewish divorce) to Seymour's Jewish remarriage. The answer was no. We were not excused. But several of the rabbis were fans of the Logo programming language, and Seymour was a rabbi celebrity. They were happy he had found joy.

In the end, Seymour and I were married by a nontraditional rabbi who did not require Seymour's formal Jewish divorce. But once again, when Seymour thought the truth would upset me, he hadn't presented it to me. It came out when he was backed into a corner. Daughter showing up at the door. Divorce papers he couldn't produce. I wondered if I gave out a signal that I could not handle the truth if the truth was hard to deal with. It was good that I asked myself these questions in analysis, because they led me back to my mother, who so often insisted on the not-truth. Was asking for the not-truth in my emotional DNA?

And then something happened that I could not bring myself to talk about in my analysis.

Seymour and I went to a downtown jewelry store and chose an engagement ring together—a small pear-shaped stone on a gold band. The one they had in the store fit perfectly, and the jeweler said that he would clean and polish it for me while we waited. Seymour stepped away to buy something at another counter. I sat down, waiting for my ring to be ready. I wondered what Seymour was looking at. Perhaps, I thought lovingly, he was getting something to mark our engagement for the two of us?

After a few minutes, I had my ring and Seymour had stepped away from the counter. I asked him what he had been doing. I forget the details, but it was something like, he had bought a charm for an ex-girlfriend who collected small gold bears on a bracelet. Now they were just friends. But she would like the bear charm. I had heard all about her. One of his many past loves.

I was hurt. Angry. Didn't I have the right to his full attention when we were shopping for my engagement ring? Seymour looked confused. "But I just bought you an engagement ring. This bear, it's nothing. I just bought you an engagement ring."

I went home alone, in a daze with my diamond ring in its box. Several hours later, Seymour showed up, distraught. I wondered where he had been. The thought crossed my mind that he had delivered his bear and sought advice about how to handle me. He was at our door with flowers. How could he make this up to me? Should we give the ring back and start fresh with a new one? I had no words. I had no confidence. I simply moved beyond. I put the pear-shaped diamond on my finger. The next day, I went to analysis disheveled and sleepless, but I did not tell this story to Dr. Holzman.

For a week I talked about many other things. Mostly I complained to Dr. Holzman about his office. When our sessions were after nine in the morning, and now they often were, I could hear his secretary chatting in the outer office, and worse, I could hear his graduate students chatting as well, many of whom I knew, since I had just recently been a Harvard graduate student myself. If I could hear them, couldn't they hear me? I told my analyst I was unhappy with this office setup: It was inhibiting my free associations. What did he think? Dr. Holzman asked: "Why are we talking about my office rather than your life?"

I went a certain distance in this analytic work and then I stalled. I was proceeding toward a marriage that I feared would not hold up to scrutiny. Yet I did not want to call it off. In psychoanalytic language, what I did is called "acting out." If you are in analysis, it is better to slow down making big decisions and talk about them first. You want to make sure you are acting with clarity. I was afraid that if I talked, I wouldn't act. I had conflicts, and instead of looking at them, I married Seymour.

RATHER THAN TALKING to Seymour about what might be on his mind, I chose to focus on our wedding. Everything fell into place. One morning, driving to work, I saw a white angora dress in a shop window in Harvard Square—a slim skirt and a simple sweater top with a keyhole detail at the neck. That same day, after I finished seeing my patients, I bought it and a pair of bone-colored leather high heels to match. Seymour's close colleague and friend at MIT, Nicholas Negroponte, offered to have the wedding in his beautiful Brookline carriage house. His wife, Elaine, knew about a place called Winston's Florists. In one visit, everything was arranged. White roses and Dutch tulips for every table. A small bouquet for me. Small corsages for my aunt and Seymour's mother, who was flying in from South Africa. Boutonnieres for Seymour and my grandfather. A chuppah made of greenery.

Seymour and I had a favorite restaurant in the Back Bay, and one night, after dinner, Seymour asked our waiter if he could speak to the chef. Right there, he told the chef that our meal had been superb and asked him if he would cook it at our wedding. The chef said, "Absolutely." If we were having forty people, he would bring some friends to help cook and serve. Done. Nicholas had a friend who was into calligraphy. So there was a beautiful wedding program—illustrated with the drawing that was on the cover of my favorite childhood version of Cinderella. Seymour and I went to Louis and bought him a wedding suit in a soft, mauve wool.

Seymour wanted to have something at the wedding that would be a reminder of our first date. He decided on puff-pastry swans, just like the swan boats in the Boston Public Garden. I didn't know swan pastries existed, but Seymour found a hotel that had them on the menu. The pastry chef decided that they needed to be preassembled and brought to our event on flat sheets. Marvin won my heart by volunteering for the job of ensuring that the swans arrived intact. He promised that if he needed to invent some contraption for transport, it would be invented.

On the day before the wedding, I had a manicure and pedicure, rare indulgences. The man who usually cut my hair at a salon on Newbury Street came to Saint Botolph Street to do my hair and put in a garland of flowers, a surprise from the elegant Elaine Negroponte. I felt beautiful in my dress. For good luck, Seymour hadn't seen it.

We did not write our own vows. Or make speeches. But there was one special thing in the ceremony. Just before the breaking of the glass, Seymour recited Shakespeare's sonnet 116. *Let me not to the marriage of true minds admit impediments.* Seymour and I had a lot of problems, and knew it, but that sonnet was how we thought about what we were doing. Every marriage has its mythology and that was ours. We hoped it would be enough.

For our honeymoon, Seymour and I spent a few days in New York.

Hugging myself with joy at my wedding, December 1977, Brookline, Massachusetts.

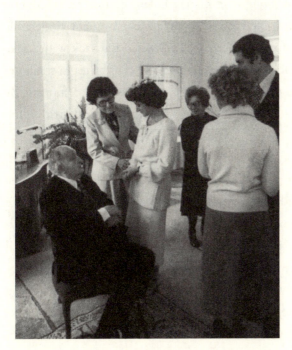

Sharing a moment with Mildred and Grandpa.

Nicholas suggested we stay at the UN Plaza because it had a swimming pool enclosed in glass on its twenty-seventh floor. On Monday morning, Seymour traveled to New York early on business. I arrived at the hotel later, at five. There was a message for Mrs. Papert.

I had decided not to take Seymour's name; by this point I had established myself professionally as Sherry Turkle. I didn't like being Turkle, but in my mind, I had made "Sherry Turkle" into a new person, the woman who studied psychoanalytic culture and computer culture. There was also this: MIT had a senior, famous Professor Papert and that was Seymour. I didn't want to be MIT's second Professor S. Papert. But seeing "Mrs. Papert" written out on the hotel stationery was thrilling.

On our final night in New York, there was an omen of trouble to come: Seymour bent over and could not stand up. For the first time, he told me that as a young man he had fallen off a ladder. Here was another story he hadn't wanted to share, an inconvenient vulnerability. I helped him into a hot bath and massaged his back with Vicks VapoRub, the only relevant medicinal thing I could find in the hotel gift shop, and we used steaming towels to make a hot compress. By morning, Seymour managed to get to our plane without a trip to the emergency room.

Within hours of our return to Boston, Marvin's wife, Gloria, found us a back surgeon at Massachusetts General Hospital. At the consultation, he said that Seymour had several herniated disks. He probably needed an operation to prevent nerve damage. But first Seymour should try an aggressive exercise program and should avoid all sitting for long periods. Back surgery, the surgeon said, should never be recommended, even by back surgeons. Seymour now wrote at a podium. We had one podium at home, another at work, and wherever he was, he greeted visitors while lying on the floor. I got used to "standing dinners." We ate at "high tables," leaning against them as you would a counter. During this time, Seymour made a lot of progress on a book he was writing on children and computers. It went through many titles. In the end, it would become *Mindstorms*. And he worked on examples of decentralized, emergent intelligence for his project with Marvin. As was always the case with Seymour, every constraint brought a greater capacity for concentration.

One day in early spring 1978, I came home to find Seymour lying on the floor of our living room, unable to move. I called an ambulance. At the hospital, he was sedated and there followed a flurry of tests, scans, blood work, and consultations. Surgery was scheduled almost immediately. Moments before Seymour was wheeled away from me to go to the operating room, I took a felt pen and wrote a note on his back: "Take care of this one. He is very loved."

SINCE IT WAS HARD for Seymour to navigate the stairs of our fourth-floor walk-up during his recuperation, he stayed at home, and for many months our South End apartment became a kind of MIT annex. Students came to discuss their research and help write proposals. Faculty to debate on current controversies about technology and children's learning.

One was Joseph Weizenbaum, an eminent computer scientist who took a philosophical stand against the field of artificial intelligence and more broadly about following computer science wherever it wants to take us. When I came to MIT, Weizenbaum was one of the first faculty members to seek me out. Given our collegial interests, Weizenbaum considered me a natural ally, and we began to teach together. Programs, argued Weizenbaum, can be written to help machines make decisions. But only people have the capacity for moral choice. This is ultimately what makes us human. And human choice is the product of judgment, not calculation. It includes nonmathematical factors, such as emotions.

Then Weizenbaum made a leap that I hadn't: It was therefore immoral to teach children to program. When he looked at the children Seymour was teaching, Weizenbaum didn't see the wonder of "powerful ideas." He saw the spread of a dangerous way of thinking to the young and vulnerable. Programming served as a primer in instrumental reason, a form of rationality that focused on the most efficient means to achieve an end but did not reflect on the values of that end. The act of programming, said Weizenbaum, encouraged programmers to live in the closed world of the machine. Where Seymour saw computers as a privileged place to learn, Weizenbaum saw a place where you could forget other people and your emotional and moral responsibilities to them.

Weizenbaum was offended that I was studying children learning to program. He believed it could only be my love for Seymour that led me to be anything but critical of such an obviously pernicious curriculum. Weizenbaum and I agreed completely on the incompetence of artificial intelligence for any role that required empathy. But I saw the effect of programming on children (and adults) as a topic for research. I saw programming as a Rorschach, a place where people expressed their very different cognitive and emotional styles. And I saw the computer as an evocative object that was provoking important conversations.

As soon as children began to consider how the computer worked, they were led to consider whether or not it was alive. Since the computer's programming made it seem "sort of alive," they wondered if people were programmed as well? How exactly, asked children, were people different from machines? The question of free will, I thought, was what sex had been to the Victorians: threat and obsession, taboo and fascination.

I thought these conversations were positive. I couldn't agree with Weizenbaum, who wanted me to say, prior to investigation, that putting children and computers together was always a bad thing.

I invited Weizenbaum to work with me; we could investigate children's responses to computers together. But where I saw empirical questions, he saw a philosophical absolute. On this, we agreed to disagree. Yet, at MIT, we were solid allies in a larger critique of the engineering culture.

Weizenbaum and I shared the view that engineering students needed to have an education open to the larger world of human experience and values. But in the MIT of the late 1970s, engineers were most likely to be taught that the products of their work were neutral tools and that feelings and social considerations had no place in the world of scientific facts.

In this culture, the pressure for perfection was enormous. The message was: If you put in the time, you can get *everything* right. There is one correct measurement and finding it is the engineer's moral responsibility. When, in all this pressure to get things right, things do go right, engineers are both celebrated and encouraged to generalize their methods. That means using the style of thinking that works in engineering to think about the world in general.

But the engineering aesthetic (you can understand everything; you can get everything to work with greater efficiency and less friction) runs into trouble when you use it to think about people and their social relationships. To understand people, the most important step often involves stopping to appreciate that you have a story with at least two points of view. There may not be measurements at all. The most relevant data may be feelings. Feelings aren't friction free but conflict ridden.

During my early days at MIT, a student committed suicide. He picked up a desk in the room he was in, used it as a battering ram to shatter the window, and, still holding onto the desk, plunged to his death through the shards of glass. Faculty were encouraged to talk with students about the incident. At the time, the chief psychiatrist at MIT and I spoke of this suicide as doubly traumatic for students. You could put yourself in the place of the desperate student. But also, the MIT landscape had been scarred by how this student expressed his pain. Others could have been killed by the falling body and desk. The student was angry at himself, MIT, we didn't know the rest.

I spoke with my classes about the incident, and in one class, a student observed that the suicidal student would have fallen at the same speed without the desk—those were the laws of physics—and his classmates seemed to like his comment. It defused tension with engineer bravado. The victim had not done the math correctly, they joked. I waited it out. Some students found their way to other feelings. About the stress of being at MIT. About their fears of never being good enough. Of being expected to be perfect. At MIT, the most admired students were the ones who took more upon themselves than anyone could possibly do. Students who felt on the edge had to look in complete control. That was the code of the engineer. Until then, I'd thought mostly about how I was being intellectually nurtured by MIT. Now I considered how these students could use a professor like me. I could help them look at their own stories with greater self-compassion.

SEYMOUR'S BACK WAS MENDING; I felt my anxiety over his recovery lifting. I was beginning to breathe again. And then things began to fall apart. One evening stays with me, but it was only one among many. Seymour and I expected company for dinner. Uncharacteristically, I was in charge of cooking.

On this particular night, the first course was a lentil soup Seymour had made in advance and I only had to reheat. Then there was a salmon course. I knew how to bake that, with some sea salt and butter. Then salad. And ice cream and cookies for dessert. Seymour was working at MIT and would buy wine on his way home. A detail remains with me. He wanted Sancerre. By seven, the guests had arrived, but Seymour had not. When an hour passed with no word from him, we decided to go ahead with dinner. Fortunately, our guests had brought some wine. Not Sancerre.

Seymour called around nine. He had forgotten our dinner altogether. But that wasn't why he was calling. He had flown from Logan Airport in Boston and was now at Kennedy Airport. He was on his way to Tunisia. As I recall, Seymour explained that a mathematician on his way to Tunis through New York had come to his office, and they began talking about a project that could perhaps bring the Logo language to the entire Tunisian school system. This, Seymour said, had always been his dream. To begin to work with large school systems.

There was nothing wrong with Seymour's dream. What was wrong was that there was nothing happening at Saint Botolph Street that he felt deserved advance notice. He later said that the fact that we didn't have children made him feel that such spontaneity should not have been a problem. The repetition of these incidents became a problem for me. There were more and more calls where Seymour announced that he had to be elsewhere. Immediately. He was in a thrilling conversation. He had seen something that swept him up, and he hoped I would understand that he could not turn away from this opportunity. Argentina. Costa Rica. London. I asked him if he was having an affair. He said no. But the spur-of-the-moment departures made what I considered a normal family life nearly impossible. A part of me felt unreasonable. I had married an artist, a pioneer, proselytizing for a cause he had worked on for decades.

I called the Boston Psychoanalytic Society and Institute to say that I was putting my candidacy on hold and would not be returning to my analysis with Dr. Holzman. I wrote him a letter, addressed and stamped it. I closed my eyes when I got to the mailbox. For right then, I chose my marriage over its scrutiny.

Seymour's psychoanalyst, Grete Bibring, had died during the summer of 1977, and, ever since, I had been trying to get Seymour back into treatment. Seymour resisted. He tried the psychiatrist to whom Dr. Bibring's patients had been referred but complained that this new therapist reminded him of a fish. I gently suggested that this might be a transference reaction, but Seymour wanted nothing to do with the fish. He apologized for his disappearances and impulsive behavior but insisted he was fine.

NOW IT WAS SUMMER 1978 and I wasn't fine. I suggested we go to Annisquam for the summer, a place we loved. At the time I thought of it as a refuge, but it was just as much a reprieve from confronting the reality of my distracted husband. That summer I shut my eyes to the trouble looming in my marriage and dove still deeper into work on children's first responses to "smart" electronic toys.

I was aware of my great privilege in having discovered this line of intellectual pursuit. Never again would I be able to hear children meeting a smart machine for the first time. I could hear with clarity what I had theorized: the computer provoking them to new thought, including about such fundamental things as what was special about being a person.

In Annisquam I interviewed children about the first generation of electronic toys and games just as they came on the market. There was Merlin (it played tic-tac-toe and other simple logic games), Simon (it asked you to repeat sound patterns), and Speak & Spell (it gave you words to spell or say). I brought all of these to a small playgroup of five-to-eight-year-olds that met in local homes and on the beach. The objects provoked striking conversations. In one, six-year-old Craig had just won a round of tic-tac-toe with Merlin and shared his "winning strategy" with his friends Robert, five, and Greg, eight.

CRAIG: Merlin doesn't know if it cheats. It won't know if it breaks. It doesn't know if you break it, Robert. It's not alive.

GREG: Someone taught Merlin to play. But he doesn't know if he wins or loses.

ROBERT: Yes, he does know if he loses. He makes different noises.

GREG: It's smart enough to make the right kinds of noises. But it doesn't really know if it loses. That's how you can cheat it. It doesn't know you are cheating. And when it cheats, it doesn't even know it's cheating.

Jenny, six, interrupted with disdain. "Greg, to cheat you have to know you are cheating. Knowing is part of cheating."

That Annisquam summer, four young children stood amid their shoreline sand castles and argued the moral and metaphysical status of a machine on the basis of its psychology: Does the machine know what it is doing? Does it have intentions, consciousness, feelings? What was important here was not the "yes or no" of whether these children thought computers cheated or even whether computers were alive. What was important was the quality of the conversation, both psychological and philosophical, that the objects evoked.

I thought of this new work as a study of "philosophy in everyday life." Over that summer, I discerned a significant shift in how children thought about life—and consciousness—from what the Swiss psychologist Jean Piaget had found in his classic studies beginning in the 1920s.

In Piaget's world, the world of traditional, nondigital objects, the idea of consciousness evolved side by side with the idea of life. As children associated life with the biological, it followed that consciousness became a property of animals and then was narrowed down to something that only people have—and maybe pets. But this was not how things were unfolding on the beach in Annisquam. The children I studied in 1978 were fine with the idea that their new toys, conscious machines, were not alive. At the time I wondered if they were the first generation to grow up with a split between the ideas of consciousness and life, the first generation who might grow up believing that human beings are not alone as aware intelligences. I was humbled.

And there were changes, too, in how children settled on what was alive. Piaget argued that in the world of traditional objects, children developed the concept of life by making finer and finer distinctions about the kind of physical activity that is evidence of life. In particular, children built the notion of life on progressive refinements of the concept of motion.

So a thing was alive if its physical motion came from within itself. Children were not always sure whether these new smart toys were alive or not alive, but it was clear, even to the youngest child, that physical movement was not the key to the puzzle. Children saw the relevant criteria as psychological and moral: Were the games aware, did they care, did they cheat?

Most remarkable, the first generation of computer toys helped children build theories of psychology. To make sense of how computers were different from people, children split the psychological. They used ideas such as "The game thinks like a person but it doesn't feel" with conviction. They were comfortable with a firm line beween the cognitive and affective.

A classical view of people as "rational animals" gave way to a new idea, people as "emotional machines."

But this categorization troubled me. It slid over the difference between what computational and human machines can experience— only people live in human bodies, have human life cycles, and are born to nurturing human mothers. Only people start out little in a world of grown-ups and grow up to be big, facing a new generation that they must nurture with what they have learned on their journey. Only people know pain and illness. Only people fear death.

When children settled on the idea that computers could think, and people could feel, I called it their "romantic reaction" to the computer presence. Computers were objects without feelings. People, in another class, had feelings, and that's what made them special. I was working on this people-are-not-objects material when I went to see Charlie and he told me that when I was an infant he had used me as a data source.

I had only recently learned that Freud had analyzed his daughter Anna, a transgression of a commonsense rule of psychoanalysis. Piaget, too, had used his children as experimental subjects. It was a time of dashed myths. I was haunted by fathers who looked at children and assumed object ownership rather than relationship.

18.

Coming Apart

At the end of the summer, Seymour came up with the idea that we should stay at the beach all year round. Our Saint Botolph Street apartment was being converted into a condominium and we couldn't afford to buy it. We had to move. Seymour suggested renting a house in Annisquam or Gloucester. I was tempted: Being near the ocean reliably takes me back to Rockaway. But there were practical considerations. As senior MIT faculty, Seymour had a light course load, mostly graduate supervision, but I was an assistant professor just starting out. I had teaching and administrative responsibilities almost every day. And although I had put my own analysis on hold, I was continuing my training as a clinical psychologist. I had patients and many hours of supervision. A three-hour commute seemed daunting. I argued for an apartment in Boston.

Now I understand that Seymour wanted a hideout as much as a home. He was easily distracted, and once distracted, life became chaotic. During the summer he promised Diane a trip to Disneyland. She joined us in Annisquam. But at the last minute, he canceled Disneyland because he remembered that he had promised computer scientist Allen Newell that he would join him at a conference in Australia. Seymour ended up making neither trip. He stayed in his room, writing, hoping that elegant work would compensate for disappointing both his daughter and an esteemed colleague.

I'm sure Seymour hoped that living out of town would help him stay grounded. But when he suggested living at the beach, he spoke only about how beautiful it was, how inexpensive the rent. Instead of helping us talk about his moods, distraction, and erratic behavior, I let him talk about lovely views and financial practicality. Previously, when I had tried to talk about our difficulties, he had apologized and disappeared. Now I was afraid of my anger. When he canceled Diane's Disneyland trip, I took her out for fried clams in Gloucester. Her eyes were down. She barely spoke. I, too, was having trouble with small talk. I felt too much in this daughter's skin. I felt left behind and disappointed. I was thinking of Charlie. Seymour was in pain. But he was causing real damage. We had a guest, a French friend, Patrick Miller, a psychoanalyst I had known since my Lacan year in Paris. Against the silence of our fish fry dinner table, Patrick said something around the idea that being a father and having a father were difficult. I remember a sense of relief at hearing this simple true thing. My eyes moistened. I began to find some words to go with my feelings.

After Disneyland, I approached Seymour in a less generous spirit than he deserved. Instead of tending to his fragility, I put my defenses up. Beauty and bargain prices at the beach? No, I told Seymour. We would live in Boston.

With the semester upon us, I quickly found the only three-bedroom apartment we could afford and called Seymour to look it over: the second floor of a house on Tappan Street in Brookline, a twenty-minute drive to MIT. The apartment had high ceilings, a dining room, a large kitchen, and a back porch. Each of us could have a study. In many ways, it was ideal. But it had scuffed linoleum and orange tiles in the kitchen and worn-out blue carpets and floral wallpaper in the bedrooms. Because it was a rental, we were not allowed to make "improvements."

On moving day, we had painters applying three coats of white paint over as much of the apartment as the owners would allow. But when I walked into our apartment and faced the baby-blue shag carpets, my breathing grew shallow. And then I felt faint. I sat on the bedroom floor and put my back to the flowery wallpaper. Even then, I understood my panic attack: With Seymour increasingly distracted, I wanted control over my space because I felt I was losing control over my life.

Seymour was gentle. Let the painters finish. Let the movers do their job. If you are unhappy in two weeks, we'll break the lease, pay some kind of penalty, and go somewhere else. I focused on Seymour. I loved him. I let myself relax. Tappan Street became our home. Seymour had a storage unit that yielded up a rough-hewn refectory table. I bought a set of reproduction bentwood Breuer chairs to put around it. I seemed to have gotten myself settled down.

IN NOVEMBER 1978, I was on the shuttle from Boston to New York, flying home for Thanksgiving, when I caught a glimpse of a book review in the *New York Times* with a stock photograph of Sigmund Freud. Someone in the row ahead of me was reading it. The title of the review was "The Psychoanalytic Tango." I wondered who had written a book about Freud in Argentina. But this review was about my book; the tango referred to the complex machinations of Lacan's Freudian School. I felt a sense of mission accomplished. Growing up, I read the *New York Times* every day. Having a book reviewed in its pages—this was something special to me.

Seymour reads me a positive review of *Psychoanalytic Politics* at Tappan Street, Brookline, toasting me with coffee, fall 1979.

So that Thanksgiving, as Mildred, Grandpa, Seymour, and I ate our Jewish/American Thanksgiving—Zabar's treats alongside turkey, stuffing, and cranberry sauce—I felt happy to bring my husband, my book, and my *New York Times* home to my family. But I was stalled by worry about Seymour. He was writing multiple books. He was barely sleeping. He was trying to start an international center. His sudden departures to "elsewhere" continued.

I felt I had let him down. I hadn't supported his desire to live at a distance from MIT. He must have understood that he needed to be at a physical remove from the pressures he felt at work. I still hadn't convinced him to go back into psychotherapy since Grete Bibring's death. And my own mind was restless. While my marriage was in crisis, I was preoccupied with finding Charlie.

The summer before, on the North Shore, my aunt Mildred had come to visit. I was happy to watch Seymour win her over. He knew that, from her point of view, he had a lot going against him as a husband. He wanted her to appreciate what he had to offer. He showered her with cooking affection (salmon in parchment, quenelles) and offered to take her flying. To my surprise, she agreed. She returned flushed but clearly pleased that she had been brave enough to try.

It was on this visit that I shared with my aunt that I had decided to find my father. No more desultory searches in telephone books for Charles Zimmermans. Only two months after I hired my New York ex-cop detective, I was sitting in the floral-papered bedroom on Tappan Street when he called to say he had found my father and gave me his address.

It was from Tappan Street in December 1979 that I wrote to Charles Zimmerman, and it's where I took the call when we made our date.

On the day before my visit, Seymour came with me to New York. For luck, we returned to the UN Plaza, the hotel where we had spent our honeymoon. We arrived on a Friday. My date with Charlie was for Saturday at noon. I couldn't decide if I wanted to meet Charlie alone or whether Seymour should be with me. I fell asleep, restless. When I woke up, at 3:00 A.M., Seymour was not in the room. He had left a note. "Out for coffee." I went to the lobby. The coffee shop was closed. I could not find him. I wandered the hotel. I felt abandoned. I had no idea if these feelings were justified. When I become angry, it always comes with self-doubt: I fear that I am too much Robert Bonowitz's grandchild. Seymour reappeared several hours later. Sleepless, he had taken his pad and paper and gone out searching for coffee and a quiet place to write. We quarreled. But it was pointless because I just wanted to be comforted. Now it was just a little past dawn. I still hadn't decided if I should see my father alone. Seymour suggested I take a swim. The gym and pool opened at six; I could decide later.

When I came out of the pool and into the gym reception area, Seymour was there, on the telephone, smiling. He was talking with one of the women he had been dating when we first met. Now she lived in New York, and he had made an appointment to meet her for lunch while I was with Charlie. He told me that he would be back at the hotel by 2:00 P.M. If I wanted him, I could call him then. I flew into a rage. I told him he must cancel his lunch. How could he be meeting with another woman? I left the hotel in a state of agitation. He didn't see the problem. She had a boyfriend. This was a friendly lunch. Why was I jealous of shadows? We managed to make a plan: I'd call and leave a message at the hotel if, when I was with my father, I wanted Seymour to join us.

Over the phone, Charlie gave me an address for our meeting and elaborate instructions for how to get there by subway from Manhattan. And detailed directions for how to walk to this address once I got out of the station. Memories came unbidden, of the very few times I have followed my father's instructions. Each time they felt like an order. Drink a cantaloupe malted. Take both oars in a rowboat. I hadn't wanted to drink the malted or row the boat alone. I had just wanted to please him. On my way to Charlie's apartment, I had to change trains twice. I had written down Charlie's directions. I hated to be in the subway, but I was happy to follow them. Doing as my father said. There had been so few times.

My destination was about a ten-minute walk from the subway. I had dressed up for the occasion, so I was walking in high heels. I would begin this meeting in pain. Charlie greeted me at the door in a sports coat and tie. This was when he asked if I had found him through his ad in the *New York Times*. It was the ad publicizing his book on Einstein. He said he had found arithmetical errors in the Michelson-Morley experiment on which Einstein's work depended. He claimed these mistakes were decisive, that Einstein's theory was incorrect.

It turned out that this was not his only book. He had written another, *Raw Food Vegetarianism and World Peace*, a petition to the United Nations to insist that all heads of state be vegetarians because this would make them less warlike. I felt a connection. I thought: *He is eccentric, true, but with intellectual passions.*

After we talked for a while, Charlie put both of his books on the table. In each he had already written: "To my daughter Sherry from Charles Zimmerman." I, too, had a book to share. I had brought him a copy of *Psychoanalytic Politics*. Now I inscribed it. I don't remember what I wrote. And then, while his girlfriend, Lila, was still working on getting our lunch ready in the kitchen, Charlie showed me a picture of him pushing me in a baby carriage.

I could understand that my gregarious, love-to-dance mother would have come to feel poorly matched with this odd, rather disconnected man. But why go to the extreme of cutting off all contact?

When I met Charlie, I was writing about children who, when they first met electronic "smart" toys, argued that people were unlike any object because people had feelings. So I was struck that one of the first things my father talked about was treating the infant me as an object. I remember making this connection at the time and thinking, *This idea is exhausting. I must return to analysis.*

As he searched for an envelope for the picture of me in the baby carriage and the clipping that announced my scholarship to Radcliffe, Charlie said that when I was a baby and my mother was not around, he experimented on me. He began to describe what he referred to as "our work."

In one experiment, he would remain in my presence but not speak to me, sometimes for hours. Or he would isolate me in a room and make no contact. Or he would sit with me but not touch me. He wanted to know how human infants responded to deprivation, he said, and how they behaved when deprivation was lifted.

With this story, my time of trying to find ways to identify with Charlie ended. Now I put myself my mother's place. For so many years I had resented her keeping my father from me; now these feelings fell away. She had fled him. She'd been trying to protect me from his appalling experiments. As soon as she found out about them, she had wanted only to escape. And with this story, I left the table to call Seymour. I needed him with me.

When Seymour arrived, I made Charlie tell his story of his experiments again. Seymour allowed his face to show only an interested, engaged look. But now that Charlie had an MIT mathematician in the house, he wanted to show off the details of his Einstein disproof. Words flew. Error. Factor. Speed of light. Seymour listened intently; he asked questions that interested Charlie. They sat side by side on the couch. Charlie handed Seymour pencils and paper. I had brought him a thing of value: a husband who could help get his Einstein news out to the world. Charlie had become all about the facts.

I thought about how both my parents had a vexed relationship with facts. My mother was willing to leave facts to the side; my father decided that extracting a set of facts from me could be equated to a relationship with me. It might be more accurate to say that Charlie thought that if he could make our relationship about our experiments, he would know what our relationship was. Now that he knew that both my husband and I were professsors, and at MIT to boot, he was hoping to make our relationship about publicizing the Einstein disproof. I had been objectified as a child. And now, again, I felt objectified. I didn't think Charlie was capable of anything else.

I saw the irony of the moment. In my work, I tried to move engineering and science students away from seeing people the way Charlie saw me.

I could hear that thirty years after the event, Charlie still sounded annoyed that on the day when I was about a year old and my mother found out about our experiments, she didn't "get it"—she didn't understand the importance of the work. Charlie said that my mother had gone out shopping and surprised him when she came home early. An experiment was in progress. When she came into the apartment, I was in a separate room from Charlie, crying. When she got upset, to appease her, Charlie offered her coauthorship when he published the findings from our studies. He said: "She wasn't even a real scientist. But I offered her credit and she turned it down!"

Instead, she returned to her parents' home in Brooklyn and took me with her.

While we were eating lunch, Charlie had put the clipping about my scholarship award into a manila envelope. After talking with Seymour, he added his books and the picture of the two of us when I was a baby. Lila took a Polaroid of Charlie and me on her living room couch. This, too, went into the envelope.

It was time to go. We promised to stay in touch, and Seymour told Charlie that he would carefully read the Einstein book. Charlie said that Seymour's help would be precious.

With Seymour, I retraced my steps and we took the subway back to the hotel. In the room, Seymour's work, his many papers, lay scattered around the room. I spent Sunday in bed. I could barely move or speak. Seymour worked in our room, in the hotel restaurant, in the lobby. On Monday morning, we were running late for our flight back to Boston and I asked Seymour to pack while I went for a swim. When I returned, the room had been tidied. Charlie's books were there and the clipping, but the photographs were missing. Hysterical, I postponed our departure. The room must be searched. The trash. Our baggage unpacked and repacked. I blamed Seymour for the missing objects, never recovered.

AWARDED SCHOLARSHIP

Cambridge, Massachusetts — Miss Sherry R. Turkle, daughter of Mr. and Mrs. Milton Turkle, of 29 Murdock Court, Brooklyn, has been awarded a scholarship to Radcliffe College in Cambridge, Mass., by the Radcliffe Club of New York. As a senior at the Abraham Lincoln High School, Miss Turkle was editor of the School newspaper, editor of the School current affairs magazine, secretary of General Organization, and a representative to the Brooklyn Borough Student Council. She received a citation from the Mayor's Committee on Scholastic Achievement. Mrs. Sidney Freidberg, 88 Central Park West, New York City, president of the New York Club, has worked with other members of the club during the past year to make this freshman scholarship possible.

The newspaper story about my scholarship to Radcliffe that Charlie had with him when I visited in December 1979.

ONLY WEEKS AFTER MEETING CHARLIE, Seymour and I were both in Dallas for work. Since New York we'd been careful around each other. I was aware that meeting Charlie had made me yearn for the kind of partner that Seymour was not. I didn't think I was being fair to him. I'd become sensitive, quick to tears. I thought of the expression "thin-skinned." I felt as though I had no skin.

Seymour and I had not been able to talk about the strain that my reunion with Charlie had imposed on our marriage. My father was an eccentric scientist. My husband, old enough to be my father, laughed about his foibles by joking about himself as an eccentric scientist. Of course, when Seymour met Charlie, what concerned him most was the story of the experiments. But there was a moment when Charlie was explaining his Einstein disproof to Seymour and had Seymour beside him on the couch, going over the math. Seymour looked up at me and knew I had been staring at them. Seymour's eyes registered pain. Later, Seymour asked if I saw the two of them as odd. As odd? Seymour was an internationally respected scientist. A chaired professor at MIT. In one way, this made no sense. But it had its own sense. When Seymour's eyes registered pain, he had seen something on my face. I had added an extra layer of fragility to our fragile marriage.

Our second anniversary had been the day after our return from New York. We were still tense. I was trying to find peaceful times for Seymour and me to be together. I envisaged Dallas as such a time. I had agreed to be on a radio show to discuss *Psychoanalytic Politics*; Seymour was going to consult at Texas Instruments. We should have plenty of time to relax. We checked into the downtown Hyatt, with its large internal atrium, and then an ice storm hit. The radio station canceled the interview. TI canceled the consulting. The airport closed. For Seymour, these were ideal working conditions. I was a favored dialogue partner and no one else could reach him.

We got down to our writing projects. I was working on a paper that would become "Computer as Rorschach," an early statement of how I saw the subjective side of this new technology. Seymour was working on *Mindstorms* and he was stuck on how to introduce its fundamental idea: Objects carry ideas; computers will bring new ideas into children's lives. I suggested that he do what I ask of my students at the start of each semester. I told Seymour he should write about an object that was important to him as a child and the ideas it carried. Something, obviously, that was not a computer. And say what it meant to him. Something personal.

Seymour did not hesitate. Gears. When Seymour was a child, he loved cars and gears. And playing with gears became a model for thinking about other things. Particularly mathematics. When Seymour told me the story of the gears, we hugged each other in joy. It was perfect. It was how his book should begin.

There was a twenty-four-hour coffee shop at the Dallas Hyatt. For three days, Seymour hardly left it. He wrote his story of gears and love and learning. Learning needs love and a connection to body and mind. An object, Seymour argued, can bring these things together. By the time Seymour met differential equations in high school, they felt like old friends because they bore a family resemblance to the gears he had been playing with since childhood. And there was this: First he played with the gears in his toy car. But then he played with the gears in his mind.

But if eager curriculum builders had said, "Let's put gears into the elementary school curriculum; they are so helpful for teaching mathematics," they would have missed the point. Different people will have their own versions of Seymour's gears. The computer is powerful as a learning object because it is protean. It can be so many different things for different people.

The coffee-shop essay expressed an idea that Seymour and I shared: We love the objects we think with; we think with the objects we love.

. . .

SEYMOUR AND I both had Guggenheim Fellowships for the academic year 1980–81. The plan was to spend the year together in New York. But our landlords at Tappan Street would not let us sublet our apartment. So our possessions once again went into storage. As always, this made me feel unmoored. This is a legacy, I think, of the night Milton threw my possessions in the garbage and told me to leave Murdock Court.

Seymour told me he wanted to rent a house in Maine for a long country summer before our year in New York. I thought this was a great idea, pleased to give him this "away" time since I had nixed the idea of our living year-round at the beach. But once I was in place in Maine, Seymour's commitments seemed to be in Boston. He said that as he was finishing *Mindstorms*, he also he wanted to work intensely with Marvin on the book they now called *The Society of Mind*. I'm sure he felt overcommitted. This meant that I was often alone in Maine, in an isolated house without a car. I didn't yet have a place to stay in New York, and we had given up our apartment in Boston.

One night in Maine, expecting Seymour, I roasted a chicken and filled the house with wildflowers. When, for perhaps the fifth time that summer, he called at six to say he was not coming home, I felt literally beside myself, observing what this jumpy, anxious Sherry would do next. Ever since meeting Charlie, I needed Seymour to be more constant. Instead, he seemed to be slipping away. And I was slipping away as well.

I heard rumors of an infidelity from a graduate student. I got unhelpfully hysterical, but Seymour denied it and I believed him. We decided that when we moved to New York, we would live in separate apartments and take it one step at a time. But after that summer in Maine, the shadow of other women trapped us in a tedious pattern. I would get angry; he would be sorry. And I wanted to have children. I think Seymour knew he would not be able to take on that responsibility, that he needed a way out. Characteristically, it was hard for us to have a real conversation.

WHILE WE WERE torn between coming apart and recommitting to a life together, Seymour took a job in Paris. Working with his MIT colleague, the digital design pioneer Nicholas Negroponte, Seymour became the scientific director for a major French government initiative, known in our family by its shorthand name, "le Centre Mondial." It promised to marry a technical and humanistic vision of what digital life could mean for education, economics, the arts, and politics. We agreed that I would live in Boston and continue to work toward tenure at MIT. We would furnish an apartment in Paris for the two of us. I would spend summers and vacations there. During the academic year, Seymour would come to Boston when he could.

We were seeing a therapist together to clarify the terms of our continuing commitment to each other. The way I saw it, the Paris commuting would work only if Seymour, wherever he was living, was faithful to me. I could support the Paris job; something like this had always been Seymour's dream. But he had to live there as a married man, faithful to me, as I would live in Boston as a married woman, faithful to him. Whatever the past, this had to be the future. I didn't come to this as a moral position. It was what I required emotionally. If this was unrealistic, the marriage would have to end. I thought that Seymour was on the same program. I may have misunderstood. Our therapist had a perspective that would be helpful to me moving forward: It doesn't always matter what people say. What matters is what you know, deeply know, your partner is capable of doing. From this perspective, Seymour had not shown a vocation to be a faithful husband to me. I had not shown a vocation to be in a fluid relationship.

I had received a publisher's advance for my book on computer culture. With Seymour's help, there was just enough money for a down payment on a small apartment on Marlborough Street in the Back Bay, my favorite part of Boston. Finally, a home from which I would not be evicted. I moved in with a sense of great relief, collecting my things from storage units in Brookline and Cambridge and Boston.

On one of Seymour's visits to Boston during the summer of 1982, we made a plan to return to Paris together. The idea of writing in our Paris apartment while Seymour worked at the Centre Mondial sounded wonderful. Seymour told me about great new restaurants he had discovered in our neighborhood. There might be a gala at the Centre Mondial. I bought an evening gown. I remember that my friend Nancy visited us before our departure to Paris. She took me aside and gently expressed reservations about my high spirits. Was I trying to match Seymour's mood? Evening gowns? Galas? Why was everything so ramped up? I knew she was right. Seymour told me not to worry. He had already gotten us two tickets on the Concorde.

Once in Paris, my mood when we got into the taxi was giddy. Seymour gave the driver the name of a small Left Bank hotel. But why? Seymour haltingly admitted that we couldn't go to our apartment because he had been living there with a woman that summer. Her books and clothes were in our apartment. He thought that seeing the apartment would upset me. As my time in Paris played out, I discovered that Seymour's daughter knew about the affair. I lost my balance. I might have been open to some kind of conversation, but Diane's presence in the story derailed me. I tried to explain to Seymour why involving Diane had crossed a line. In my mind, he must have known. He must have wanted our relationship to end. Reflecting back, I'm less sure. I think he saw Paris as a different world. The way he made decisions was to act and then see how he felt. He said that by the time I arrived, he realized he had a wife he loved and wanted to return to. The French have an expression. *Et encore.* And yet.

Everything that was wrong with our marriage is in this story: my high spirits because I lived in a fantasy world in which we could make this Paris plan together. Seymour's ability to spin a fantasy world for me to live in. How the fantasy was sustained by his ability to behave as though it were real. Seymour had the capacity to run several convincing story lines of what our life was about. And I was a woman you could lie to.

By fall 1982, it was clear that things were not working out at the Centre Mondial as Seymour and Nicholas had hoped. Seymour returned to Boston. Over time, painfully, we decided to divorce. I was relieved. For so long, I had been trapped in anger and a sense of betrayal. And now, with this decision, it didn't matter what I could forgive or not forgive. I could appreciate all that Seymour had been to me but move on with my life. And Seymour was free. He didn't need my forgiveness.

In the end, Seymour and I were better friends to each other when our divorce was a certainty. Knowing it was going to happen allowed us to care for each other as we separated our lives. Seymour accompanied me to a surgery to protect my fertility and tended to me during my recuperation. I helped him explore whether psychiatric medication, more sophisticated than only a few years before, might be helpful to him. Now he was thinking of some of his difficulties in terms of mood swings. Perhaps that was the state he was in when he got on a plane because he was in a compelling conversation. Perhaps that was why he promised total commitment to three or four projects. He went on a trial period of medication. We both held our breath. We had an understanding that if medication helped, we were both willing to reconsider our decision to divorce. I considered a Seymour without his flights to faraway locations, without his constant changes of plan. I didn't know what that might look like. The medication seemed to help, briefly, but Seymour said that drugs made him incapable of holding theorems in his head. He once joked that he chose mathematics over our marriage. I helped Seymour find a new therapist in Boston.

And, back in Boston, I was finally in a psychoanalysis I didn't run away from. And in which I told the truth. As best I could.

19.

The Last Experiment

Academics have a rule called "up or out." If you are on a tenure track, your university has to either promote you or deny you tenure. They can't just keep you around year to year. I began at MIT as an assistant professor in fall 1976. In fall 1983, my department considered my case while *The Second Self*, my book on computer culture, was in manuscript. I felt I had a strong case. Nevertheless, MIT said they wanted to take an additional year to consider, time to have my book published and reviewed. This wasn't a good sign. Since I had arrived at MIT, two other junior faculty members in my department had already been denied tenure because, I heard, their work had been seen as going "too far" and being "too critical" of technology. I worried that the same would be said of my book. All of this was unsettling because it didn't sound like criticism from an academic community; it was more like the defense of a tribe.

For *The Second Self*, I had interviewed hundreds of MIT students and faculty. I sat in on MIT lectures and seminars. I ate early-morning breakfasts and late-night Chinese food with computer hackers. I took programming courses at Harvard and MIT. I went to meetings of hobbyist computer clubs on the East and West coasts. And of course, there were my studies of children meeting computer toys and children learning to program. I wrote many true things about how the engineering culture sees the world. But instead of looking at my work as ethnography, where the working premise is that the researcher sits, listens, has conversations, and observes, the group of faculty judging my case was asking for information on my "data sets" and "experimental methods." They wanted questionnaires, surveys, coded interview protocols. If there were interview transcripts, how many linear feet of printout did I have on file? Of course, I had gone into my interviews with a set of questions for each community I studied (children with electronic toys, children using Logo computers, home-computer users, AI scientists, hackers, engineering students). This is what ethnographers do. But ethnographers also leave themselves open to what is happening in the moment, particularly in that moment when the interview is "officially" over but the conversation truly begins. I worried that these inquiries about my experimental protocols and linear feet of interview transcripts were a signal that my style of inquiry was not being accepted on its own terms.

The Second Self was systematic new work, pursued over six years. But at MIT, one way to dismiss work was to say that it was not "scientific." To make matters worse, I had signed a publishing contract with a large commercial press—Simon & Schuster. I thought this was wonderful. I wanted my book to reach as many readers as possible. And the advance relieved a financial pressure: I used it to help support my family. But I discovered that from the point of view of those at MIT judging my work, I should have been publishing my book with an academic press.

I had a tense conversation about this with my colleague Thomas Kuhn. A historian of science and the author of the pathbreaking *The Structure of Scientific Revolutions*, Kuhn had near godlike status in my department. Now, on the phone in the living room of my Boston apartment, my eyes filled with tears as Kuhn told me that publishing with Simon & Schuster had been a terrible mistake. I think he understood that something fundamental dogged my case.

In my interviews with MIT students and faculty closest to computer science and artificial intelligence, I had discerned that a value proposition accompanied their descriptions of their technical goals. Namely: It was good if people thought of themselves as digital machines, because that way, ambivalence could be avoided. You could experience the world in absolutes. People were ultimately data. Information objects. As Marvin Minsky had once put it, "the mind is a meat machine." My work highlighted this value proposition and challenged it.

WHEN I FIRST ARRIVED at MIT, I'd turned to the study of computer culture because it extended the themes of my earlier work—how ideas about mind break out into the popular culture. After I met Charles Zimmerman, I recognized deeper connections. Discovering how my father had seen me as an object to study helped me see this world of values in my own story.

While I was in suspense about my tenure case, I visited Charlie at his Queens apartment for the first time, a dark, unfurnished studio. He told me that he had something very important to say. He had never taken this tone before, and I was terrified.

He had come to a decision, Charlie said. He was going to distribute his disproof of Einstein at MIT. The one that began with the supposedly bad arithmetic in the Michelson-Morley experiment. Charlie had printed seventy new copies and was now making a list of who should get them. Certainly the president of MIT, the provost, and the deans. Certainly all the physicists. "What about the psychologists?" he asked me. He wanted my input.

Charlie once told me that when he tried to correspond with great physicists about his disproof of Einstein, it wasn't so much the rebuff that angered him as the suggestions of some that he write to another person who had also written to them with an objection to Einstein. In other words, my father should write to someone these eminent scientists viewed as a fellow member of Charlie's fraternity of crank scientists.

Once, at a dinner, I heard Victor Weisskopf, the legendary MIT physicist who had studied with Niels Bohr, regale the table with how he handled the many letters he received from oddball scientists: "They are so intense. So well-meaning. I put their letters in folders according to their interests and try to match them. But it can backfire. Sometimes they write back to me, outraged that I have set them up with a crackpot."

Charlie felt the scorn of being one of Weisskopf's outraged "crackpots." I had wanted to feel like Charlie's legacy, that I had brought him the academic legitimacy he could not accomplish for himself. But as he saw it, MIT had not taken him seriously and I was his revenge.

Though I had seen Charlie several times a year since our first reunion, I had never seen him happy or excited. Not even on that first day we met. Now, in his studio, there was the beginning of something, not a smile but a kind of grimace. He explained that he had taken care of all the details, including the purchase of the necessary stationery—I glanced over at a pile of manila envelopes. And he had written a cover letter. He was going to have it printed and he would sign all the copies. He pointed to the screen of his computer monitor so that I could read his letter to the MIT faculty. It was short. He introduced himself as a scientist who had been distributing his dis-proof of Einstein for fifteen years. He had already sent it to numerous members of the MIT faculty, he wrote, but they had not adequately responded. Now his daughter was on the faculty and he was dedicat-ing his book to her. He was enclosing it with this letter.

I felt like a child with an all-powerful adult, a sure sign that I was not being altogether rational. In the moment, all I remember saying was that I was sorry, but I wasn't feeling well and had to cut my visit short. I asked him to please not do anything with the books until we discussed this further. Sending them was not a good idea, I said. I didn't get anything out of him. I don't remember our good-bye. I flew home to Boston immediately. I wanted to talk to my friends, my ana-lyst, and my MIT dean, Harry Hanham, who had been so helpful during the Lacan visit.

I told Dean Hanham that I had recently found my biological father and unfortunately, he was not altogether well. I told him a bit about Charlie's history and shared his current plan. I waited for the dean to smile. I was hoping he would tell me to put this distraction out of my mind. After all, MIT was a sophisticated place. A crank-scientist father was not worth worrying about. The dean didn't say that. He understood that the opposition to my appointment had to do with my not being "on board" with the MIT ethos, with my running against the grain. This kerfuffle would not be helpful. If they already saw me as a woman they didn't want around because I didn't do science—and why shouldn't MIT have social scientists who did science?—then this told them that I was connected to something bogus and unseemly.

Dean Hanham was clear: I should try to stop my father from sending those books.

But how? My friends' suggestions were projections of their personalities. Threaten to never see Charlie again if he sent out the books. Forcibly, physically pick up the books and destroy them. Take them away from Charlie and say I had mailed them to the relevant people; then have a few friends pretend to be physicists and write him responses on MIT stationery. Seymour and I were now separated, but we were still close. He thought we should cajole Charlie. He offered to approach him, all smiles, and tell him that it was never good to send out scientific materials "cold." Seymour would promise to prepare the ground with influential figures. Charlie and he could discuss the Einstein disproof and strategize about possible intellectual partnerships. Nothing would come of it, but Charlie would be diverted past the tenure vote. I was impressed at how like Seymour this strategy was. Seductive. Confident in his powers of complicity.

Finally, my psychoanalyst gave me advice, in something of a departure from neutral analyst mode. She had a strong clinical opinion: My father had never sought me out. He had been content to be out of my life. I had pursued him, stimulated him. I remember a phrase she used. "You activated him," she said. He had been inert for over thirty years and I "activated" him. As she spoke, the image that came to mind, unbidden, was of electrons in their orbits. If I dropped out, she said, he would be deactivated. That's the word she used: "deactivated." It seemed so telling—she used an object word. What I had to do now was *nothing*. And he would do nothing. I did as she suggested. In response to my inaction, my father did indeed deactivate. He never sent the books.

I didn't hear from my father for a year, until he once again wanted a favor from me. He wrote to say he was ill and that he had refused all standard treatment. He believed only in macrobiotic healing. The Kushi Institute, the center of such healing, was in Boston. He wanted my help.

I told Charlie I would find him a macrobiotic cook in Queens who would deliver meals to him, and I set us up on a schedule of regular visits to check in. But soon he was too frail for this plan. He was in a nursing home and calling to complain about the food. When I arrived at his bedside, his cheeks were sunken, his voice shaky. We didn't talk much of the past or the future, of MIT or Einstein. I brought macrobiotic food and sat by his side.

After he died, I was there to bury my father and, according to his wishes, had a rabbi perform the traditional Orthodox service at his graveside. He didn't know how to be a father, but while I was growing up, my connection to the idea of him, to a fantasy that he had somehow been special, a scientist father, had given me courage. That was worth a lot.

And Charlie brought something unexpected: a reconciliation with my long-dead mother. She'd faced the reality of Charlie's deprivation experiments and said no. And I now understood why she had devoted herself, clumsily but passionately, to keeping me from him. She had protected me.

IN FALL 1984, I received a letter from my department head saying that I had been denied tenure.

When I looked at this letter, I thought: This was not right. *Psycho-analytic Politics* and *The Second Self* were significant. At MIT, I had found new ways to write about the inner history of technology. And I had begun to investigate the new field of computers in education: With my colleague Donald Schön and a small research team, I was studying Project Athena, the introduction of educational software across the MIT curriculum. How did using simulation technology in classrooms and laboratories change how students and faculty approached their subjects and one another?

But I had a lot going against me. My work was not in the formal, experimental tradition that MIT was comfortable with. I was critical of the engineering mind-set. There were few women at MIT and none other than me in my department. My all-male department colleagues were cordial but barely spoke to me outside of faculty meetings, perhaps to avoid any appearance of impropriety. They, on the other hand, played squash together. They went out to lunch and drinks together. They socialized with one another in couples. I would learn about these events only when I would walk into faculty meetings and overhear stories of yesterday's fun.

When my tenure case was on the line, I was surprised and moved when a colleague who had just read the manuscript of *The Second Self* came into my office and said: "I had no idea. Your work is wonderful. I don't know anything like it. I just had no idea." In our many years of working together, this man had not hit on me or belittled me. He had nothing against me. I was just invisible to him. And then he read my work and liked it. My story is not unusual. It's the less sordid side to gender discrimination in academics. And so many other places.

Still, I believed I had the resources to put up a fight for my tenure. The dean, Harry Hanham, and the former provost, Walter Rosenblith, were on my side. My case had been approved in my department and in the School of Humanities and Social Sciences. Things had stalled further up. Because of this, I think, my department head, Carl Kaysen, gave me a great gift. He broke the rules of confidentiality that normally would have surrounded my case and gave me a copy of the reference letters that had been filed to make (and break) my promotion. There were positive letters but others that definitely could be used against me. Not surprisingly, I saw that if you asked experimentalists to evaluate ethnographers, they pointed out that ethnographers don't do experiments and made this seem like a black mark.

I also discovered that a new rule loomed over my case: For tenure, MIT wanted me to be in two departments and not just the one department, Science, Technology, and Society (STS), in which I had my appointment. That rule would apply to me and to all future appointments in STS. My troubles seemed part of a larger challenge to critical studies of science and technology at MIT. If every faculty member in STS also belonged to another department, this meant that if you someday wanted to disband STS, everyone would have a place to go.

I summoned my courage and made an appointment to see the provost of MIT, the physicist Francis Low. He offered me coffee and a seat on his sofa. I thanked him and said that I didn't want to be too comfortable and sat at his conference table in a straight-backed chair. I told him that I thought the Institute should reconsider my case.

One of the reasons to deny me tenure, I said, seemed to be because of a new Institute rule that required me to have a joint appointment in my home department and a *second* department. But when I was hired, I was not informed that I needed a joint appointment. This was a *new* rule. It was surely unfair to create a new rule just as I was coming up for tenure. Also, there was a man in my department who was coming up for tenure. MIT had quickly found him a second department in order to comply with this new rule and then had promoted him. I'm sure he deserved his promotion. But why could MIT not promote and find a place for a successful woman while doing the same for her male peer? Before we discussed any assessments of my work, I told Provost Low, I would like to get this matter cleared up. The meeting ended. We shook hands. No smiles.

Shortly afterward, I was in my office when I received a hand-delivered letter from Low saying that the decision on my tenure had been reversed.

I had been brought up to succeed by turning in my best work, and now my best work was an institutional irritant. It's hard to accept an in-house critic, no matter how clever. My department had supported me but did not protect me when a new rule meant that I would certainly be dismissed.

I learned some things from this fight.

It's hard to be a difficult woman, but sometimes you have to step up. I didn't like working in a community that didn't want me, but I chose to stay on because MIT nurtured me intellectually—I was in the right place to study the psychology and ethics of digital culture. I wanted my job and thought I deserved to have it.

Fight first on the ground you share with your opponent. In my conversation with my faculty colleagues, with the dean, and with Francis Low, I didn't lead with the gender argument or rebut the criticisms of my work as antitechnology or qualitative. I knew that if I stayed at MIT, I would be fighting these battles for decades to come. Instead, I fought on ground where it was easiest for MIT to admit an oversight that then allowed me to stay there and do the work.

Don't underestimate the price of a fight. I "won," but for many years, at least in my mind, my case confirmed me as an outsider. I was not admired for my defiance. Women who are dispensed with and come back to make trouble are not likable, even when they win on their merits. And instead of feeling proud that I had stood up for myself, I felt ashamed that I had been forced to do so. I exiled myself. I attended departmental meetings, taught my courses, did my research, and immersed myself in my students' writing. I chose to stay off the larger MIT stage.

We experience our lives as segmented until, in a moment of crisis or decision, things start to come together. So even when I got MIT's imprimatur, I never had a sense of belonging. Real daughters don't have to argue their case before a jury. Real daughters don't get legalistic letters that tell them to be gone and that they then need to reverse by the power of their wits. Nor, it crossed my mind, do real daughters have to hire detectives to track down fathers who have disappeared for decades. This is not a good way to think about success at work. Or about belonging to a community of peers. But it was how I felt.

MIT treated me as an inconvenient object. And I was part of an inconvenient department that could be made more convenient if everyone in it could also be placed somewhere else. When it came time to deal with me, MIT made a rule that made no sense given why I had been hired and what I had been asked to do, but the institution applied the algorithm anyway. And everyone seemed to go along. Rule-based thinking could be used to avoid considering the person at hand. What I was studying at MIT had become lit from within.

20.

The Assault on Empathy

I t had taken me nearly a decade since my arrival in building 20, but by spring 1985, I had claimed my professional ground. *The Second Self* had been published—I had begun to tell the story of how computers change the way we think, especially about ourselves. At MIT, both the technology and the values of a new era were taking shape in front of me.

Now that I had tenure, I faced Thomas Kuhn's objection to Simon & Schuster with composure. I was happy with my decision. I thought that everyone should be concerned about the emotional and social aspects of computer culture. I was committed to writing both for the academy and beyond it, for educators, parents, policy makers, and the business world. We were all in this together. I was speaking to Girl Scout troops (computers weren't just for boys) and clinical psychologists (they needed to get involved with computers; these machines were going to change their patients' lives).

During a media interview about *The Second Self,* I had a life-changing moment. A reporter profiling me for *Esquire*'s "40 under 40" issue wanted to include some personal background. What did my father do for a living? He knew my mother had died. But what about my father? There was no thank-you to a father in the acknowledgments of my book. Had he died?

Panic silenced me. I had omitted Milton from my acknowledgments because, well, he hadn't helped. I hadn't practiced a smooth public version of "I am not close with Milton Turkle." Nor was I ready to mention any other father. As far as I knew, Susan and Bruce, my half siblings, knew nothing about any other father. I had kept my mother's secret. A magazine article was not the place for big revelations. So in this *Esquire* interview, I ventured into the ridiculous. "This interview can only be about the substance of my work, not my personal life," said the woman who stood for the idea that thought and feeling are one. In the published story, the interviewer notes that I am reduced to silence when he pursues the simplest personal question. Perceptively, he asks: "Why choose masks unless you're more comfortable with the third person than the first?"

That was December 1985. Immediately afterward, I spoke with Susan and Bruce about Charlie. They told me that Milton had recently told them about my adoption. His decision seemed tied up with my not thanking him in the acknowledgments of *The Second Self*. Then I spoke with Milton. That went much like our final conversations on Ocean Parkway. He told me what I owed him: a thank-you in my book and a public statement that he was my father. I made no progress on getting him to see things from my point of view. I wished him health. And told him I was glad that Susan and Bruce now knew the truth.

I owe a lot to that writer from *Esquire*. By that spring, I could tell people the story of my life. And the liberation that came from my getting tenure meant that I no longer lived in fear of Charlie and his pile of preaddressed envelopes or of MIT finding me out as too much a humanist or too much a Freudian. When *Ms. Magazine* had named me a Woman of the Year the previous fall, I hid it from my colleagues. Now I could relax, and I was free to study what I found most compelling.

As a *Ms. Magazine* Woman of the Year, January 1985.

I was at MIT when the first Macintosh computer—the spiritual descendant of the Alto from Xerox PARC—arrived at Seymour's research group. People stood around just to watch it be unwrapped. And then to stare. Fonts. A mouse. Windows. Pull-down menus. Icons.

The personal computers of the 1970s and the IBM PC of the early 1980s presented themselves as potentially reducible to their underlying mechanisms. When you typed commands, you understood that you were talking to the operating system, so you knew that there was one. And if you wanted to, you could customize your user experience, getting closer and closer to the machine's hardware. This new Apple presented the user with a simulated desktop and icons on a screen—representations of file folders, documents, a trash can—that offered nothing to suggest how their underlying structure could be known. The system told you to stay on the surface and to take things at interface value. When the world comes to us in simulation, we lose a sense of what lies beneath.

And we learn to not care. The Macintosh gave more than a sleeker path to get things done. It introduced a new way to think. Apple called its interface "transparent." But this transparency was what we used to mean when we said "opacity."

My earlier question—how does technology change the way we think?—was back in a new form. I had begun with the shift from meaning to mechanism. Now, in the context of computing, I would look at the move from mechanism to simulation. From transparency to opacity. When I first came to MIT, I taught against the fantasy that technology could solve every problem. Simulation burnished another fantasy: the idea that technology would solve the problems it caused. If we are lonely, we will meet in virtual reality.

In the new world of online communities, you could show up as an aspect of yourself, a younger self, a self of a different gender, or any other self you could plausibly create. In the early 1990s, people "cycled through" their real and virtual lives. Boundaries blurred. "RL," real life, as one young man told me, was "just another window." But even as he and I had that conversation, we were talking about a dying way of life—people "visiting" their online lives when they "went" to their computers. Soon we would all be connected to our machines and each other, all the time. With mobile connectivity, there would be no sharp distinction between the virtual and the "real." We would accept what we did on our screens as real enough.

I found myself in the center of technology's perfect storm: When we chatted with online programs, we were alone but could create the illusion of being together. With our always-on digital connections, we were together with other people but could end up feeling strangely alone. The computer offered the illusion of companionship without the demands of friendship. You could interact but never feel vulnerable to another person.

Technology has always promised efficiency, control, and certainty. Now technology suggested it would minimize social friction, the human interactions that caused emotional stress. You can hide behind a screen or behind a conversation with a program.

In either case, you have more efficiency because you have less vulnerability. With technical mediation, the emotionally rough becomes smooth, that which had friction can become friction-free. But who thinks that a life without conflict, in which we don't have to face the choices we've made or deal with troublesome people, is a better life? Apparently, technology does.

Technology was not wise. It proposed one thing, but life taught another. On our screens we became eloquent but edited our thoughts. Face-to-face, when we stumbled and lost our words, we revealed ourselves most to one another. Online, we preached authenticity but practiced self-curation. We were constantly in touch yet lonelier than before. And when we are lonely, we are tempted.

I studied the cost of our tethered lives as I dealt with the emotional fallout of meeting my father. The importance of defending the human ability to show empathy of an authentic kind had been underscored by conversations with Charlie, who had not seemed capable of empathy of any kind.

And my work was marked by becoming a mother. I married soon after my divorce from Seymour. An avid reader, a lover of classical art and rock and roll, Ralph Willard charmed me with his energy and appetite for life. What we shared most of all, during our decade together, was our commitment to family. Our daughter, Rebecca, was born in 1991. By 1995, when I wrote *Life on the Screen* about the implications of online identity for intimacy and empathy, I was no longer just an academic studying digital technology; I was a mother of a preschool child who wanted to play games on my computer. And who soon wanted to go online. My research and personal life had to align—I couldn't write my books one way and live another.

Rebecca was thirteen when Mark Zuckerberg launched Facebook. Before Facebook, my work had been of interest to some, but now the culture caught up with my professional concerns. I was continually pressed for my opinions on parents, children, and social media. On a personal level, having a child brought my values into focus. Considering the human is always the

I am reimagined as a cyberdiva (and trying to look like my mother in her glamour shot) for the book jacket of *Life on the Screen*, summer 1995.

best guide for how to build technology. Our first question must always be: What are we trying to maximize with our inventions?

I wanted to raise an empathic child. And I knew that without the ability to spend quiet time alone, that would be impossible. But that was where screens began to get us into trouble. Our capacity for solitude is undermined as soon as we introduce a screen. Screens not only distract us but encourage us to look to others for our sense of self. What is lost when this new circle draws us in? Attention to others. Attention to oneself. The capacity for solitude without stimulation— which is where the capacity for empathy is born. We can't relate to others until we are comfortable with ourselves. That's a psychoanalytic first principle: If you don't teach your children to be alone, they'll only know how to be lonely.

When we speak face-to-face, we attend to more than the content of the conversation. We also attend to one another. Communicating on screens makes us feel less vulnerable, but empathy requires vulnerability. And it's our capacity to be vulnerable that makes us most human. Finally I came to this: Technology makes us forget what we know about life. As it confronts us with the question of what we most value about life.

When Rebecca started high school in 2005 and began using Facebook, I was several years into studying adolescents and social media, interviewing students about their attitudes about privacy. One young woman, an early Facebook enthusiast, told me she wasn't much concerned. She said: "Who would care about me and my little life?"

Now we know the answer: When we are online and when we are tracked by our devices our lives are bought and sold in bits and pieces to the highest bidder and for any purpose.

When I first considered that question—"Who would care about me and my little life?"—it led me to ask whether we could have intimacy without privacy and whether we could have democracy without privacy. I argued that the answer was no, but I thought of them as two separate questions. I had a lot to learn: The social-media business model evolved to sell our privacy in ways that fracture both our intimacy and our democracy.

But even after people could see this, they didn't want to talk about it. We had a love affair with a technology that seemed magical. And like all magic, it worked by commanding our attention so that we took our eyes off what was actually going on.

Today we can no longer ask, "Who would care about us and our little lives?" Now the question is "How much do we care about one another?"

As I finish this book in the fall of 2020, we find ourselves alone

My TED talk: "Connected, but Alone?" Vancouver, March 2012.

together, exactly there. In the crucible of an enforced isolation, we explored the limits of where our screens can take us. As technology became our lifeline, we realized how much we missed the full embrace of the human.

I think often of my lessons in *dépaysement*: To see more clearly, make the natural seem foreign. The amazing thing about living through dramatic change is you are right there when something that once seemed odd begins to seem natural. The trick is to remember why it once seemed odd, because that might be a reason worth remembering. We must remember when it felt most natural to communicate by text or Zoom or online post instead of having face-to-face conversations. Even when sharing intimate sentiments. Or condolences.

People Are Not Objects

G rowing up, I was part of my family but felt that something was off. Silence about my father and my name was taken for granted, but it wasn't right. So I viewed everything that *was* there with special attention. I had to go rooting around in musty cupboards to figure out who I might be.

Since the rules never seemed natural, I believed things could be another way. I developed an outsider's clarity. I carried it with me beyond childhood. I was a stranger at Radcliffe, certainly. And in France. I grew into a braver woman, developing strengths through a life lived more as a visitor than as someone who feels at home. I learned that loneliness is not fatal. I found solitude, the kind of being alone that allows you to discover your own company. All of this sustained me at MIT, where my academic work made me something of a killjoy in the American love affair with technology.

I devoted myself to exploring my own life in practices that asked me, essentially, to become a stranger to my own voice in order to hear it in a different way: I did this in psychoanalytic work of the classical kind, where my analyst sat behind me and I, as a patient, reclined on a couch and free-associated four days a week. And I continued in psychoanalytic psychotherapy, where the patient and analyst are face-to-face.

Writing this book was another kind of displacement and brought its own discoveries, among the most precious a new appreciation for my mother's complexity. She had to face that Charlie used me for his experiments, deprived me of his voice, attention, and touch. Did she feel that by not learning of them sooner, she bore responsibility? After she left him, perhaps she began to lie to herself about them or endeavored to forget them. Little by little, other lies and other kinds of forgetting may have seemed acceptable as well. Whenever I think about her being alone with this secret, I feel a pull toward her, a wish to comfort her, and something inside me becomes undone.

I've reconsidered the other secrets that she and I shared—especially my never-repeated "educational" shower with a naked Milton on our first morning as a new family in Rockaway. My mother had so recently removed me from one set of experiments and then, with a new husband, was complicit in another.

And yet I remember her dressed and coiffed outside the shower stall, bridal, smiling, happy to be embarked on a new life. I think she wanted to include me in her success. We were going to be a different kind of family from her parents. She was trying to assert herself as the sister who acted on new ideas. Not as intellectual as Mildred, but perhaps more advanced. She and Milton might have been reading articles or books on progressive child psychology. This is something that no one in her Bonowitz family would do. But this is the kind of thing that Milton, I would later learn, loved to do—to feel that he had consulted the experts. The shower was to educate me, yes. But also it was to make my mother feel that, although this time she hadn't married a chemist, she was with an intellectual man. She's living across a set of pavers from her parents and sister in Lafayette Court and trying to feel special. On that first morning, she wanted to feel that she was on her way, with me, to something new.

I have kept our pact. I dream of her holding my face. Even when I am as old as Grandpa and as old as Grandma, I'll always love you. My love for her has expanded as I've learned more about her, thought more about her.

My mother had her own temptations. For elegant things. For social status. My mother, I think, would not only have wanted a Facebook page; she would have wanted to be an Instagram influencer. But when it came to the crunch, she blew up the marriage that she thought made her appear successful. She called an end to the experiment. What she moved us to was far less than what she had dreamed it might be. But she knew that a child could not flourish in Charlie's Bayside laboratory.

THE WAY WE LIVE NOW is an experiment in which we are the human subjects—treated as objects by the technology we have created. Our apps use us as much as we use our apps.

We are treated as objects when we are swept up as data to be bought and sold on an international market. Or when our attention is manipulated by our devices, not just to keep us glued to them but to determine what we read, what images we see, and what programs get to see us. We reduce ourselves to objects when we are addressed by machine-generated text or voices, because to be understood, we can only respond in ways that such objects can understand. When we are treated as objects, we are encouraged to objectify one another and, of course, ourselves.

A virtual assistant or chatbot that offers friendship reduces a person to lines of code, because that's all it knows how to do. But now technologists argue that to get the most out of such programs, we should treat them as the people they're pretending to be. However, if we put ourselves on the level of the machines we've created, we elevate them and diminish ourselves. We start to say that relationships between people and machines are "interpersonal." There's no sense to that.

But once people say it and once children hear it, we forget that it has no meaning. It just starts to be how we talk. That's the unacknowledged experiment. How we talk changes how we see ourselves. I remember when, in the late seventies, my colleague Joseph Weizenbaum came to tell me how upset he was that his secretary and graduate students wanted to be alone to chat with a computer program he had written, a simple program called ELIZA that could fake a conversation in the style of a Rogerian psychotherapist. Everyone in his laboratory knew that ELIZA didn't understand them, but it didn't seem to matter. Today our technology is fancier. Our vulnerability is the same.

It's time for us to call an end to the experiment. It's not too late to say enough is enough. The first step is distancing ourselves from this new normal to reclaim our complex selves. We are people with bodies and emotional and social histories. The more we appreciate all of that, the less likely we are to think that we should be made machine readable.

To fix our crisis of intimacy and privacy, of empathy and human connection, we don't need more apps. We need one another. We are the empathy app. And we have the potential to do the right thing when it counts. It's not too late to reshape the digital to serve the human.

My mother got us from Bayside to Murdock Court, from something toxic to something imperfect with which I could negotiate. And that's why she remains my heroine.

That she put me on a difficult path seems like a metaphor for what lies ahead when we challenge technology's status quo. I could navigate the Turkle household because the troubles I faced there involved people in their emotional complexity—including jealousy and irrationality. I grew up talking my way through it. In contrast, if you're the object in an experiment, there's no talk-back. As we face down a suite of technologies that objectify us, we can insist on a future where we can construct new terms, a new way of living with our inventions. Technology presents itself as opaque, impenetrable, inevitable as it has been delivered. It is none of those things. It can be analyzed, made transparent, modified, and brought under control. Technology proposes a noble leap that will bond us so tightly to objects that we become as one with them. To resist that takes hard work. Because not only does technology offer the friction-free as where it wants to take us, but it makes the path to getting there the one of least resistance. But it's the other path that politics and human relationships have in common: the uncertain glory of a stumbling climb. It's not the world of the friction-free. It's the world of negotiating with people—unknown, disappointing, transcendent. It's ours.

It's June 2018 and I'm in Barcelona, a city in which I have little history. I've been a tourist here twice. Once I came to see the wonderful Gaudí buildings and once I visited friends with Rebecca, who was ten at the time. Rebecca had torn a ligament in her ankle in a playground accident a week before our planned departure. But we took off for Barcelona anyway, planning to take taxis and eat tapas. My friends had young children. If we couldn't do a lot of sightseeing, at least we would have the benefit of a new place, new food, deepening connection.

Over the weekend, we took a road trip to Barcelona's PortAventura, a Spanish version of Disneyland. At the entrance, Rebecca was issued a wheelchair—her "invalid" status meant that everyone in our party automatically went to the front of every line, even the ones with two-hour wait times. We were thrilled by what felt like a guilty pleasure.

Twenty years later, these happy associations come back to me. I have finished the first draft of this book, and I text Rebecca my good news. We've been texting back and forth, working on details for her wedding, planned for the following summer.

I'm in Barcelona to give a speech about new trends in artificial intelligence. I've called my talk "The New AI—Artificial Intimacy." Now machines are not content to show us they are smart; they pretend to care about our love lives and our children.

When computer toys first wowed children with their ability to play games, children not only saw the toys as "sort of alive" but actually changed how they talked about what was special about being a person. When they met computer toys, children saw people as special not because they were smart (these new machines were smart as well) but because they had feelings. Young children essentially described people as emotional machines. It seemed an unstable category. Even then, my computer-scientist colleagues dreamed of creating robots and screen avatars that could be our companions of the heart—machines with as-if feelings and as-if empathy. I wondered: Once people were in the company of these new "emotional" machines, the artificial ones, how would we distinguish ourselves from these pretenders? More important, would we want to? Would pretend empathy seem empathy enough?

I came up with this troubling formulation: We nurture what we love, but we love what we nurture. After taking care of an object, even one as simple as a digital pet that lived in a plastic egg and wanted to be fed and amused on schedule, children (and their parents) got attached to it emotionally. This finding did not have to do with the intelligence or empathic qualities of the digital objects that asked to be taught or tended. It had to do with the vulnerability of people. When machines ask us to care for them, we become attached to these machines and think that the machines care for us. "Pretend empathy" had an awesome weapon: the deep psychology of being human.

And now we were beyond human vulnerabilities and projections. Now the machines were outright declaring their affection.

This is the original sin of artificial intelligence. There is nothing wrong with creating smart machines. We can set them to all kinds of useful tasks. The problem comes up when we create machines that let us think they care for us. "You are the wind beneath my wings," says Siri in response to "Siri, I love you." These "empathy machines" play on our loneliness and, sadly, on our fear of being vulnerable to our own kind. We must confront the downside of living with the robots of our science-fiction dreams. Do we really want to feel empathy for machines that feel nothing for us?

As I prepare the final notes for my talk on the dangers of artificial intimacy, I suddenly remember a night in 1982.

Seymour and I had gone to the Boston premiere of *Tron* with Marvin Minsky. We were excited. The film depicted the mind as a society of programs—this was the theory that Marvin and Seymour were writing about! After the film, we stood outside the theater while

Marvin regaled us with his ideas about our object minds. The film, said Marvin, was on the right track. Everyone should take their kids to this film and avoid more traditional fare.

In his mind, Walt Disney's *Bambi* was the worst. I took the bait. What was wrong with *Bambi*? Every kid sees *Bambi*. Marvin's response has stayed with me for half a lifetime: "*Bambi* indoctrinates children to think that death matters. Someday we will conquer death by merging with computers. Such attachments—Bambi's attachment to his mother, for example—will be unimportant. People need to learn to give that stuff up." I knew Marvin to be a loving father and husband. But in his mind, attachment would only be an impediment to progress in a world where people and machines evolved together.

Marvin Minsky died in 2016. But I'm still fighting his idea, now more than ever part of the cultural mainstream, that it is good to have devices that can wean us from our dependency on one another. For Marvin, the burdens that come with human bonds were unnecessary and inefficient because an engineering solution was on the horizon— we are ultimately going to mate with machines or evolve into machines or become one with machines.

These ideas are seductive. Of course we want technology to bring us sharper wits and a cure for Parkinson's. We like the idea that some kind of artificial intelligence can help monitor the safety of isolated elders. And then we are caught short. There is a red line—one I have seen so many people cross. It's the line when you don't want children to get attached to their mortal mothers because they should be ready to bond with their eternal robot minders. It's the line where you take your child as your experimental subject and ignore her, registering her tears as data. It's the line you cross when one of your classmates commits suicide by jumping out a window and you joke about the laws of physics that were at work in his descent. It's the line you cross when you know that the car you manufacture has a design flaw and a certain kind of impact will kill its passengers. You'll have to pay damages for their lives. What is the cost of their lives in relation to that of redesigning the car? This is the kind of thinking that treats people as things. Knowing how to criticize it is becoming more pressing as social media and artificial intelligence insert themselves into every aspect of our lives, because as they do, we are turned into commodities, data that is bought and sold on the marketplace.

At the very moment we are called to connect to the earth and be stewards of our planet, we are intensifying our connection to objects that really don't care if humanity dies. The urgent move, I think, is in the opposite direction.

With my daughter, Rebecca, September, 1991.

The evening before my talk in Barcelona, I thought about Marvin and *Tron*. I remembered that when Rebecca was small, I went out and bought her all the Disney movies I had seen as a child. Of course, I bought *Bambi*. In my home, there would be no shortage of stories with mother-child bonds.

And now Rebecca is twenty-seven. Only a few weeks before, she helped me choose my gown for her wedding. I had a favorite, but wasn't the neckline too low? Studiously, patiently, my daughter stood opposite me, putting herself in my place, taking me seriously. My empathic girl. No, she said. The neckline is perfect.

Acknowledgments

This book began its life in a conversation with my friend and mentor Jill Ker Conway. Once, at dinner, Jill and I were talking about our mothers, both fragile and strong. I told Jill that as a child I had to decipher how my mother interpreted reality. Keeping up required a kind of detective work. Jill encouraged me to write about how this personal story meshed with my professional journey. Thank you, Jill, for that decisive encouragement. Katinka Matson helped me frame these initial thoughts and was an exemplary reader of a book in development.

Participants in the events I describe read drafts, made corrections, and confirmed details: Bernard Goldhirsch, my junior-year English teacher; Catherine Weill of rue du Bac days; Radcliffe classmates Amy Gutmann, Judith Lieberman, Ann Zimmerman Russell, Deborah Fiedler Styles, Nancy Lipton Rosenblum, and Emily Spieler; Chicago friend Merilyn Salomon; David Riesman alumnus Michael Schudson; Bonowitz/Bearman

cousins Donna Bearman, Tod Bonowitz, and Andi de Palma; and Professor Loren Graham, Professor Kenneth Manning, and Dean Harry
Hanham, all at MIT during my tenure case. A special thanks to Alan Kay
for a check in on Xerox PARC; to Professor Nicholas Negroponte for his
notes on the chronology of the Centre Mondial; to Seymour's brother and
sister-in-law, Alan and Gloria Papert, for Papert family fact-checking; and
to Susan and Bruce Turkle for help on significant details. Reunions of
the PS 216 sixth-grade class of 1960 were precious, as were reunions of the
Lincoln High School class of 1965 and the Harvard/Radcliffe class
of 1969.

Other friends provided full readings and chapter notes, some including
the proper use of French idioms and the correct spelling of Paris streets.
I've had this project in mind a long time so there are sure to be people I'm
leaving out. I beg forgiveness in advance. I thank Claire Baldwin, Roberta
Baskin, Melia Bensussen, Rachel Botsman, Emily Carlin, Marlene Cof-
fey, Judith Donath, David Dreyer, Helen Epstein, Kelly Gray, Edward
Greer, Bernard Gustin, Douglas Hopkins, Maggie Jackson, John LaFre-
niere, Kent Lawson, Terrence McNally, Nilofer Merchant, Terry Moore,
Artemis Papert, Jacqueline Rose, Ben Sherman, Susan Stern, Susan Su-
leiman, Mary-Kay Wilmers, and Veronica Windholz. The students in
my pandemic-interrupted seminar on Memoir mentored me over Zoom.
When I was taken aback by the sheer heft of my first draft, Katie Hafner
gave me an unsentimental demonstration of how to use a red pencil. Jane
Wolfson offered wise counsel.

I have three final debts, my greatest. To Virginia Smith Younce and
Caroline Sydney at Penguin, who over many years helped me see the
book that this book wanted to become. They were meticulous and committed and—something that is important for all of us, always, and,
unsurprisingly, turns out to be crucial when you are editing a memoir—
deeply kind.

And I thank the reader whose literary taste has been one of my life's unexpected joys: my daughter, Rebecca Sherman. In the history of this book, as in everything else, when I needed her, we had the conversations I needed.

ST

Provincetown, Massachusetts

September 2020

Notes

These are not comprehensive bibliographical citations for the books and papers I mention in this memoir, either those I have read or those I have written. My goal here is modest: there were a few places in the text where it seemed that more information about a reading or other detail would help the reader retrace my steps.

INTRODUCTION: *LE NOM DU PÈRE*

xx **"My mother was my first":** Nayyirah Waheed, "Lands," in *Salt* (self-published CreateSpace, 2013).

CHAPTER 1: SUMMER PALACE/WINTER PALACE

27 **My grandparents told me:** It wasn't until long after the war that it became known that the U.S. State Department had concealed from FDR the extent and severity of what was happening to the Jews in Europe—in fear that if he understood it, he might be moved to intervene more forcefully than he already had in Europe, something that my grandparents were not aware of in these childhood conversations.

CHAPTER 2: THE MEMORY CLOSET

32 **song called "Serenade":** It was Enrico Toselli's "Serenade," which sometimes comes to me unbidden when I close my eyes.

CHAPTER 4: *DÉPAYSEMENT*

82 **I answered no to all:** Some North House residents told me they chose those dorms because of their excellent music-practice facilities and that private-school graduates also chose North House for this reason.

86 **To see your own culture:** And it helps, too, to underline how groundbreaking was work such as that of Carol Gilligan, who challenged the presumption that psychological tests, to be valid, should be done on men—that whole "baseline" argument. I first came across Gilligan's work when I was at MIT. Kenneth Keniston, a colleague, said I must read it. I devoured it. C. Gilligan, "In a Different Voice: Women's Conceptions of Self and of Morality," *Harvard Educational Review* 47 (1977): 481–517; and C. Gilligan, "Woman's Place in Man's Life Cycle," *Harvard Educational Review* 49, no. 4 (1979): 431–46. In 1982, Gilligan published her findings in the classic, *In a Different Voice: Psychological Theory and Women's Development* (Cambridge, MA: Harvard University Press). On *dépaysement* specifically, see Claude Lévi Strauss, *Structural Anthropology* (New York: Basic Books, 1963).

CHAPTER 8: NEWSPAPERS AND VINEGAR

152 **"objects to think with":** See *Totemism* (Boston: Beacon Press, 1963) and *The Savage Mind* (Chicago: University Press, 1966).
154 **Totalitarianism thrives on it:** Hannah Arendt, *The Origins of Totalitarianism* (New York: Harvest, 1994), 474 ff.
163 **call its "third places":** The sociologist Ray Oldenburg talks about third places in *The Great Good Place: Cafés, Coffee Shops, Bookstores, Bars, Hair Salons, and Other Hangouts at the Heart of a Community* (New York: Paragon House, 1989).
164 **Prisunic, one of the first:** Prisunic was acquired by Monoprix in the 1990s.
166 **not eager to hear:** See, for example, "Epistemological Pluralism: Styles and Voices within the Computer Culture" (with Seymour Papert) *Signs: Journal of Women in Culture and Society* 16, 1, Autumn 1990.

CHAPTER 9: THINGS FOR THINKING

179 **a few of Freud's classic works:** Unsurprisingly, the most important to me was Sigmund Freud, "Mourning and Melancholia" (1917). *The Standard Edition of the Complete Works of Sigmund Freud,* James Strachey et al., eds. (London: Hogarth Press, 1953–74).
180 **Erikson described identity:** My introduction to Erikson was his classic *Childhood and Society* (New York: W.W. Norton, 1950).

CHAPTER 10: GREAT BOOKS

189 **"nourishing raisins in a cellular mass":** Victor Turner, *Dramas, Fields, and Metaphors: Symbolic Action in Human Society* (Ithaca: Cornell University Press, 1975), 23.

CHAPTER 11: THE LACANIAN VILLAGE

193 **ethnographer and subject:** For a review of four theories of psychoanalytic interpretation, see Victor L. Schermer (2011), "Interpreting a Psychoanalytic Interpretation: A Fourfold Perspective," *The Psychoanalytic Review,* 98(6): 817–42.

196 **Foucault was with me:** My first book on digital culture, *The Second Self: Computers and The Human Spirit* (New York: Simon and Schuster, 1984), addressed people facing a stand-alone object. My second, *Life on the Screen: Identity in the Age of the Internet* (New York: Simon and Schuster, 1995), examined the networked and now potentially multiple self.

196 **Wylie's vexing theorists:** The theorists I was reading in Wylie's class are now available in excellent English translations. For a brief introduction to the experience of that heady course, I would start with Jacques Lacan, "The Mirror Stage as Formative of the I Function, as Revealed in Psychoanalytic Experience," in *Ecrits* (New York: W.W. Norton, 2002), 93–100; Jacques Derrida, *Writing and Difference* (Chicago: University of Chicago Press, 2017); and Michel Foucault, "Doctors and Patients," in *Madness and Civilization* (New York: Vintage, 1988), 159–98.

200 **in America, people see themselves:** David Riesman, Nathan Glazer, and Reuel Denney, *The Lonely Crowd: A Study of the Changing American Character* (New Haven: Yale, 1950), revised abridged edition, 2001. "Prestige, status, [and] success are a substitute for the genuine feeling of identity," said Fromm. Erich Fromm, *Man for Himself* (New York: Owl, 1990 [Holt, 1947], 73.

201 **I wrote my book:** *Alone Together: Why We Expect More from Technology and Less from Each Other* (New York: Basic Books, 2011); *Reclaiming Conversation: The Power of Talk in a Digital Age* (New York: Penguin Press, 2015).

CHAPTER 12: *CHÈRE-CHEUR*

217 **"reveal in the innermost":** Theodor Adorno, "Die revidierte psychoanalyse," cited in Russell Jacoby, *Social Amnesia: A Critique of Contemporary Psychology* (Boston: Beacon Press, 1975), 34.

218 **there is a problem:** Wladimir Granoff, *Filiations* (Paris: Éditions de minuit, 1974); François Roustang, *Un destin si funeste* (Paris: Éditions de minuit, 1976).

CHAPTER 15: THE XEROX ROOM

248 **founders of artificial intelligence:** This definition of AI is usually attributed to AI pioneer John McCarthy, who coined the term in 1955.

262 **artificial intelligence and psychoanalysis:** These ideas would gel into a 1988 paper. Two scientific traditions that thought they had little in common actually had the most important things in common. Sherry Turkle, "Artificial Intelligence and Psychoanalysis: A New Alliance," *Daedalus* 117, no. 1 (Winter 1988): 241–68.

CHAPTER 16: BUILDING 20

270 **the psychoanalyst Donald Winnicott:** I asked my students to begin where I had, with "Transitional Objects and Transitional Phenomena," in D.W. Winnicott, *Playing and Reality* (New York: Tavistock, 1971).

270 **I repaid my debt to the memory closet:** The "object" books I edited were published by The MIT Press: *Evocative Objects: Things We Think With* (2007); *Falling For Science: Objects in Mind (2008); The Inner History of Devices* (2008).

274 **It was designed to transparently:** Seymour had written Logo at Bolt, Beranek and Newman, a Cambridge consulting firm, with two colleagues— Wallace Feurzeig and Cynthia Solomon—in 1967, soon after he first came to the United States. "Logo" is not an acronym. It was Feurzeig who named the language, taking it from the Greek *logos*, meaning "word" or "thought." The basic idea of the language was that using it would teach you the most powerful ideas in computer science. It would make computation transparent. By the time I met Seymour eight years later, he was the head of MIT's Epistemology and Learning Group. Logo and what it meant for the future of education were at the center of his work.

276 **computer screen evoked:** The computer pioneer Douglas Engelbart had pioneered this idea in the late 1960s, and in 1973, Alan Kay at PARC had invented the Alto, the first computer that fully demonstrated the desktop metaphor and graphical computer interface. It never became a commercial product, but several thousand units were built and used at PARC, which is where I met one when Seymour and I visited in January 1977.

282 **lose a great privilege:** And indeed, these two great friends worked together on this project until it was clear that if *The Society of Mind* was to be completed, it would have to be without Seymour. Then they pursued their work separately. Seymour wrote multiple books on the future of children and computing, beginning with *Mindstorms: Children, Computers, and Powerful Ideas* in 1981 (New York: Basic Books). Marvin published *The Society of Mind* in 1986 (New York: Simon & Schuster) and then *The Emotion Machine* in 2006 (New York: Simon & Schuster).

Chapter 17: The Marriage of True Minds

293 **philosophical stand against:** Joseph Weizenbaum, *Computer Power and Human Reason: From Judgment to Calculation* (San Francisco: Samuel Freeman, 1976).

299 **The objects provoked:** I analyzed this conversation in depth in *The Second Self: Computers and the Human Spirit* (New York: Simon and Schuster, 1984; twentieth anniversary edition (The MIT Press: Cambridge, MA), 1995, my MIT "tenure book."

Chapter 18: Coming Apart

316 **by its shorthand name, "le Centre Mondial:** Its full name was Centre Mondial Informatique et Ressource Humaine.

Chapter 19: The Last Experiment

328 **Using simulation technology:** At the time, my critique of simulation software in education was unwelcome at MIT, but it pointed to larger and persistent problems. I discuss my original MIT studies in the context of later developments in *Simulation and its Discontents* (The MIT Press: Cambridge, MA, 2005).

Chapter 20: The Assault on Empathy

334 **"Why choose masks":** David Hellerstein, "Computers on the Couch," *Esquire*, December 1, 1985, https://classic.esquire.com/article/1985/12/1 /computers-on-the-couch.

339 **our lives are bought and sold:** The literature here is vast, but most recently, see Shoshana Zuboff's *The Age of Surveillance Capitalism: The Fight for a Human Future at the New Frontier of Power* (New York: Perseus, 2019).